New Challenges for UNICEF

Also by Yves Beigbeder

INTERNATIONAL MONITORING OF PLEBISCITES, REFERENDA AND NATIONAL ELECTIONS: Self-determination and Transition to Democracy

*JUDGING WAR CRIMINALS: The Politics of International Justice

LE HAUT COMMISSARIAT DES NATIONS UNIES POUR LES REFUGIES

*THE INTERNAL MANAGEMENT OF UNITED NATIONS ORGANIZATIONS: The Long Quest for Reform

THE ROLE AND STATUS OF INTERNATIONAL HUMANITARIAN VOLUNTEERS AND ORGANIZATIONS: The Right and Duty to Humanitarian Assistance

THE WORLD HEALTH ORGANIZATION (*with the collaboration of Mahyar Nashat, Marie–Antoinette Orsini and Jean–François Tiercy*)

also from the same publishers

New Challenges for UNICEF

Children, Women and Human Rights

Yves Beigbeder

palgrave

© Yves Beigbeder 2001

First published 2001 by
PALGRAVE
Houndmills, Basingstoke, Hampshire RG21 6XS and
175 Fifth Avenue, New York, N. Y. 10010
Companies and representatives throughout the world

PALGRAVE is the new global academic imprint of
St. Martin's Press LLC Scholarly and Reference Division and
Palgrave Publishers Ltd (formerly Macmillan Press Ltd).

ISBN 0–333–80047–8

This book is printed on paper suitable for recycling and made from fully managed and sustained forest sources.

A catalogue record for this book is available from the British Library.

Library of Congress Cataloging-in-Publication Data
Beigbeder, Yves.
    New challenges for UNICEF : children, women, and human rights / Yves Beigbeder
        p. cm.
    Includes bibliographical references and index.
    ISBN 0–333–80047–8 (cloth)
    1. UNICEF. 2. Children—Legal status, laws, etc. 3. Children's rights. 4. Child welfare. I. Title.

    K639.B45 2001
    362.7—dc21
                                            2001035792

10   9   8   7   6   5   4   3   2   1
10   09 08 07 06 05 04 03 02 01

Printed and bound in Great Britain by
Antony Rowe Ltd, Chippenham, Wiltshire

Contents

List of Figures and Tables

Figures

Tables

Foreword

The United Nations system had been on a roller-coaster ride in the post-Cold War era. Initial euphoria about the construction of a 'new world order' went up in smoke, literally, with the downing of Black Hawk helicopters and the unseemly display of dead American marines in Mogadishu. The ill-informed, yet understandable, giddiness about the expansive possibilities for international cooperation turned quickly into a day-after hangover that was still in effect as we blithely watched the Rwandan genocide. The 'end of history' debate ended as quickly as it had begun. And yet, 1999 was the *annus mirabilis*, or *horribilis* depending on your point of view, with vigorous international responses in Kosovo and East Timor.

The point here is not to discuss the relative successes or failures of these high-profile efforts, but rather to suggest the requirement to move beyond the ups and downs of today's headlines, to grapple seriously with the low-profile details of multilateral cooperation in every arena. Well publicized efforts to foster peace and security are essential but so too are the day-to-day and often invisible struggles to improve lives and to enforce international norms. Eradicating poverty and disease, improving education, and providing succor to children and women around the world are as much the 'stuff' of multilateral cooperation as blue-helmeted soldiers.

In this respect, I commend Yves Beigbeder for analysing the 'New Challenges for UNICEF'. The organization is unusual among UN agencies in that it is well-known among the public in both rich and poor countries. Not only was UNICEF awarded the Nobel Peace Prize in 1965, its goodwill ambassadors and other celebrity supporters help burnish its reputation for seriousness and cost-effectiveness. Its $1 billion annual budget comes from voluntary contributions – from governments, charities, businesses and the sale of popular greeting cards.

This volume is not, however, a puff piece or an official story. It fills an important void in the literature, not only about the study of the institution charged with the promotion of children's and women's rights and welfare but about international organization more generally. To put it simply, we know precious little about the functioning of intergovernmental secretariats in contemporary world affairs. How does a body like UNICEF operate among a myriad of state and non-state actors, aiming to fulfil its mandate by working in collaboration with governments, corporations, grass-roots groups, the military and non-governmental organizations? Does leadership matter, and if so how? Is the Convention on the Rights of the Child another piece of paper or a wedge for change and a meaningful tool for new projects?

The honest student or practitioner of international relations should be willing to admit that everyone is groping and coping to understand the contemporary world in which international organizations and we ourselves operate. Yet, there are mainly grand theories and how-to manuals, but little between the abstract analyses emanating from scholars and the mundane matters of bureaucrats. The common ground between them is too rarely ploughed.

One of the reasons is that too few observers understand academic and practitioner preoccupations. A trained lawyer who began his career at Nuremburg and spent almost 35 years in UN service before returning to teaching and writing, Yves Beigbeder is able, however, to speak to both officials and scholars. Both will find satisfying interpretations of over half a century of UNICEF's efforts. He paints convincing portraits of strong leaders (Henry Labouisse and Jim Grant), of an international agency whose field efforts in development and humanitarian relief have been complemented by normative efforts to protect and enhance children's and women's rights. At the same time, one of the few institutions within the UN system that has an almost universal reputation for effectiveness and rectitude has its shortcomings. And the author does not shy away from criticisms. One that I would have emphasized is the tensions and competition with other international agencies, the turf-consciousness that plagues the UN system generally.

For all of the goodwill and public recognition surrounding UNICEF, few objective studies of the organization have been undertaken. This is why the present volume is essential reading for students and practitioners of international organization.

Thomas G. Weiss, November 2000
Presidential Professor, Co-Director, UN Intellectual History Project
The Graduate Center, The City University of New York
New York, NY, USA

Preface and Acknowledgements

Most organizations in the United Nations system have been subjected since the 1980s to recurrent attacks. Industrialized countries want them to be more efficient, less costly, better coordinated among themselves and with other bodies working in the same field. The US lead in these criticisms and the US refusal to pay their dues to the UN proper and other UN bodies has proved a counterproductive blackmail which has paradoxically hampered the organizations' efforts to reform and has reduced their programmes. Developing countries want the organizations to spend more on development and less on peacekeeping, while they reject any attempt to erode their national sovereignty through humanitarian interventions.

UNICEF is one of the few privileged UN agencies which is well-known among the general public in both rich and poor countries and enjoys a reputation for efficiency as the only global institution providing humanitarian, emergency and development assistance to children. Its name is often cited favourably in press and radio reports and its 'good works' are visible on TV screens.

The agency was awarded the Nobel prize for peace in 1965. Its financing through voluntary contributions by governments, other organizations and foundations, and by individuals, its sales of greeting cards and the well-publicized presence on war or poverty scenes of goodwill ambassadors and other celebrity supporters also contribute to its popularity.

While UNICEF has generally escaped most of the criticisms addressed to the 'political' UN and to some specialized agencies or bodies such as UNESCO, UNIDO or UNCTAD, one of its challenges is to maintain its identity and its activities as a UN children's agency among other UN organizations having a broader mandate, which includes children, in their own field: can UNICEF have its own separate programmes in public health, WHO's domain; in food and nutrition, part of the FAO's concerns; in education, a substantial part of UNESCO's programmes; in child labour, one of the ILO's activities? Or, more generally, are UNICEF programmes too extended and diffuse, is UNICEF trying to embrace too much at the risk of being ineffective?

The problem of rivalry with the specialized agencies is not new: they tried unsuccessfully to 'abort' the birth of UNICEF in 1946, and some tensions have occurred between them and the agency from time to time.

Is UNICEF apolitical? Like the specialized agencies, UNICEF has been created as a specialized body in principle separate from the 'political' UN. However, UNICEF is an intergovernmental body subject to the pressures or instructions given by members of its governing board, representatives of their own governments. The position of these governments is naturally influenced by national and international politics. UNICEF works in a number of countries in consultation with or with the consent of the governments concerned: the agency's work in those countries cannot but be also subject to internal national politics and international politics. Finally, UNICEF has at times taken position publicly to deplore or blame international or national decisions which affected the welfare of children in specific countries or areas. Hence the difficulty for UNICEF, shared with many other intergovernmental and non-governmental organizations (IGOs and NGOs) working in relief and development assistance, to be or to appear to be above politics.

Another challenge to UNICEF is fighting donor fatigue, in so far as its resources come exclusively from voluntary contributions by governments, governmental agencies, IGOs and NGOs, foundations, business firms and individuals. This is linked to the visible cost-effectiveness of UNICEF, to the constant demonstration that it has comparative advantages over other IGOs and NGOs, or that it necessarily and usefully complements or supplements their activities.

This raises the issue, applicable to UNICEF and to many other IGOs and NGOs, of the difficult (or impossible) assessment of the impact of the agency's work on the real world: have UNICEF's programmes exerted an effective influence on countries' leaders, government, administrations to the benefit of children's health, nutrition and education in their countries? Have they played a role other than rhetoric in this or that country's development? Can UNICEF really fight poverty in developing countries, without direct and effective role in the economy of these countries?

Finally, the success or failure of UNICEF's programmes is dependent not only on their applicability to regional, national and local conditions, on the availability of financial and other resources and on the energy, enthusiasm and integrity of the agency's staff, but on broader political, military, economic, social and cultural factors. The best soil would ideally be good governance, a healthy economy, civil peace and peace with neighbouring states: there would then be no need for international assistance. In the real world, help is needed in countries where more money goes to arms than to health, where ethnic and other strife oppose citizens, where civil or external war exhausts resources, where AIDS and malaria weaken or kill part of the population. Can UNICEF help in such circumstances?

Early in August 1999, two teenage Africans from Guinea died in flight in the open landing gear of an airliner between Conakry and Brussels. A letter was found in their clothes addressed to 'the excellencies and officials of Europe':

> We suffer enormously in Africa. Help us. We have problems in Africa. We lack rights as children. We have war and illness, we lack food ... We have schools, but we lack education ... If you see that we have sacrificed our lives it is because we need your help to fight against poverty and to end wars.[1]

This tragic appeal may be the best justification for UNICEF's efforts. Even if the agency's effective assistance is limited by its limited resources, it does provide useful advice and material assistance to governments and people in need, and, importantly, it gives hope to many. What cause is more valuable and attractive than that of helping babies and children to survive, grow and develop into useful citizens through support in health, nutrition and education?

This book tries to keep a balance between praise where it is due, i.e. in most areas, and a few criticisms which have been expressed of some of its operations and management. The latter should not be hidden, any more than some of the conflicts or tensions with other UN agencies or NGOs: no organization is perfect and transparency is required by donors and supporters. Problems should be exposed and their causes explained, so that prevention and correction may be timely applied. These few 'shadows' should not detract from the many 'lights', UNICEF's useful contribution, at the global level, to the protection and welfare of children of all countries, and particularly in developing countries.

The book recalls UNICEF's predecessors, its creation in 1946, its original mandate and the evolution of its programmes, its structure, management and funding. It describes the agency's work in public health, food aid and nutrition, education and sanitation, and its role in natural and man-made emergencies. Its advocacy for the adoption of the Convention on the Rights of the Child and its assistance to governments in the implementation of the Convention is also reviewed. Internal management issues are also discussed while the final chapter summarizes current UNICEF challenges.

The book is based on UNICEF reports and internal documents, press releases as well as periodical publications for the general public, relevant books and articles. It is also based on a number of interviews with UNICEF serving or retired staff and other colleagues of UN agencies. Reference is often made to Maggie Black's two extensive, well documented historical books on the agency's life and activities from its creation in 1946 to the mid-1990s – *The Children and the Nations: The Story of Unicef* (1986), and a sequel, *Children First: The Story of UNICEF, Past and Present* (1996), both sponsored by UNICEF. Clearly, the present essay does not attempt to compete with Black's detailed reviews of UNICEF's work which constitute a unique reference source for the period covered.

The essay is written as an individual, independent research work, not sponsored or guided by UNICEF. As such, the book does not claim to be a comprehensive review of all the agency's programmes and achievements. Its purpose is to present in a relatively brief form some of the important events in the agency's life, its main programmes, the challenges and problems faced and what solutions, if any, were found.

Thanks are addressed to staff in UNICEF in New York and in Geneva who helped me in obtaining relevant documentation and information, to retired colleagues for their useful advice, and to the helpful and patient staff in the UN and WHO Libraries in Geneva. Due credit is also given to UNICEF for giving permission to make references to and use a few excerpts from Maggie Black's book *Children First: The Story of UNICEF, Past and Present* (Oxford: Oxford University Press for UNICEF, 1996). The editing skills of Mandy Eggleston are gratefully acknowledged.

Finally, the author has written this book in a personal capacity: views and assessments are his own responsibility – they do not necessarily reflect the views of, nor commit in any way, UNICEF and the other organizations referred to in the following chapters.

Notes:

- The use of the word 'agency' in reference to UNICEF in the present book follows the same use in UNICEF publications. It does not affect the status of UNICEF as a Fund, a subsidiary body of the UN General Assembly: UNICEF is not a specialized agency of the UN.
- The sign $ in the text refers to US$.

List of Abbreviations

ACABQ	Advisory Committee on Administrative and Budgetary Questions
ACC	Administrative Committee on Coordination
ARI	acute respiratory infections
CCH	WHO/UNICEF/UNFPA Coordinating Committee on Health
CDD	control of diarrhoeal diseases
CEDC	children in especially difficult circumstances
CERD	Convention on the Elimination of Racial Discrimination
CIDA	Canadian International Development Agency
CRB	Commission for Relief in Belgium
CSI	Christian Solidarity International
CVI	Children's Vaccine Initiative
ECHO	Humanitarian Office of the European Union
ECOSOC	Economic and Social Council
EPI	Expanded Programme on Immunization
FAO	Food and Agriculture Organization of the UN
FGM	Female genital mutilation
FLS	Financial and Logistic System
GAVI	Global Alliance for Vaccines and Immunization
GOBI/FF	Growth monitoring, Oral rehydration therapy, Breastfeeding, Immunization/ Food supplements, Family planning
GPA	Global Programme on AIDS
GPV	Global Programme for Vaccines and Immunization
IBFAN	International Baby Food Action Network
ICCB	International Catholic Child Bureau
ICESCR	International Covenant on Economic, Social and Cultural Rights
ICPR	International Covenant on Civil and Political Rights
ICRC	International Committee of the Red Cross
IDD	iodine deficiency disorder
IDEAL	Intensive District Approach to Education for All
IFAD	International Fund for Agricultural Development
IGO	Inter-governmental organization
ILO	International Labour Organization

IMCI	Integrated Management of Childhood Illness
IMF	International Monetary Fund
IPEC	International Programme on the Elimination of Child Labour
IYC	International Year of the Child
JCGP	Joint Consultative Group on Policy
JCHP	Joint Committee on Health Policy
LRA	Lord's Resistance Army (Uganda)
MICS	Multiple Indicator Cluster Survey
MNT	maternal and neonatal tetanus
MSF	Médecins sans Frontières
Nats	Niños y Adolescentes Trabajores
NGO	non-governmental organization
NPO	National Professional Officers
OAS	Organization of American States
OAU	Organization of African Unity
ODA	Official development assistance
OECD	Organization for Economic Cooperation and Development
OIA	Office of Internal Audit
ORS	oral rehydration salts
ORT	oral rehydration therapy
PAHO	Pan American Health Organization
PHC	primary health care
PROMS	Programme Manager System
RRTs	Rapid Response Teams
RUF	Revolutionary United Front (Sierra Leone)
SCF	Save the Children Fund
SIAR	Scandinavian Institutes for Administrative Research
STD	sexually transmitted disease
UCI	Universal Children's Immunization
UK	United Kingdom
UN	United Nations
UNAIDS	Joint UN Programme on HIV/AIDS
UNAMET	UN Mission in East Timor
UNCTAD	UN Conference on Trade and Development
UNDP	UN Development Programme
UNESCO	UN Educational, Scientific and Cultural Organization
UNFPA	UN Fund for Population Activities
UNGA	UN General Assembly
UNHCR	UN High Commissioner for Refugees
UNICEF	UN Children's Fund

UNIDO	UN Industrial Development Organization
UNIFEM	UN Development Fund for Women
UNIMIS-HR	UN Integrated Management Information System – Human Resources
UNITA	National Union for the Liberation of Angola
UNITAR	UN Institute for Training and Research
UNRRA	UN Relief and Rehabilitation Administration
UNRWA	UN Relief and Works Agency for Palestine Refugees in the Near East
USA	United States of America
USAID	US Agency for International Development
VAD	vitamin A deficiency
WFP	World Food Programme
WHO	World Health Organization
YWCA	Young Women Christians Association

1
The Creation of UNICEF

Do the world's children need UNICEF? The care for children is, or should be, a natural concern for all parents and relatives, and for the local community. At the national level, governments should ensure that children receive proper health care, adequate nutrition, and basic education and training, and that they are safeguarded from violence, exploitation, poverty and discrimination. The problems faced by families and nations in providing adequate care and protection to children in certain areas and particularly in times of conflict have caused, in the twentieth century, the creation of international organizations needed to complement or even assume entirely these tasks, generally on a temporary basis. Some of the organizations which preceded UNICEF were either fully dedicated to children's welfare or included children as beneficiaries, together with their family, in their relief action. Some organizations were (and some still are) non-governmental – the Commission for Relief in Belgium, the Save the Children Fund – some were intergovernmental – the League of Nations and the United Nations Relief and Rehabilitation Administration. The latter's demise led directly to the difficult birth of UNICEF, with the determining influence of such individuals as Dr Ludwig Rajchman and delegates of 'like-minded' countries against the opposition of the USA and the other western countries and of the UN specialized agencies fearing the competition of an intruder in their domain.

Organizations which preceded UNICEF

UNICEF is the first intergovernmental organization (IGO) concerned only with children. The League of Nations expressed interest in child welfare 'as an essential subject of international study' and adopted in 1924 a Declaration of the Rights of the Child. Its action in favour of refugees did not separate children from adults. Similarly, non-governmental organizations (NGOs) created before the Second World War gave succour to victims, adults and children, without focusing exclusively on children, with one exception: the Save the Children Fund.

The International Committee of the Red Cross was created in 1863. Under its fundamental principles, the International Red Cross and Red Crescent Movement brings assistance without discrimination to the wounded on the battlefield and endeavours to prevent and alleviate human suffering wherever it may be found. The principles refer to the suffering of individuals, who, as wounded soldiers and prisoners of war were in principle adults. However, war victims clearly include families, men, women and children, although the latter are not identified as the sole or even preferred object of assistance.

The Commission for Relief in Belgium (CRB)

The Commission for Relief in Belgium was created by Herbert Hoover in 1914, with the agreement of the USA, France, the UK and Germany. The CRB was a temporary international NGO with some IGO attributes: it negotiated and concluded agreements with states, enjoyed immunities granted by the belligerents, flew its own flag and issued its own passports.

This large international humanitarian operation was undertaken on behalf of the civilian populations of occupied Belgium and northern France in response to the threat of famine in that region. Its beneficiaries were Belgian and French civilians, thus including children together with adults. Between 1914 and 1919, the Commission procured, shipped and supervised the distribution of relief supplies sufficient to maintain the protected population at subsistence levels, and it also supported welfare services. This extraordinary venture gave assistance to a civilian, non-combatant population in an enemy area, with the approval of the enemy. As noted by Macalister-Smith:

> In particular, the Commission's political neutrality and operational independence, and its director's capacity to negotiate directly and impartially with all sides involved, indicate minimum requirements for any relief operation or relief organization. The level of international cooperation developed by the CRB in its global network of procurement offices and supporting charitable organizations was also a valuable precedent for the conduct of future relief programmes.[1]

The leadership role of Herbert Hoover resumed after the Second World War: in 1946, he was asked by President Truman to propose measures to alleviate the postwar famine which extended over two-thirds of the world.

Following visits to 38 countries, he made a number of public declarations exposing children's starvation and poverty, suggesting that their 'redemption' be entrusted to the newly created UN.

The League of Nations

Before the League was established, a Convention of 1910 undertook to punish the procuration of women under twenty, even with consent. Article 23(c) of the Covenant entrusted the League 'with the general supervision over the execution of agreements with regard to the traffic in women and children'. Accordingly, the League convened an international conference in 1921 which led to a new convention raising the age of protection to 21 for persons of either sex, and which secured support for international action from practically all the Members of the League. In 1924, at the instance of the Save the Children Fund, the Declaration of the Rights of the Child, commonly known as the Declaration of Geneva, was adopted by the League's Assembly (see below).

The League then took over the work of the International Association for the Promotion of Child Welfare which had been established in Brussels. The Council appointed an Advisory Committee on Child Welfare which, combined with the Advisory Committee on Traffic in Women and Children, became the Advisory Committee on Social Questions. The Committee had a limited task: it was to study those problems on which the comparison of the methods and experiences of different countries, consultation and exchange of views between the officials or experts of different countries or international cooperation were likely to assist the governments in dealing with such problems. The Committee set up a Child Welfare Information Centre and published a number of reports, in liaison with the ILO and the Health Organization of the League.[2]

The League took a more active role when it appointed, in 1921, Dr Fridtjof Nansen, the Norwegian scholar, explorer and philanthropist, as the High Commissioner for Russian Refugees. Most original refugees resulted from the Bolshevik Revolution of 1917, but additional numbers from other European sources converted the, initially, temporary programme into a permanent activity. The competence of the Commissioner was later extended to cover Armenians, Assyrians, Assyro-Chaldeans and Turks, and to refugees from the Near East.

The Red Cross Societies and other charitable organizations, as well as a number of governments, had initiated international refugee work during the First World War. A Conference of such NGOs, convened by the ICRC and the League of Red Cross Societies then brought the question of refugee protection to the attention of the Council of the League.

On the death of Dr Nansen in 1930, the Nansen International Office for Refugees was created by the League's Assembly, an autonomous body responsible for the exercise of functions of humanitarian assistance.

While the League had identified traffic in women and children and, later, child welfare as suitable objects of concern and study, its operational assistance was addressed to refugees and not specifically to children.

Save the Children Fund (SCF)

The Fund preceded the creation of UNICEF as a non-governmental organization entirely dedicated to the relief and welfare of children. From its birth in 1919 as a British charity collecting funds to provide food and clothes to foreign children in European war-devastated countries, it has now developed into the International Save the Children Alliance, grouping 26 national Save the Children organizations. The Alliance focuses on coordination in emergency situations and on providing long-term sustainable solutions for children and their communities in more than 100 countries. In 1999, the Alliance had a combined annual budget of almost \$400 million, almost half of UNICEF's annual budget. An independent NGO, the SCF also works as one of UNICEF's many operational partners.[3]

In 1913, at the request of the Macedonian Relief Fund in London, Eglantyne Jebb, an English woman of 37, went to Macedonia to deliver relief money following the Balkan wars which had stricken the area. Jebb's distress at the finding that so many children were abandoned and suffering was at the origin of the creation of the Fund in 1919. The SCF first embarked on a programme of feeding starving children in Europe, including ex-enemy countries whose populations had suffered from the Allied blockade. It worked through existing organizations with similar aims. Large grants were made available to feed and clothe children in Austria, Germany and Hungary, but also in France, Serbia and Armenia.

In January 1920, Jebb created the 'Save the Children International Union' in Geneva with the International Committee of the Red Cross, SCF/UK and a Swiss Committee as members. The Swedish Rädda Barnen and the French Comité de secours aux enfants joined the Union, followed by organizations in South Africa, Australia, Canada, Ireland, Germany, the Netherlands, Italy and Turkey. In an effort to fight the Russian famine of 1921, the SCF sent its own teams who acted as agents to administer relief for 14 different national member organizations of the Union. Over two years, up to 300 000 children had been fed. The Union originally instituted relief action, with the emergency distribution of food. It later set up homes, clinics and hospitals, and provided qualified social workers to help in planning and establishing national child welfare councils. It established the system of child sponsorship, now applied by many organizations in different regions, and established the central clearing station for information known as the Child Welfare Information Center, originally placed under the authority of the League of Nations.

In 1944, the Union amalgamated with the 'International Association for the Promotion of Child Welfare' to form the 'International Union for Child Welfare', which was disbanded in 1946. The International Save the Children Alliance was created in 1979. Its current seat is in London.

In 1923, Jebb drafted her 'Charter of the Rights of the Child', known as the 'Declaration of Geneva' (see Figure 1.1). Jebb wanted to give a focus and broad unifying principles to a growing interest in international child welfare. In substance, her rationale was that children are the most important part of mankind, as the nations of tomorrow. In her words:

> If they are allowed to grow up stunted or neglected or strangers to moral values, or are ignored in their misery by the more fortunate, they will inevitably grow up to hate and destroy, and tomorrow's world can only end up in disaster, politically and economically.

By the present Declaration of the Rights of the Child, commonly known as the Declaration of Geneva, men and women of all nations, recognizing that Mankind owes to the Child the best it has to give, declare and accept it as their duty to meet this obligation in all respects:

  I. THE CHILD must be protected beyond and above all considerations of race, nationality or creed.
  II. THE CHILD must be cared for with due respect for the family as an entity.
  III. THE CHILD must be given the means requisite for its normal development, materially, morally and spiritually.
  IV. THE CHILD that is hungry must be fed, the child that is sick must be nursed, the child that is physically or mentally handicapped must be helped, the maladjusted child must be re-educated, the orphan and the waif must be sheltered and succoured.
  V. THE CHILD must be the first to receive relief in times of distress.
  VI. THE CHILD must enjoy the full benefits provided by social welfare and social security schemes, must receive a training which will enable it, at the right time, to earn a livelihood, and must be protected against every form of exploitation.
  VII. THE CHILD must be brought up in the consciousness that its talents must be devoted to the service of its fellow men.

Source: Kathleen Freeman, *If Any Man Build: The History of Save the Children Fund* (London: Hodder & Stoughton, 1965), Appendix A, pp. 147–8. Declaration drafted in 1923 by Eglantyne Jebb, revised in 1948.

Figure 1.1 The Declaration of Geneva

In 1924, the Declaration was adopted by the League of Nations and became the 'Charter of Child Welfare of the League of Nations'. As will be seen later (Chapters 2 and 7), the UN proclaimed its own Declaration of the Rights of the Child in 1959, followed by the Convention on the Rights of the Child in 1989.

As a pioneer in this specialized field, the SCF had early on adopted policies and practices which may have guided or helped the founders and the leaders of UNICEF.

An important principle, contained in the Geneva Declaration, was that children should be helped beyond and above any consideration of race, nationality or creed. One of Jebb's revolutionary ideas was that modern charity 'must have the same clear conceptions of its objects and seek to compass them with the same care, the same thoroughness, the same intelligence as are to be found in the best commercial and industrial enterprises': in other words, compassion should allow for, or be supported by, good management. Another innovation was Jebb's firm belief that the message should be sent through 'wide, systematic and persevering propaganda' in order to attract more funds. Jebb employed a professional publicist whose policy was to adapt to the needs of philanthropy methods which had hitherto been reserved for the publicizing of 'patent medicines': 'charity business' had been invented, for a good cause.

The principles of Jebb have been summarized as follows:

- that aid should be given in a planned, scientific manner;
- that aid should be preceded by careful research;
- that it should be directed towards the family;
- that it should be given on the basis of need and not on any sectarian basis;
- that it should be constructive, self-sustaining;
- that it should stimulate self-help;
- that it should be pioneering, and able to develop models for others to follow.

These principles have been updated by the present SCF to include a commitment to the realization of children's rights and an opposition to any form of discrimination on the basis of age, belief, political views, gender, culture, ethnicity, sexuality and disability. The SCF is also committed to balance a response to short-term needs (e.g. in relief work) with longer-term development work, and to maintain a careful balance between working where it can be most effective in achieving influence and impact and a special commitment to the poorest and most marginalized children. Finally, SCF is determined to protect its independence as an organization, both in funding and in programming.

Save the Children/US received in March 2000 a $50 million, five-year grant from the Bill and Melinda Gates Foundation to save newborn lives worldwide. The grant will support the first phase of the ten-year Saving Newborn Lives global initiative to reduce the estimated 5.4 million annual deaths of newborn (infants in their first month of life). This award represents the largest private grant to Save the Children/US in its 68-year history. Save the Children/US will lead this initiative in partnership with prominent technical and academic institutions, NGOs and government agencies in at least six to eight developing countries, particularly in Asia and Africa.[4]

Has Save the Children become a competitor to UNICEF, rather than only an occasional partner? Whatever the case, this development shows the growing relevance and impact of NGOs in the field of children's welfare, as in others, in relation to intergovernmental organizations and governments.

The United Nations Relief and Rehabilitation Administration (UNRRA)

UNRRA was created in November 1943 in Washington with a membership of over forty countries and dominions as a temporary intergovernmental organization, the term United Nations being used to describe the war alliance between the USA, the UK and the USSR. The agency's mandate was to help the war-devastated countries of Europe and Asia to meet their immediate relief needs for food, clothing and medical supplies and to rebuild their economic and social fabric. Supplies were delivered to governments, which were responsible for internal distribution to their population. UNRRA's relief assistance was not specifically addressed to children, although they were, with their families, among the beneficiaries.

However, the link to international children's welfare is that UNRRA's sudden demise, in 1946, was at the origin of the creation of UNICEF, due to a large extent to the determined action and leadership of Dr Ludwik Rajchman.[5]

Dr Rajchman (1881–1965), a Polish national, was a pioneer in international public health. As Medical Director of the Health Organization of the League of Nations from 1921 to 1939, he earned a high reputation as a medical visionary with unparalleled experience in the international politics of health, in the words of Maggie Black.[6] Dr Wallace Aykroid, who had been on his staff and later became the Director of the Nutrition Division in the FAO of the UN, described him as the 'most remarkable human being' he had met. Ideally suited to play an important part in setting up the World Health Organization (WHO) he was considered by some of his US colleagues as a 'doctrinaire left-winger': many found him too radical in his ideas and too efficient in their realization. They ensured his rejection from the creation of WHO. WHO's loss, however, proved to be UNICEF's gain, as Dr Rajchman decided to place his experience, his talents and his energy at the service of children worldwide. He played a major role in the creation of UNICEF and in the orientation of its policies and programmes, ensuring that its functions would extend to more than just feeding hungry children.

During the three and a half years of its life, UNRRA provided essential relief and rehabilitation supplies to around 25 countries in Central and Eastern Europe, Asia and Africa. One priority was to rebuild communications and transport systems so that relief could be distributed. The agency provided supplies of fats and cereals, seeds, fertilizer and agricultural machinery, cattle and livestock, raw materials and tools. UNRRA was also active in public health: it was particularly successful in controlling typhus, malaria and cholera.

In 1945 and 1946, the peak period of its operations, UNRRA had 15 000 international staff and 35 000 local employees on its payroll, and had spent nearly $4 billion in aid. In spite of its achievements, the agency was exposed to constant criticism from the US. There were accusations of mismanagement, both among its own officials and among the officials of governments who received UNRRA supplies. The main problem was, however, political, resulting from the incipient Cold War: most of the agency's beneficiaries were Eastern European countries under Soviet influence or domination, while the US provided over 70 per cent of UNRRA's income – together with the UK and Canada, the joint proportion amounted to over 90 per cent. Political confrontation had taken place in relation to displaced persons: Eastern European governments claimed that their nationals had no choice but to return to their home countries, while UNRRA, under western influence, maintained that the individual alone could decide what he or she wished to do.[7]

In 1946, President Harry Truman asked Herbert Hoover to survey the world food situation. Following a tour of 38 countries in 82 days, Hoover found that the first expression of famine was to be found in children.

In a radio address in June 1946 from Ottawa to the people of America, he declared:

Disease and mortality among the little ones are over the sensitive barometers of starvation and poverty. Several nations have done the best they could ... and the scattered charitable agencies are doing the best they can in limited areas. But they are only touching the fringe of the problems ... There are somewhere from twenty to thirty million physically subnormal children on the Continent of Europe, and there are other millions in Asia ... I would like to suggest that the redemption of those children be organized at once by the Emergency Food Council of the United Nations and that all nations be called upon to contribute to its cost ...[8]

At the fifth session of the UNRRA Council, held in Geneva in August 1946, Fiorello LaGuardia, its new Director-General, had to announce that the US was withdrawing, which meant the demise of the agency. Plans were then made for the dissolution of UNRRA and the transfer of its activities and funds to UN specialized agencies: health to the Interim Commission of the future WHO, agriculture to the FAO, displaced persons to the Preparatory Commission of the International Refugee Organization and other functions to the UN or UN bodies responsible to its Economic and Social Council.

However, Dr Rajchman, who had opposed UNRRA's dissolution, proposed using the residual funds to help children, the primary victims of the war, with the support of the UK. The Council finally approved Rajchman's motion, in spite of objections that such a fund would upset the organizational pattern of the UN system.

Among other resolutions concerning other UN agencies, the Council recognized that 'The rehabilitation of the children and adolescents of countries which were the victims of aggression is of paramount importance for the achievement of recovery' and that international assistance would be desirable for the completion of national programmes and for the coordination of the work of governments and voluntary agencies. The Council then resolved, in part:

1. That such assets as the Central [UNRRA] Committee may determine to be available after the completion of the work of UNRRA shall be utilized for the benefit of children and adolescents.

2. That such purpose might effectively and appropriately be served by the creation of an International Children's Fund to which such assets would be transferred together with any gifts for this purpose and for child health purposes generally, which may be made by governments, voluntary agencies, individuals and other sources.[9]

Was this Fund to be a UN specialized agency? If so, long delays were to be expected, with the setting up of an interim commission and the drafting of a treaty, convention or constitution, then to be ratified by a set number of countries. Alfred Davidson, legal advisor to UNRRA, reassured Rajchman that the UN General Assembly could create a subsidiary body under its own authority (under Article 7.2 of the UN Charter). Furthermore, Davidson argued that women and children, i.e. a civilian population, constituted an 'apolitical' domain, and it would be difficult for UN delegates to raise objections.[10]

The 14-nation Standing Committee on the Rehabilitation of Children and Adolescents, created by the UNRRA Council, drew up a draft constitution for the Fund, in consultation with ECOSOC and the UN secretariat. On 30 September 1946, LaGuardia officially presented the proposal to ECOSOC with his full and convincing support: he felt sure that the proposed activity, the care of children of the world, would meet with the enthusiastic unanimity of the Council and the General Assembly. He did not hide the fact that such work would be costly: 'You cannot provide for millions of children without necessarily entailing great expenses.' However, it was the 'very best investment that the concerted efforts of nations could possibly make'. Realistically, he said that scientific and technical knowledge and assistance must be complemented with food, medical supplies and clothes, everything that is needed to protect that child or to save its life. He thanked Dr Rajchman for sponsoring and guiding the proposal through the Central Committee of UNRRA and the Standing Committee. The proposal was approved, on the understanding that no specialized agency would be established, but only a simple machinery to collect funds and distribute material.[11]

The Council decided that a draft resolution could be submitted to the General Assembly before the end of the year. Rajchman and John Charnow, a young State Department official who joined UNICEF later, worked on the draft resolution and its justification. The justification for the final proposal stated in part:

> The children of Europe and China were not only deprived of food for several cruel years, but lived in a constant state of terror, witnesses to massacre of civilians, to the horrors of scientific warfare and exposed to a progressive lowering of standards of social conduct. The urgent problem facing the United Nations is how to ensure the survival of these children. Millions of adults have emerged from the war not as fit to meet the grave problems of the day as they were in 1939. The hope of the world rests on the coming generation ... War has destroyed

numerous children's institutions and services and their technical management. In some cases physicians and nurses have been reduced to one-half of pre-war strength on account of extermination by aggressors, by warfare, and lack of training facilities.

Undernourishment, nutritional and social diseases are rampant among children and adolescents. Infant mortality was doubled or trebled in numerous areas. Millions of orphans are being cared for under most deplorable conditions, crippled children in untold thousands are left with the scantiest care or no care at all.[12]

The creation and mandate of UNICEF

On 11 December 1946, the UN General Assembly endorsed ECOSOC's recommendation in adopting unanimously Resolution 57 (I) creating an International Children's Emergency Fund. The Fund was to be utilized and administered, to the extent of its available resources:

(a) For the benefit of children and adolescents of countries which were victims of aggression and in order to assist in their rehabilitation;
(b) For the benefit of children and adolescents of countries at present receiving assistance from the United Nations Relief and Rehabilitation Administration;
(c) For child health purposes generally, giving high priority to the children of countries victims of aggression.

The Fund was therefore in part a successor to UNRRA in the specific field of child support, but its scope was broader in this field, first in extending its assistance to children and adolescents not receiving UNRRA assistance, and second in being made responsible for child health generally.

The Fund would finance or arrange for the provision of supplies, material, services and technical assistance and coordinate related activities. Its assistance would be provided on the basis of need, without discrimination because of race, creed, nationality, status or political belief. The Fund was not to engage in activity in any country except in consultation with, and with the consent of, the government concerned. The Fund would cooperate with all voluntary relief agencies, and appeal to them to continue and intensify their activities.

An Executive Director, appointed by the UN Secretary-General in consultation with the Executive Board, would administer the Fund. The

Executive Board was to be composed of representatives of 25 governments, including the five permanent members of the Security Council,
in accordance with an unwritten rule applying to most UN bodies. The
Board would elect its own Chairman and Vice-Chairmen. A link was
established with specialized agencies and in particular with the future
WHO: to the maximum extent feasible, these agencies' staff and
technical assistance should be requested with a view to reducing to a
minimum the separate personnel requirements of the Fund. Principally,
WHO's technical domain was to be protected from the possible
expansion of the new Fund's activities and staffing. Its resources were
to be provided by remaining UNRRA assets and voluntary contributions
from governments, voluntary agencies, individual or other sources. The
Fund was given most of UNRRA's residual resources, $31 538 436 out of a
total of more than $48.2 million. In addition, out of the $4 million given
to WHO, $1 million was a trust to be used for a relief programme for
children run by UNICEF.[13]

On 19 December, at its first meeting, the Executive Board elected Dr
Rajchman as its Chairman. In January 1947, Maurice Pate was appointed
as UNICEF's first Executive Director. Pate was Rajchman's choice, with
Hoover's support: in order to gain and maintain US support for the Fund,
the candidate had to be an American, a humanitarian and a Republican:
Pate fitted all categories. He had served on Hoover's staff in Belgium
during the First World War, he had been active in Polish relief during the
Second and he had been one of Hoover's assistants during the latter's
world mission in 1946. Pate accepted the appointment 'on one condition,
namely that it include all children of ex-enemy countries: Japanese,
Finnish, Austrian, Italian, and German', following Eglantyne Jebb's
contention that there was no such thing as an 'enemy child'. This
condition was privately agreed to by the members of the UNICEF
Executive Board. A few days after his appointment, Pate wrote to the US
Secretary of State asking for one hundred million dollars 'to provide a glass
of milk and some fat to be spread on bread – the bread to be furnished by
the aided countries – for six million hungry children in Europe and
China'. The US gave UNICEF $15 million, 'a fair initial payment' in Pate's
words.[14]

The disputed extension of the Fund

The fate of UNICEF remained uncertain until December 1950, when its
life was extended for three years. Three years later, in 1953, the General
Assembly lifted any time limit to its mandate.

In December 1949, the General Assembly seemed to legitimize the Fund by recognizing the important role it had been playing in the structure of the UN. Its resolution also congratulated the Fund, then in its third year of operations, for its great humanitarian effort in Europe and in the Middle East, being extended to Asia, Latin America and Africa, in bringing substantial aid of lasting value, through feeeding, medical and related programmes, to millions of mothers and children. It approved the decision of the Fund's Executive Board to devote a greater share of the Fund's resources to the development of programmes outside Europe.[15]

However, the four permanent specialized agencies directly concerned with UNICEF's programmes, ILO, FAO, UNESCO and especially WHO, were opposed to the extension of the Fund. In May 1950, their Directors-General made it clear at the seventh session of the Administrative Committee on Coordination (ACC) that, apart from relief, every aspect of a long-term programme outlined in a report of the UN Secretary-General already formed part of the programmes either of their respective agencies or of the UN. While the Directors-General subscribed fully to the importance of maintaining a UN fund-raising and supply organization, it was (for them) clearly necessary to avoid any long-term arrangement which would involve overlapping responsibilities for the formulation and execution of programmes on behalf of children. It would be undesirable to establish a machinery which would in fact constitute a specialized agency. ACC emphasized that the creation of international organizations with wide responsibilities for a particular age group or other special section of the population would cut across the whole of the existing organizational structure of the UN and the specialized agencies.

The four agencies wanted to replace UNICEF by a subsidiary intergovernmental body within the UN proper, a programme-making and coordinating committee consisting of the executive heads of the UN and agencies concerned, and an 'administrative unit' to direct the campaign for 'contributions and other functions'. UNICEF was in fact to be liquidated as an autonomous, separate agency.

Already in July 1948, the First World Health Assembly had found that UNICEF's health projects fell within WHO's competence and declared that WHO was ready and willing to handle these projects as soon as suitable arrangements could be made. In May 1949, the WHO members of the Joint Committee on Health Policy (UNICEF/WHO) had expressed some concern over the expansion of technical staff and health activities within UNICEF, and concern that a second UN agency, operating in WHO's field, might develop from UNICEF.[16]

On the other hand, in April 1950, the Social Commission of the General Assembly took a pro-UNICEF position. It considered that UNICEF had been one of the most promising achievements of the UN and that it had extended the influence of the Organization by contributing effectively to the betterment of the situation of children in the world. It recommended to ECOSOC to ensure the uninterrupted continuation and development of UNICEF's activities.[17]

On 11 August 1950, ECOSOC proposed in Resolution 310 (XI) the replacement of UNICEF by a UN International Children's Endowment Fund with a new structure somewhat similar to that recommended by ACC. More specifically, the specialized agencies would develop and give technical approval, in their field, to all programmes of assistance to governments to be presented to the new UN Children's Board, an intergovernmental body. The administration of the new Fund would be assisted by an advisory committee composed of representatives of the UN and of the specialized agencies in order to coordinate cooperation with these organizations. Central administrative expenses would be covered by appropriations in the UN regular budget. Operational expenses would be financed by voluntary contributions. As requested by ECOSOC, the Secretary-General prepared a draft resolution incorporating these proposals, to be effective on 1 January 1951, for presentation to the General Assembly.

The debates at the Third Committee of the General Assembly on the proposed substitution of a UN International Children's Endowment Fund to UNICEF started on 6 October with an introduction by the (French) Assistant Secretary-General in charge of the Department of Social Affairs. When presenting the draft resolution,[18] he raised one of the sensitive points at issue, i.e. whether the establishment of an endowment fund simply meant a change of name and terms of reference, or whether it involved dissolution of one body with the necessary winding up of its finances and the creation of a new body.

The US delegate, Mrs Roosevelt, supported the draft resolution. She recalled that the US government had contributed two-thirds of the $148 million received by UNICEF, plus private contributions by US citizens exceeding this sum. However, as early as June 1949, the US government had expressed the view that the emergency for which UNICEF had been created was drawing to a close, and that the long-range needs of the children should be studied in order to determine which of those needs could be met on a continuing basis within the UN structure. The US opposition to an extension of the Fund could be explained in part by internal political and financial reasons, and in part by the antagonism of a few key US officials towards Rajchman. It was rationally based on the assumption that UNICEF's work could and should be taken over by the specialized agencies. Most western countries initially supported the US position.

Different views were expressed by other delegates. In particular, the delegate from Yugoslavia wanted UNICEF's assistance to continue. Its organizational structure had proved to be efficient and its administrative apparatus was cheaper than that of any of the other international organizations. There was no need to establish a new body or to reorganize UNICEF's existing machinery. UNICEF had become the common property of millions of ordinary men and women all over the world who regarded the problem of children as a common problem of modern society. The delegate from Pakistan was blunt: the draft resolution was in the nature of a funeral oration for UNICEF. The main point raised by the US delegate that the emergency was over was an illusion. The UK delegate proposed that the Fund, which had worked efficiently and promptly in emergencies without bureaucratic delays, be continued for two years. The Indian delegate felt it would be a pity that UNICEF be transformed into an advisory organ. The Fund did not need more coordination. It gave food to the hungry and medical aid to the sick, it saved the lives of children and gave fresh hope to mankind that by a joint disinterested effort the world could be made a better place to live in. Several other delegates wanted UNICEF to continue its work in a wider field, or to become permanent.

On 16 October, the Yugoslav delegate proposed two amendments to the draft resolution and other proposed amendments, which reversed its initial intent: the General Assembly would again consider UNICEF's future in three years' time, 'with the object of continuing the Fund on a permanent basis'. The adoption of the Yugoslav amendments (by 35 votes to 8, with 5 abstentions) saved UNICEF's life, at least temporarily. It was also agreed to change the title of the agenda item and of the draft resolution to read: 'Continuing needs of children. United Nations International Children's Emergency Fund', the word 'Emergency' replacing 'Endowment'.[19] On 1 December 1950, the General Assembly adopted Resolution 417 (V). UNICEF was to continue its activities for another three years on the same principles as previously prescribed by the Assembly. The Assembly approved the policy of the Executive Board of the Fund to devote a greater share of its resources to the development of programmes outside Europe. The only change was to reconstitute the Fund's Executive Board as from 1 January 1951 to consist of the governments of the states represented on the Social Commission and the governments of eight other states, not necessarily members of the UN – this to allow the nomination of Switzerland.

However, a number of Third World countries and UNICEF staff were careful about not publicizing the extension of the Fund as a defeat for the US, whose renewed support and funding were essential for the future of UNICEF.

Three years later, the climate of the debate in the General Assembly had totally changed. Following a unanimous recommendation of ECOSOC that UNICEF should continue its work on a permanent basis, it was then decided to refer the item 'Continuation of the United Nations International Children's Emergency Fund' directly to the General Assembly without reference to the Third Committee. All delegations heaped high praise on the work of UNICEF and adopted unanimously the nine-Power draft resolution. Resolution 802 (VIII) adopted on 6 October 1953 removed any reference to time-limits in previous resolutions and decided to change the name of the organization to the United Nations Children's Fund, retaining the symbol UNICEF.[20]

Conclusion

UNICEF was finally given permanency. Attempts to end its activities had been based on two points. One, the emergencies for which it had been created were over, so the agency should be disbanded. Two, setting up a UN agency dealing with an age group made no sense: it cut across the mandates of specialized UN agencies, potentially causing duplication and conflicts, a waste of human and financial resources. UNICEF promoters had no problems proving that emergencies continued, albeit in other regions than Europe. The new agency's expansion into other areas than relief work also justified its role.

On the other hand, the specialized agencies' 'concern' was justified. WHO's functions include, in part, 'to promote maternal and child health and welfare'[21] – why set up another UN agency to deal with children's health? The ILO's mandate includes the protection of children at work, UNESCO's work in education is mainly addressed to children, and the FAO's functions in the field of nutrition do not exclude children. The theoretical justification to create a separate UN children's agency on a permanent basis could only be to give it functions separate, complementary to those of the specialized agencies, or functions for which the specialized agencies were not well equipped or willing to assume. In the first seven years of its activities, UNICEF fulfilled these unwritten requirements by being mainly an operational agency. Instead of giving sound public health advice to ministries of health, as WHO does, UNICEF gave material assistance to countries in the form of food, clothing, medicines, health and other equipment. Other arguments in favour of the continuation of the Fund included its capacity to collect voluntary funding, its effectiveness, its light and flexible management and its low administrative costs.

Besides these rational and practical arguments, the birth of UNICEF as a separate agency, following UNRRA's demise, was mainly due to the support and initiatives of a number of individuals, first to the support of Herbert Hoover, then to the political skills and technical competence of Dr Rajchman and the support of British diplomat Philip Noël-Baker, of New York Governor Herbert Lehman, of Professor Robert Debré, a renowned French paediatrician and others. UNICEF's growth and continuation as a permanent agency was primarily due to the success of the agency's programmes, itself due to the devotion and efficiency of its first Executive Director, Maurice Pate, and his staff, under the leadership and guidance of Rajchman as Chairman of the UNICEF Executive Board. The praise lavished on UNICEF by many delegates of Third World countries during the 1950 debates at the Third Committee contributed decisively to the decision to extend UNICEF for three years, which led in 1953 to making its status permanent.

The final and weightiest argument is that the cause of children is universally recognized as a priority and essential concern. Who would vote against children's welfare and health?

2
An Expanding Mandate

The 1946 resolution of the UN General Assembly which created UNICEF defined its beneficiaries as 'children and adolescents of countries which were victims of aggression' and of countries receiving assistance from UNRRA. The assistance of the new institution would consist of the provision of supplies, material, services and technical assistance on a non-discrimination basis. Its mandate would include the rehabilitation of children and child health generally. The 1950 resolution, which extended UNICEF's life for three years, approved the geographic expansion of its programmes 'outside Europe' and placed the Fund in the category of the UN development agencies: it was to support national programmes designed to aid children within the framework of existing UN activities for promoting the economic and social development of underdeveloped areas. In addition to emergency work and the provision of supplies, UNICEF was to provide training and advice, meet the long-range needs of children particularly in underdeveloped countries and strengthen the permanent child health and child welfare programmes of the countries receiving assistance. The 1953 resolution, which made UNICEF permanent, also linked its activities to the long-range economic and social programmes of the UN.

UNICEF is now a well-established, universally recognized and prestigious institution, the sole UN body devoted only to children, a development agency with relief assistance functions. In 1998, financial contributions to its budget amounted to $966 million, its programmes extended to 161 countries, and it employed approximately 5600 persons, including national officers, at its headquarters in New York, its 8 regional offices and 125 country offices worldwide. Its current programmes cover health, including reproductive health, nutrition, safe water and sanitation, education, child labour, child victims of armed conflicts and discrimination against women. UNICEF is also the lead UN agency helping governments to implement the Convention on the Rights of the Child.

UNICEF's original mandate explicitly refers to children and adolescents: UN General Assembly Resolution 57(1) of 11 December 1946 establishing UNICEF does not set an age limit for its beneficiaries. A 1969 resolution referred to the unmet needs of 'one thousand million children under fifteen years of age living in developing countries'. The UNICEF Executive Board confirmed this age range in 1969. Article 1 of the Convention on the Rights of the Child defines a child as 'every human being below the age of 18 unless, under the law applicable to the child, majority is attained earlier'. Later General Assembly resolutions and decisions of the UNICEF Executive Board extended the mandate of the Fund to women, especially mothers and poorer women.[1]

This chapter is an overview of the evolution of UNICEF from its difficult birth as an unwanted UN body to a successful, highly visible UN institution with extensive activities. Specific programmes are reviewed in more detail and assessed in later chapters.

This evolution is presented in four periods corresponding to the terms of office of its four Executive Directors. While changing programmes were due to an extent to the leadership of the Executive Directors with the support and advice of their staff, the orientation of the Fund's programmes was often initiated and promoted by Presidents of the Executive Board, such as Ludwik Rajchman, Robert Debré and Zena Harman. The approval of programmes is dependent on decisions by the UNICEF Executive Board. They are also contingent on resolutions of the UN General Assembly and of governing boards of other UN agencies. More generally, UNICEF's evolution was triggered by, accompanied or followed broad political, military, economic, social and scientific changes. These have included, among others, decolonization, the Cold War and its end, international and civil conflicts, natural emergencies, evolving development and public health concepts, medical and technological progress, globalization and the increasing role of the new 'civil society' partners. A number of these changes are illustrated by International Conferences or International Days or Years – they were the object of international conventions, or were publicized by catchy slogans. Note should also be taken that initiatives credited hereunder to one Executive Director may have been the result of previous efforts of the preceding Executive Director before the end of his term of office.[2]

Maurice Pate – 1947–1965

Maurice Pate, born in Nebraska (USA) on 14 October 1894, was briefly a banker and businessman. He went to work for Herbert Hoover's Commission for Relief in Belgium during the First World War. At the end of the war, Hoover assigned him to head the child-feeding operation which the American relief operation was undertaking in Poland. During the Second World War, he organized the privately operated Commission for Polish Relief and, later, joined the American Red Cross as director of relief to prisoners of war. Pate accompanied Hoover on a survey of the world food situation in 1946. In January 1947, Pate was appointed as UNICEF's first Executive Director.[3]

Relief and mass disease campaigns – from 1947 into the 1950s

The original *raison d'être* of UNICEF was emergency relief. In the period 1947–50, its assistance was limited to war-devastated Europe, with some work involving Chinese children who were the victims of the civil war. At the peak of its operations, some six million children received daily food supplements in 50 000 centres spread over 12 countries.

In April 1948, $5 million was approved for China by the Executive Board, out of which $500 000 was to be used in Communist-held areas. Relief was therefore to be provided on both the Nationalist and the Communist sides, on the principle that children are above the political divide. In October 1949, the People's Republic of China was declared but not recognized by the UN. UNICEF operations in China were suspended in December 1951. The same principle of equal treatment for all children applied to assistance provided to children in defeated Germany and Austria, and in eastern European countries. For the latter, their takeover by Communist regimes and the Cold War caused the closure of UNICEF assistance and missions.[4]

In 1947, the Scandinavian Red Cross Societies sought assistance from UNICEF for an international tuberculosis campaign aimed at immunizing all uninfected European children. Eight million children were vaccinated in conjunction with WHO. WHO gave technical advice while UNICEF provided vaccines, syringes and vehicles. This was both the largest vaccination campaign ever undertaken and the first one to use the BCG vaccine outside the controlled circumstances of the clinic. The TB campaign had extended UNICEF's role from war-related relief into public health. Further mass campaigns to control or eradicate epidemic diseases extended beyond Europe to other continents. By the mid-1950s, 3.5 million children worldwide were being tested for TB every month and over 1 million vaccinated. The use of long-acting penicillin preparations in one single injection made it possible to cure millions of persons suffering from yaws. UNICEF was closely involved in a yaws campaign in Indonesia. By 1955, local teams of health professionals and lay workers were locating and treating over 100 000 yaws cases a month, while in Thailand nearly 1 million cases had been cured.

In May 1955, the World Health Assembly launched the malaria eradication programme with which UNICEF became associated. By the end of the 1960s, it was apparent that the programme had failed on account of a number of political, financial, managerial and technical problems. It was later replaced by a more modest control programme. By the end of the 1950s, almost half of UNICEF's aid – $12.2 million out of $25 million a year – was committed to mass campaigns against epidemic diseases, including malaria, TB, yaws, trachoma and leprosy.

In the early 1950s, investigations among children in Africa revealed widespread malnutrition. The prescribed medicine was protein through the provision of milk. In 1957, UNICEF used supplies of surplus skimmed milk offered without cost by the US as part of its programme to provide milk via schools and health facilities to 4.5 million children and to pregnant and nursing mothers. In Europe, UNICEF helped countries to develop their own conservation plants.

The UN Declaration of the Rights of the Child – 1959

Following the lead of Eglantyne Jebb and of the League of Nations, at the urging of the International Union for Child Welfare, the UN adopted on 20 November 1959 this non-binding Declaration, followed in 1979 by a binding Convention.[5] The new Declaration updated and expanded the 1924 Declaration. Among its ten Principles, it reaffirmed that the child, by reason of his physical and mental immaturity, needs special safeguards and care, including appropriate legal protection, before as well as after birth, and that every child was entitled to all rights without discrimination. It added that the child 'shall be entitled from his birth to a name and a nationality'. The child should enjoy the benefits of social security, adequate nutrition, housing, recreation and medical services. Special treatment, education and care should be given to physically, mentally or socially handicapped children. The child is entitled to receive free and compulsory education. He should be protected against all forms of neglect, cruelty and exploitation. He should not be employed before an appropriate minimum age. A link with UNICEF was set by another resolution adopted by the General Assembly on the same day, recognizing that 'the aid provided through the Fund constitutes a practical way of international cooperation to help countries to carry out the aims proclaimed by the Declaration of the Rights of the Child'.[6] This implicitly expanded UNICEF's role beyond emergency relief and general child health to child nutrition, education and protection.

The 1960s: the First Decade of Development

In January 1961, the General Assembly designated the 1960s as the UN Development Decade and called upon all member states to unite in a sustained effort to break through the cycle of poverty, hunger, ignorance and disease which afflicted much of the world. This was also the decade of decolonization: 17 former colonies in Africa achieved independence in 1960, and most newly independent countries, also exposed to the explosion of their population, needed development assistance.

In June 1961, Pate presented to his Executive Board a report, *Children of the Developing Countries*. The report was based on a survey initiated by UNICEF in 1960 which included state-of-the-art reports from the specialized agencies on children's needs in their specific field: WHO for health needs, the FAO and WHO for nutritional needs, UNESCO for educational needs, the UN Bureau of Social Affairs for social welfare needs, the ILO for work and livelihood needs. The report argued that children's needs should be built into national development plans. Henceforth, UNICEF would consider the needs of children along with those of their parents and would take into account the 'whole child'.

In order to join the development agencies' group, UNICEF had to prove that it was not only providing food and nutrition, and maternal and child health care. Its programmes extended into education, women's issues, water supplies and sanitation. In these areas, UNICEF provided material assistance in the form of equipment, drugs, vehicles and training stipends.

The year 1961 saw another key policy decision, that of adopting a flexible 'country approach'. The UNICEF Executive Board had applied policies to administer funds according to globally applicable principles and standards. In order to be eligible for assistance, a country had to meet several criteria that it often considered inappropriate. Pate reported in April 1961 that certain governments, when consulted on the different types of assistance currently offered by UNICEF, had indicated that they would like UNICEF policy to be deliberately directed towards what they themselves regarded as priority needs (i.e. needs considered not on a world scale but purely in their own domestic context), within the general context of a national policy of economic and social development. Pate said that UNICEF would be ready to assist countries in making surveys of children's needs and planning comprehensive long-term programmes. This meant that there would be a wide variety of country plans for children, ranging from comprehensive five- or ten-year plans to short-term and incomplete plans. UNICEF should respond sensitively to each unique situation.[7] Each project would be weighed on its own merits and according to the wishes of the receiving country. Priority would be given to those projects in which action had been determined to be both vitally necessary and feasible by the beneficiary country. The result of that decision was that programmes were considered by the administration to be more effective when they demonstrated an understanding of the interdependence of issues of health, nutrition, community development, education and social welfare. As noted by Weiss,[8] UNICEF's dynamism and flexibility were reflected in the decision on country programming, which anticipated in programmatic terms ten years ahead of its time the content of General Assembly Resolution 2626 (XXV). The Second Development Decade, starting in January 1971, was to be guided by the principle of country programming. It was only then that UNDP replaced its old system, under which projects were proposed and decided upon individually, by the country programming method.

In April 1964, a round table conference was convened under UNICEF's auspices at the Rockefeller Foundation Center in Bellagio, Italy bringing together a number of leading development economists and planning specialists and a high-level representation from developing countries to discuss planning for children in national development. It marked the formal introduction of UNICEF into the development community as a full-fledged member.

Maurice Pate died on 20 January 1965 in New York City. In 1965, UNICEF was awarded the Nobel Prize for Peace, a recognition for the agency and for the pioneering work of Pate.

Comments

As UNICEF's first Executive Director, Maurice Pate, a modest man and a man of integrity, played a crucial role in the firm establishment of the institution and of its credibility. In the words of Charnow:

> Pate imbued the organization with three main characteristics – a spirit of self-criticism, a willingness to learn from experience, and a deep sense of trusteeship for the funds contributed to it. In addition he firmly established UNICEF as a field-oriented organization, keeping the headquarters role to the minimum necessary.[9]

Another characteristic, unusual for a UN body, is its flexibility, which enabled it to make timely adjustments.

Pate initiated UNICEF's geographical expansion beyond Europe and its progressive conversion from a humanitarian to a development institution. He introduced the innovative country approach and planning for the 'whole child' in national development. He loosened the subordinate links between a dependent UNICEF and the UN specialized agencies, helping the new body to become an institution in its own right. Pate initiated the use of celebrities in a public relations campaign for UNICEF in enlisting the comedian Danny Kaye for a popular film, a television show and field tours, without costs to the agency.

Pate can also be credited for providing relief assistance to children in both sides of a civil conflict, and to children in Communist countries, even if this assistance was limited in time, exposed to criticisms from dominant donors and, in due time, rejected by the recipient authorities. These precedents set UNICEF apart from other UN bodies as an institution which attempted to circumvent the tight limits of national sovereignty in order to ensure that children's needs prevail over international or national politics. Finally, Pate created a strong motivation in his staff, an *esprit de corps* which the present UNICEF has maintained.

During Pate's term, UNICEF income from voluntary contributions varied from $59 million in 1948 (the high point in relief operations in Europe), to a low of $10.2 million in 1952, to $32.8 million in 1964.[10]

Henry R. Labouisse – 1965–1979

Henry R. Labouisse (US) was born on 11 February 1904 in New Orleans. He was Director of UNRWA from 1954 to 1958, and Director of the UN International Cooperation Administration in 1961. From 1962 to 1965, he served as US Ambassador to Greece. On the recommendation of Maurice Pate, he was appointed as Executive Director of UNICEF in 1965. He left UNICEF in 1979 and died on 25 March 1987 in New York City.[11]

Non-partisan relief

Following Pate's example, Labouisse maintained UNICEF's tradition of non-partisan relief to children and mothers in distress on both sides of civil conflict, albeit with careful diplomatic handling, in order not to upset governments or donors. During the Nigerian civil war (1967–70), UNICEF's assistance was to be channelled through the International Committee of the Red Cross with the utmost discretion. The needs of 'all Nigerian children' were to be given proportionately equal attention, and the agency was not to be perceived as supporting the rebels' cause.

Assistance had been given to Vietnam, then South Vietnam, since 1952. In 1967, Labouisse was instructed by the Executive Board to 'study ways and means whereby the help of UNICEF could be extended with the cooperation of Red Cross organizations, in emergency situations, to both parts of Vietnam'. Some assistance was provided to North Vietnam through channels opened by the League of Red Cross Societies. Following the forced reunification of Vietnam, a UNICEF mission was established in Hanoi.

After the successful intervention of the Vietnamese army in Cambodia in December 1978, the retreating Khmer Rouge forces took refuge in forest sanctuaries along the Thai border. The pro-Vietnamese government installed in Phnom Penh as the People's Republic of Kampuchea was not recognized by the UN. On 9 September 1979, the UN Secretary-General designated UNICEF as the lead agency in the UN system for the delivery of relief to Kampuchea. This extension of the UNICEF mandate beyond assistance to children and mothers, unwanted by the agency, circumvented the lack of UN recognition and allowed relief assistance to be provided to those in need by the World Food Programme and FAO, among other agencies, under the joint UNICEF/ICRC umbrella. In October, the Secretary-General asked UNICEF and the WFP to provide food and water to the populations under the control of the Khmer Rouge just across the Thai border.[12]

The Second Development Decade – 1971

On 24 October 1970, the UN General Assembly proclaimed the Second UN Development Decade to begin on 1 January 1971, and adopted an international development strategy for the decade. Member states pledged to pursue policies and measures to reduce the gap between rich and poor nations and to create a 'just' world economic and social order. While developing countries were primarily responsible for their own development, they were to be assisted through increased financial resources and more favourable economic and commercial policies on the part of developed countries. Several of the goals of the decade were of direct interest to UNICEF: all children of primary school age should be enrolled; illiteracy should be reduced; each country should formulate a coherent health programme; levels of nutrition should be improved with special emphasis on the needs of the vulnerable population groups; the well-being of children should be fostered; the full participation of youth in the development process should be ensured; and the full integration of women in the total development effort should be encouraged.

In spite of these exhortations, the gap between the industrialized countries and the developing countries continued to increase. The Bretton Woods monetary system instituted in 1944 had broken down in 1971. Soon after the outbreak of hostilities in the Middle East in October 1973, oil prices rose ending the era of cheap energy and cheap industrialization. In 1972 and 1974, two disastrous world harvests brought about a global food shortage. Increased prices of other commodities and manufactured goods and the growing burdens of external debt contributed to unstable conditions. The non-aligned countries declared in September 1973 in Algiers that the Second Development Decade had failed.

In 1974, the General Assembly adopted a resolution promoting a 'New International Economic Order'.[13] In part, the resolution called on WHO and its sister agencies to intensify the international effort at improving health conditions in developing countries by giving priority to prevention of diseases and malnutrition and by providing primary health care services to the communities, including maternal and child health and family welfare. This was of direct interest to UNICEF.

Also in 1974, the UNICEF Executive Board made a formal declaration of an 'Emergency for Children'. It was believed that even before the crisis struck, some 10 million children worldwide suffered severe dietary shortage.

A new public health policy – 1978

Following a survey by small teams mostly from UNICEF and WHO in nine countries, a joint UNICEF/WHO study, *Alternative Approaches to Meeting Basic Health Needs in Developing Countries*, was issued in 1975. The report declared: 'Firm national policy of providing health care for the under-privileged will involve a virtual revolution in most health systems.' It recommended that WHO and UNICEF 'should adopt an action programme aimed at extending primary health care to populations in developing countries'. It went so far as to advocate that 'the primary health care workers should be selected, when possible, by the community itself, or at least in consultation with the community – acceptability of such workers [being] in fact a crucial factor of success'. The study was endorsed in 1975 by the UNICEF Executive Board, which accepted its principles as UNICEF policy. In 1976, the Board committed itself to the basic services approach, which would be flexible enough to be adapted to and within the community. This approach had been tested in a number of community-based programmes in Guatemala, Indonesia and Tanzania, which had incorporated a spirit of volunteerism along with traditional systems of mutual self-help. UNICEF had trained and motivated lay members of the community to perform simple tasks such as baby weighing, early childhood stimulation and basic water handpump maintenance. These volunteers could thus act as 'barefoot' workers delivering local services.

In September 1978, an International Conference was convened jointly by UNICEF and WHO in Alma-Ata (USSR). Representatives of 134 countries participated, along with 67 delegates from the UN and some of its specialized agencies and NGO representatives. Henry R. Labouisse and Dr Halfdan Mahler, Director-General of WHO, had prepared a 49-page document that proved to be an invaluable reference tool and a source of inspiration for the Declaration of Alma-Ata, which was approved by acclamation at the final plenary session of the Conference. The Declaration affirmed that primary health care was the key to the attainment by all peoples of the world by the year 2000 of a level of health that will permit them to lead a socially and economically productive life, as part of development in the spirit of social justice. In May 1979, the World Health Assembly unanimously endorsed the Alma-Ata Declaration and adopted the strategy of Health for All as the main priority for WHO. In November 1979, the UN General Assembly also endorsed the Declaration, considering that cooperation among nations on vital health issues can contribute importantly to peace.

Primary health care is based on eight elements:

1. education concerning prevailing health problems and the methods of preventing and controlling them;
2. promotion of food supply and proper nutrition;
3. an adequate supply of safe water and basic sanitation;
4. maternal and child health care, including family planning;
5. immunization against the major infectious diseases;
6. prevention and control of locally endemic diseases;
7. appropriate treatment of common diseases and injuries;
8. provision of essential drugs.

Criticisms followed praise of the 'Health for All' declaration. Labelled as a utopian slogan without substance, Health for All was considered by some as a target which could not be reached by the year 2000. Were the leaders of member states ready to introduce radical changes in the existing health delivery systems, and ready to fight the political and technical battles required to overcome any social and economic obstacles and professional resistance to the universal introduction of primary health care? The periodic evaluations of the progress of the strategy revealed that problems were mostly economic.[14] In reality, major obstacles were national politics and governance (see also Chapter 4).

The International Year of the Child – 1979

The International Year of the Child (IYC) was first proposed in 1973 by Canon Joseph Moerman, a Belgian priest, Secretary-General of the International Catholic Child Bureau (ICCB). He obtained the enthusiastic support of a number of NGOs, including the International Union for Child Welfare, the YWCA and the World Council of Churches. It was first discussed by the UNICEF Executive Board in 1975. Its members were at first diffident, as was Labouisse himself. Moerman was able to convince Labouisse of the value of his proposal, generally for the cause of children and also in the direct interest of UNICEF. The Vatican was reticent towards the scheme initially although the Pope later congratulated UNICEF for its initiative. With the strong backing of NGOs, the proposal finally won support from governments, from the UN itself and UN agencies. In 1976, the UN General Assembly proclaimed 1979 as the International Year of the Child, on the twentieth anniversary of the Declaration of the Rights of the Child. It designated UNICEF 'the lead agency of the United Nations system responsible for coordinating the activities of the International Year of the Child'. In 1981, the General Assembly reaffirmed the role of UNICEF as 'the lead agency in the United Nations system responsible for coordinating the follow-up activities of the International Year of the Child related to the goals and objectives concerning children set forth in the International Development Strategy for the Third United Nations Development Decade'.[15]

The IYC is credited with creating greater interest in children at the international level, bringing UNICEF's attention to children's needs and special situations of which it had not previously taken much notice (for instance, the problems of street children), and drawing attention to the needs of children in industrialized countries as well. It broadened the scope of the Fund's advocacy and led to greater receptivity on the part of governments and funding agencies. It brought a substantial increase in NGO advocacy and action at international, national and local levels, and initiated the cooperation of NGOs not previously associated with UNICEF and the UN.[16] When he had launched this initiative, Moerman had felt that children, and those who care for them, were not considered important by politicians, other leaders and academics. For him, the main positive outcome of the IYC was to give worldwide recognition and respect to those who serve and care for children in various capacities.[17]

Comments

It was probably not easy for Labouisse to be a successor to the first Executive Director, who had firmly led UNICEF from infancy to adulthood. In the event, the successor was as quietly successful as Pate in assuring the healthy development of the agency. James P. Grant, his own successor, described him as a 'gentleman, an aristocrat, a humanitarian, a democrat and an egalitarian', qualities which he brought to bear in the cause of human development and child welfare.

The major conceptual and pragmatic innovation during Labouisse's tenure was the 'social revolution' in public health through the joint proposal and adoption by WHO and UNICEF of the Health for All strategy and of the primary health care process, stressing the importance of community participation and the integration of all health activities into an infrastructure of basic health services. As a useful clarification, Labouisse told the Executive Board in May 1966 that UNICEF's role in the field of development planning was not to duplicate the work of other organizations nor to advocate separate sectors for children. It was rather to focus attention on the important place of children and youth in development efforts, to encourage countries to take fuller account of them in their national plans, and to make sure that UNICEF's own assistance was in line with and gave full support to the priorities established in these plans. UNICEF was to be a catalyst, focusing attention on children's needs and providing aid that had a multiplier effect. What was needed was greater flexibility, ingenuity and exploration of unconventional methods.[18] This advice was taken to heart and successfully applied by his own successor, James P. Grant.

During Labouisse's terms of office, UNICEF's income from voluntary contributions increased from $33 million in 1965 to $285 million in 1979.

James P. Grant – 1980–1995

James P. Grant (US) was born in China on 12 May 1912. In 1946, he was a representative for UNRRA's relief programme to Communist-held areas in China. Grant worked for the US International Cooperation Administration, then the US Agency for International Development (USAID) in the 1950s and 1960s. In 1969, he became President of the Overseas Development Council in Washington, a private think-tank. UN Secretary-General Kurt Waldheim, after years of hesitation, finally appointed Grant, on the recommendation of the UNICEF Board, as Executive Director of UNICEF in 1979, as the US candidate to succeed Labouisse, in preference to a Swedish candidate. Sweden had insisted on the appointment of its candidate, in view of the high level of its financial contributions, and of contributions from Nordic countries, to the agency. This was the first, but not the last time, that the appointment of a US candidate to the post of Executive Director was challenged by European governments.

Grant resigned from his post on 23 January 1995 and died five days later, on 28 January 1995.[19]

The International Code of Marketing of Breast-Milk Substitutes – 1981

In 1981, the World Health Assembly adopted this Code as a recommendation under Article 23 of the WHO Constitution, by 118 votes in favour, 1 against (the USA) and 3 abstentions. The Code was the outcome of a joint WHO/UNICEF initiative, a challenge to important commercial interests, which caused violent polemics between NGOs and infant food-industry multinational companies, and subjected both WHO and UNICEF to US opposition and criticisms.

Since the 1950s, there had been an increase in industrialized countries in the shift from breast-feeding to artificial feeding of infants. The trend had spread to developing countries. NGOs were claiming that each year 10 million serious cases of malnutrition or infectious diseases could be directly attributable to improper bottle-feeding, and 10 per cent would result in deaths. Against the well-established advantages of breastfeeding, bottle-feeding may be dangerous in developing countries when the formula is mixed in unclean water. Furthermore, mothers may not be able to afford to buy and use an adequate amount of the product. In this context, the baby-food industry was accused of unethical aggressive marketing practices promoting excessive use of baby-food to the detriment of breast-feeding, thus creating an artificial demand.

Following a joint WHO/UNICEF meeting on infant malnutrition held in Bogota, Colombia in 1970, the two organizations convened a Meeting on Infant and Young Child Feeding in Geneva in 1979 which was attended by 150 representatives of WHO member states, UN organizations, professional associations and scientists, the infant food industry and NGOs. One of the recommendations of the meeting was to request WHO and UNICEF to prepare, in consultation with all the parties concerned, an international code of marketing of breast-milk substitutes.

The 1981 Code prohibits improper marketing practices of breast-milk substitutes. It forbids advertising or other forms of promotion of breast-milk substitutes or bottle feeding to the general public and mothers. It forbids the use by the health care system of 'mothercraft nurses' paid by the manufacturers or distributors. Labels on infant formula containers should include a statement of the superiority of breastfeeding. Governments should actively promote sound infant feeding.

The adoption of the Code was criticized in some health circles as an ideological move, not properly based on scientific data and ignoring many relevant factors. It was alleged that some of the activist NGOs who supported the Code were not trying to resolve the nutrition problems of the Third World's infants but rather the image of the infant food industry. UNICEF was criticized by the US government, which voted against the Code with the support of US manufacturers of breast-milk substitutes, in the name of free trade. According to a conservative US group, the Heritage Foundation, 'UNICEF had strayed from its primary path by collaborating with the WHO ... in monitoring the ... Code. This makes UNICEF a quasi-international regulatory agency, a function not authorized by the 1946 resolution that established the Charter for UNICEF.'[20]

In fact, the Code was voted as a recommendation, not as a regulation, and monitoring is essentially carried out by NGOs (see also Chapter 4).

The child survival and development revolution – 1982

In December 1982, Grant launched this other 'revolution' which was intended to reduce by half the estimated annual 15 million deaths of children under five.[21] He suggested a direct attack on infant and child mortality as an instrument of development. UNICEF proposed to fight against common infections of early childhood using simple medical technologies. From the eight elements of primary health care, four techniques were proposed in a package called GOBI: 'G' for growth monitoring to keep a regular check on children's health, nutrition and development; 'O' for oral rehydration therapy to treat diarrhoea, the largest cause of children's deaths; 'B' for breastfeeding as the perfect nutritional start in life; and 'I' for immunization against the six vaccine-preventable childhood diseases, tuberculosis, diphtheria, whooping cough, tetanus, poliomyelitis and measles. These technologies or practices are low-cost, except for the costs involved in promoting all the elements of the revolution. To GOBI were added two 'F's: food supplements and family planning, and, later, a third 'F', female education.

A round table conference was held at the Rockefeller Foundation Center in Bellagio (Italy) in April 1984, under UNICEF's auspices. The conference was called 'Children and Youth in National Development'. It included a number of leading development economists and planning specialists. One of the outcomes of the conference was the formation of the Task Force for Child Survival and Development, which associated UNICEF with

UNDP, WHO, the World Bank and the Rockefeller Foundation, and whose executive secretariat was provided by the Centers for Disease Control in Atlanta. The initial mandate of the Task Force was to accelerate immunization activities in a number of countries, to look at unresolved issues and to mobilize financial resources.[22]

The GOBI campaign (and later UNICEF programmes) was supported by a strategy of social mobilization. UNICEF enlisted the media and advertising industries, religious leaders and Goodwill Ambassadors, from heads of state to town mayors, from sports personalities to parliamentarians, from professional associations to trade unions, to join the movement and spread UNICEF's messages.

Initial opposition to GOBI from international health sectors, including WHO, is discussed in Chapter 4.

The silent emergencies – 1987

In the UNICEF report on the 1987 *State of the World's Children*, Grant described as 'silent emergencies', in contrast with more visible natural or man-made emergencies, the less dramatic continuum of death and human suffering imposed by poverty and ignorance, disease and malnutrition. He noted that over the previous two years, more children died in India and Pakistan than in most nations of Africa combined. 'In 1986, more children died in Bangladesh than in Ethiopia, more in Mexico than in the Sudan, more in Indonesia than in all eight drought-stricken countries of the Sahel.' The report added that by far the greatest emergency facing the world's children today was the silent emergency of frequent infection and widespread undernutrition: 'No "loud" emergency, no famine, no drought, no flood, has ever killed 280,000 children in a week.' The 'good news' was the provision by UNICEF and WHO of the proven low-cost technologies which can defeat infection and undernutrition among the world's children.

The report also argued for adjustment 'with a human face' which would incorporate debt rescheduling, improved aid flows, increased lending and 'greater access to the rich world's markets for the poor world's goods'. Economic adjustment policies of bodies like the International Monetary Fund have had a heavy impact on the poor. The report stressed that adjustment policies 'which allow children to be sacrificed for the sake of financial stability' were unacceptable.

The Bamako Initiative – 1987

This Initiative was announced by UNICEF in September 1987 in Bamako, Mali, at a meeting of African Ministers of Health sponsored by the WHO

Regional Office for Africa and UNICEF.[23] Its basic concept was to strengthen primary health care by financing it through selling drugs.

Grant played a direct and influential role in launching the Bamako Initiative, which provoked initial opposition from several public health sectors, including WHO. WHO was finally convinced to associate itself with the Initiative (see also Chapter 4). In practice, governments and donors generally provide the equipment, drugs, vaccines, salaries and training of health workers required to deliver a basic package of integrated services to Bamako Initiative health centres. Communities pay for at least part of the drugs and services they use, and many have taken over the purchase and management of drug supplies. The fees go into a revolving fund that can buy more supplies and services or go towards other community projects. Bamako principles are applied flexibly. UNICEF reported that in 1999 some 35 countries had adopted the basic strategy, mostly in Africa, plus a few countries in Asia and Latin America.

The eradication of poliomyelitis – 1988

In May 1988, the World Health Assembly declared the commitment of WHO to the global eradication of poliomyelitis by the year 2000. The Assembly thanked especially UNICEF for its overall efforts and Rotary International for its 'Polio Plus' initiative. UNICEF had been associated with WHO's Expanded Programme on Immunization since its creation in 1974, particularly in mobilizing political and financial support at international and national levels, and in providing vaccines and material for the cold chain (see Chapter 4).[24]

The Convention on the Rights of the Child – 1989

The initiative to draft a Convention on the Rights of the Child came mainly from NGOs and from a few governments. Grant and UNICEF were initially reluctant to be associated with its drafting: they were then more interested in the delivery of concrete benefits to children than in rights issues. As from 1987, Grant was finally convinced to join the promoters of the future Convention and UNICEF amended the draft by adding mention of 'the child's right to survival' and reinforcing rights to health care, food and nutrition, education and minimum standards of social provision, the mainstays of UNICEF's programmes of that period. Grant then started a determined campaign to convince delegates in UN intergovernmental fora, individual governments, parliamentarians, NGOs, the press and television media in both the industrialized and the developing worlds to give their support to the Convention.

The Convention was adopted by the UN General Assembly on 20 November 1989, and it entered into force in 1990. In 2000, it had been ratified by 191 out of 193 governments: the USA was a signatory but not a State Party, and Somalia (a failed state) had not signed or ratified the Convention. Although UNICEF was not given a monitoring role by the Convention, its adoption marked a significant evolution in the mission of UNICEF: by the mid-1990s, the Convention had become the unofficial constitution of the agency, with all its programmes directed towards the promotion of specific children's rights. It was the beginning of a strong orientation of UNICEF towards children's rights, in parallel with its more traditional functions.

More details on the Convention are given in Chapter 7.

Operation Lifeline Sudan – 1989

In April 1989, the UN launched Operation Lifeline Sudan. This operation was based on an agreement negotiated by the UN with the government of Sudan and the Sudan People's Liberation Movement and Army to allow humanitarian assistance to pass through 'corridors of tranquillity' to civilians on either side of the conflict. UN Secretary-General Perez de Cuellar appointed Grant as the leader of the operation, while he continued as Executive Director of UNICEF. The fact that Grant headed a relief effort, the major component of which was food, was an anomaly. One justification was that UNICEF had experience of working in civil war settings without giving diplomatic recognition to rebels. The UN staff assigned full-time to the operation numbered 175 – 86 from UNICEF, 78 from the WFP and 11 from UNDP. Grant made eight trips to the region to launch the operation and keep it moving. By the end of September 1989, when Grant handed over the leadership of Lifeline to Michael Priestley of UNDP, 88 per cent of the relief supplies – 103 000 tons of food and 4000 of medical and other non-food supplies – had been delivered to their destination. According to Larry Minear, 'Lifeline reflected the passionate commitment and boundless energy of James P. Grant who, as Personal Representative of the UN Secretary-General, was perhaps its single most influential force'.[25]

World Summit for Children – 1990

The Summit was held at the UN headquarters (though it was not a UN conference) on 29–30 September 1990, the result of Grant's initiative and efforts to obtain the agreement of heads of state and organizations to health, education and development goals for children. UNICEF had proposed the Summit in December 1988 to address problems and opportunities for children and to rally the political will and resources to meet their needs. In August 1989, the heads of state or governments of six countries agreed to convene the meeting. The planning committee was composed of representatives of WHO, UNESCO, UNFPA, the World Bank, the ILO and the UN, as well as 25 member states. 'Only something as dramatic and unprecedented as a summit meeting of world leaders to discuss the subject of children could significantly upgrade the priority which the world will give its children', noted UNICEF in describing this initiative. UNICEF hoped for a summit agreement on a plan for 'doing the things', nationally and internationally, 'we know can be done to save children's lives and protect their healthy growth and environment'.[26]

At the Summit, 71 world leaders and 153 governments and UN agencies committed themselves to achieving 27 specific health, education and development goals for children by the year 2000. National leaders jointly signed the summit's Declaration on the Survival, Protection and Development of Children and Plan of Action. The goals included targeted reductions in infant and maternal mortality, child malnutrition and illiteracy, as well as targeted levels of access to basic services for health and family planning, education, water and sanitation. The 27th goal was to provide improved protection to children in especially difficult circumstances (CEDC), and correction to tackle the root causes leading to such situations. UNICEF had taken an interest in this problem in the mid-1980s.

The funding strategy for attaining the Summit's goals was called the '20/20 initiative': a call for developing countries to direct at least 20 per cent of their budgets to basic needs, and for industrialized countries to earmark 20 per cent of their development assistance for the same purpose.

The Children's Vaccine Initiative was launched at the Summit by five sponsoring agencies: UNICEF, UNDP, the Rockefeller Foundation, the World Bank and WHO. In 1991, Grant told an interviewer that the commitments made at the Summit had produced increased support for the Convention and had led a considerable number of states to formulate national programmes of action to address children's needs, with the immediate effect of giving the WHO/UNICEF Expanded Programme of Immunization the boost it needed to reach a five-year goal right on target.[27]

International Conference on 'Education for All by the Year 2000' – 1990

This conference, co-sponsored by UNESCO, UNICEF, UNDP and the World Bank, was held in Jomtien (Thailand). The participants unanimously adopted a World Declaration and a Framework for Action to meet the basic learning needs of every person – child, youth and adult – in the world. Grant had tried already in 1982 to persuade UNESCO to collaborate on a major initiative to promote 'primary education for all'. It was only in 1989 that a Joint Committee on Education, consisting of representatives of the Executive Boards of UNESCO and UNICEF, was set up to promote collaboration between the two organizations.[28]

The Baby-Friendly Hospital Initiative – 1992

This Initiative was launched by UNICEF and WHO as a way of achieving goals outlined in two important documents: the 1990 Innocenti Declaration on the Protection, Promotion and Support of Breastfeeding and the World Summit for Children Declaration and Plan of Action. The Innocenti Declaration called for countries to promote breastfeeding by working towards four targets: appointment of a national breastfeeding coordinator; designation of 'baby-friendly' hospitals; enactment of laws to enforce the International Code of Marketing of Breastmilk Substitutes; and establishment of 'imaginative legislation' to ensure the breastfeeding rights of women employed outside their home.[29]

Comments

The three terms of office of Grant were filled with spectacular changes or advances in UNICEF's programmes and approach, which he carried out in spite of inter-agency hurdles and political opposition from a few member states. He designed and promoted the child survival and development revolution, with its clear and effective techniques easily understood and practised by health workers. He launched the Bamako Initiative, and pursued the WHO/UNICEF goal of immunizing 80 per cent of the world's children against six preventable diseases by the end of 1990. He pioneered the establishment of 'days of tranquillity' and the opening of 'corridors of peace' to provide immunization and other assistance to children in areas of armed conflict. Grant was a passionate and effective advocate of the Convention on the Rights of the Child and pushed for its universal ratification. He then reorientated UNICEF towards a 'rights' agency, in addition to its original role as an emergency and development organization. The 1990 World Summit was his crowning achievement, which defined specific, measurable goals to be reached by countries by the year 2000. Grant played a critical role in convincing the financial institutions of the need to build into adjustment programmes measures to safeguard the poor and the children.

Grant was a humanitarian crusader, a practical man of action and a skilful public relations man who used marketing techniques to promote children's welfare. He argued that the only way to make countries adopt better policies was to address their top people, chiefs of state and heads of government. He always carried in his pocket a small sachet of oral rehydration salts, which he readily showed in his meetings with his high-level hosts or guests.

On the negative side, Grant was criticized for launching too many new schemes too quickly and without proper consultation with other agencies, creating problems of implementation at country level for his staff. He was also deemed to be authoritarian, and less participative with his staff than his two predecessors.

US conservative circles criticized him for some of his initiatives: the narrow focus of the Marketing Code, UNICEF's 'creeping politicization' in discussing disarmament and the New International Economic Order, a reflexive anti-western rhetoric and anti-free market arguments which, in US views, has undermined other UN agencies. Grant received honours from many countries, including the US Medal of Honor, the highest civilian honour conferred by a US president. Boutros Boutros-Ghali, the former UN Secretary-General, said appropriately:

> There are hundreds of millions of children in the developing world who may never know the name of James P. Grant, but whose survival, health, growth and education have benefited, practically and measurably, from his extraordinary efforts on their behalf.[30]

During Grant's terms of office, UNICEF's income from voluntary contributions increased from $313 million in 1980 to $1006 million in 1994.

Carol Bellamy – 1995–(2004)

Carol Bellamy was born on 14 January 1942 in Plainfield, NJ, USA. Bellamy had been a US Peace Corps volunteer before becoming a Wall Street lawyer and financier. She served five years in the New York State Senate and was the first woman president of the New York City Council. President Clinton appointed her as head of the Peace Corps in 1993. Her appointment as Executive Director of UNICEF in May 1995 was preceded by a second heated dispute between the Europeans and the USA. Although the UN Secretary-General, Boutros-Ghali, had invited the Europeans to put forward a candidate, they were divided between a

Finnish former defence minister, Elisabeth Rehn, backed by 10 European countries, a Belgian candidate, A. M. Lizin, and a British candidate, Richard Jolly, Grant's deputy. The US first proposed Dr William H. Foege, a former director of the Centers for Disease Control in Atlanta. When Boutros-Ghali insisted that the post should be filled by a woman, the US then forcefully proposed Bellamy. The Europeans felt that the UNICEF post should not be given to a US national, as Americans were already heads of UNDP, UNFPA and WFP. While the US government was the largest single contributor to UNICEF – approximately 12.7 per cent of its income for 1995 – for the same year, 14 European governments and the European Union contributed 41.2 per cent. Boutros-Ghali finally gave in to US pressure in an attempt to counter the US Congress criticisms and withholding of US contributions to UN organizations' budgets, to maintain US support for the agency and to support his own bid for a second five-year term as Secretary-General.

UN Secretary-General Kofi Annan reappointed Bellamy for a second five-year term with effect from May 1999[31].

Ongoing programmes and new initiatives

Following the flamboyant tenure of Grant, Bellamy's term of office came at a difficult juncture for the agency. Its income, and that of other humanitarian and development organizations, was affected by donor fatigue. As a UN agency, it was threatened by the anti-UN campaign of the US Senate. In spite of the popularity of its mandate, its integrity had been tainted by a scandal revealed in 1994, where approximately $10 million had been lost to serious fraud and mismanagement in its Kenya office (see Chapter 8). The consulting firm Booz-Allen Hamilton found, in a management study carried out in 1994, a great deal of staff discontent, focused on processes, not on aims: 82 per cent of the staff wanted change.[32]

In response to the management study, Bellamy initiated a Management Excellence Programme in 1995 to strengthen management throughout the agency. One of its first activities was to redefine UNICEF's mission to provide the framework for the management reforms to come. The UNICEF Executive Board adopted a statement on the mission in January 1996: its text is given in Figure 2.1.

In September 1995, UNICEF's Executive Board approved a new health strategy framework for the agency's work. In its health policy, UNICEF would encourage privatization of health services if such would improve quality, equity and cost-efficiency, the establishment of community financing mechanisms, measures to ensure that the poorest people benefit

UNICEF is mandated by the United Nations General Assembly to advocate for the protection of children's rights, to help meet their basic needs and to expand their opportunities to reach their full potential.

UNICEF is guided by the Convention on the Rights of the Child and strives to establish children's rights as enduring ethical principles and international standards of behaviour towards children.

UNICEF insists that the survival, protection and development of children are universal development imperatives that are integral to human progress.

UNICEF mobilizes political will and material resources to help countries, particularly developing countries, ensure 'a first call for children' and to build their capacity to form appropriate policies and deliver services for children and their families.

UNICEF is committed to ensuring special protection for the most disadvantaged children – victims of war, disasters, extreme poverty, all forms of violence and exploitation and those with disabilities.

UNICEF responds in emergencies to protect the rights of children. In coordination with United Nations partners and humanitarian agencies, UNICEF makes its unique facilities for rapid response available to its partners to relieve the suffering of children and those who provide their care.

UNICEF is non-partisan and its cooperation is free of discrimination. In everything it does, the most disadvantaged children and the countries in greatest need have priority.

UNICEF aims, through its country programmes, to promote the equal rights of women and girls and to support their full participation in the political, social, and economic development of their communities.

UNICEF works with all its partners towards the attainment of the sustainable human development goals adopted by the world community and the realization of peace and social progress enshrined in the Charter of the United Nations.

Source: UNICEF Document: http://www.unicef.org/mission.htm

Figure 2.1 The Mission of UNICEF

from quality care and the removal of financial, cultural and geographic barriers.[33]

UNICEF's programmes over the years 1995–99 were essentially a continuation of previous programmes: primary health care, nutrition, basic education, water supply and sanitation, child protection, emergency programmes. Special emphasis was given to the achievement of the goals of the World Summit for Children. However, the major innovation was that its overall approach was now based on rights: the Convention on the

Rights of the Child was to serve as the essential framework for advocacy and programme development.

The programme priorities for 1998–2000 were defined as follows:

1. Reducing young child mortality and morbidity, an approach to be implemented in the context of the Integrated Management of Childhood Illnesses initiative, spearheaded by WHO in collaboration with WHO and other partners. UNICEF would continue to support the Bamako Initiative for community management and co-financing of local health facilities, especially in sub-Saharan Africa.
2. Improving early childhood care for child growth and development. The Baby-Friendly Hospital Initiative would be supported and expanded, and UNICEF would support local compliance with the International Code of Marketing of Breast-Milk Substitutes.
3. Preventing child disability, including a reduction of vertical transmission of HIV.
4. Improving access to and quality of basic education.
5. Improving adolescent health and development.
6. Protection from exploitation, violence and abuse. This includes promoting the elimination of child labour, reducing the impact of armed conflict on children and prevention of family separation, and preventing sexual abuse and exploitation of, and trafficking in, children. UNICEF has co-sponsored the World Congress against the Commercial Sexual Exploitation of Children, held in Stockholm in 1996, which established a global strategy to tackle this problem.
7. Prevention of gender discrimination and promotion of gender equality.
8. Reducing maternal mortality and morbidity.

The mix of activities would continue to vary from country to country as determined by the country programme process.[34]

UNICEF is one of the co-sponsors of the Joint UN Programme on HIV/AIDS with UNDP, UNFPA, UNESCO, WHO and the World Bank. The Programme was created in Geneva in January 1996 (see Chapter 4).

In December 1997, 123 countries signed in Ottawa the Convention on the Prohibition of the Use, Stockpiling, Production and Transfer of Anti-Personnel Mines, and on Their Destruction. Since 1992, UNICEF had cooperated with, and provided support for, the International Campaign to Ban Landmines, a coalition of more than 1000 NGOs. UNICEF has since been asked to assume lead responsibility for the efforts to promote ratification of the treaty (see Chapter 6).

Also in 1997, a UN Development Group was created by the UN consisting of UNDP, UNFPA, WFP and UNICEF to facilitate joint policy-making and decision-making. Bellamy resisted the original proposal of the UN Secretary-General that UNICEF and the other funds and programmes should be merged in the Group under UNDP direction and that an Office of Development Financing be created that could solicit voluntary contributions jointly to all funds and programmes, in the fear that UNICEF might lose its independence, its own characteristics and income mobilization capacity. The Secretary-General then made clear that the creation of the Group would in no way dilute or compromise the distinctive character or identity of participating organizations or the accountability of their heads vis-à-vis the Secretary-General or their respective governing bodies.[35]

UNICEF joined the WHO campaign 'Roll Back Malaria' in 1998 together with UNDP and the World Bank.

Comments

It would be premature, at the end of Bellamy's first term of office, to try to assess her professional and personal influence on UNICEF's image and effectiveness. She has maintained essential programmes initiated by her predecessors, she has been an articulate and courageous advocate for children's rights in conflict situations and for girls' and women's rights, and she has associated UNICEF with a few important inter-agency programmes. Her reputation as a tough manager has helped her to restructure the agency, to reform its management and to adjust to income reductions while staff relations were affected.

UNICEF's income in 1995 was $1011 million, and decreased to $966 million in 1998.

Staffing levels were sharply reduced from 7600 in 1995 to 5594 in 1998.

Conclusion

This short overview, necessarily incomplete, does not do justice to all the developments and achievements of UNICEF, nor to the many problems and obstacles met by the institution and its staff. Selected developments and problems are reviewed in the following chapters.

The overview does, however, show both continuity and innovation in the scope of UNICEF programmes under the leadership of its first four Executive Directors, under changing world conditions.

Continuity applies to the mandate of UNICEF, primarily the survival, protection and development of children. Emergency relief, the original cause of UNICEF's creation, is still an important part of its activities, in view of the recurring natural calamities and the growing man-made crises. Global immunization campaigns, including efforts at the eradication of a few diseases, follow the early BCG campaigns against tuberculosis. Support for safe motherhood and breastfeeding has been steadfast. UNICEF has early expanded its role from child health to nutrition, environmental sanitation and education.

UNICEF has not ceased to be a vocal and strong advocate for the cause of children and mothers in all circumstances, including those involving sensitive political implications.

The first significant innovation is UNICEF's conversion to a development, rather than a humanitarian, agency, although its popular image, as widely publicized in the media, has remained essentially humanitarian.

Its second major innovation is that of having adopted a 'children's rights' approach, based on the Convention on the Rights of the Child: the UN General Assembly welcomed this approach in December 1998.[36] The ratification of the Convention by 191 countries provides UNICEF with a broad and sound normative basis for its work. UNICEF has also shown its active interest in other international treaties, such as the Ottawa Convention on anti-personnel landmines. It has participated in the drafting of the Statute of the International Criminal Court.

UNICEF has also expanded its activities in some specific areas: its Peace and Security Agenda for Children, including support for children affected by armed conflict, its Baby-Friendly Hospital Initiative, and its work to prevent gender discrimination and promote gender equality, including its clear and strong opposition to female genital mutilation. Finally, UNICEF's participation in a number of joint UN programmes together with other UN organizations and bodies, foundations and the private sector, have led to better cooperation and use of resources, replacing earlier hostility from or competition with some organizations.

However, questions remain which cannot be answered at this stage: is UNICEF over-extended? Should its limited resources be more focused on fewer essential programmes? Are its expenditures properly controlled?

3
Structure and Finances

UNICEF is linked to the UN and to the UN General Assembly through its creation: UNICEF was created in 1946 by a resolution of the UN General Assembly in accordance with Article 55 of the UN Charter. Other resolutions have extended the duration of the agency, and then made it permanent. The agency's mandate, structure and the composition of its Executive Board were also defined in resolutions of the General Assembly. Periodical resolutions may approve the agency's policies, give it policy guidance or praise UNICEF, among other UN organizations, for its contribution to programmes related to children. Another link with the UN lies in the fact that the Executive Director of the Fund is appointed by the Secretary-General of the UN, in consultation with the Executive Board.

UNICEF is, however, not an autonomous specialized agency, such as the FAO or WHO. It was not formally established as a subsidiary organ of the General Assembly in accordance with Article 22 of the UN Charter as were UNHCR and UNFPA. Its creation in accordance with Article 55 does not define its status: it refers generally to the 'creation of conditions of stability and well-being ... necessary for peaceful and friendly relations among nations ... ' The reference to Article 55 and not to Article 22 was no doubt voluntary. By not specifically referring to a subsidiary organ of the General Assembly but only to a Fund, the drafters of Resolution 57 I, Rajchman and Charnow, were circumventing the opposition of the specialized agencies and a few governments to the creation of a Children's Agency. However, this needed administrative clarification. In a memorandum dated 30 June 1947, the UN Secretary-General, Trygve Lie, qualified the Fund as a subsidiary organ of the General Assembly and decided that its Executive Director would report directly to him.[1] UNICEF has a degree of autonomy within the UN system by having its own governing body, the Executive Board, its own secretariat and its own financial resources. However, its Executive Board is subject to the authority of the Economic and Social Council (ECOSOC), one of the six principal organs of the UN. Its secretariat reports to ECOSOC, not to the General Assembly.

UNICEF's formal structure consists of its Executive Board and its secretariat, to which should be added its 'extended family' – its expanded constituency – consisting of National Committees, NGOs closely associated with the agency's work and goodwill ambassadors.

Formal structure

The Executive Board

The composition of the Board is subject to decisions by the UN General Assembly. The Board was originally composed of representatives of 25 governments. In 1950, the Board was enlarged to consist of the members of the Social Commission and the governments of eight other states, not necessarily UN members, to be designated by ECOSOC, with due regard to geographical distribution and to the representation of the major contributing and recipient countries. In 1956, the General Assembly decided to separate the membership of the Executive Board from that of the Social Commission in order to provide for the direct election of all members to the Board. In 1957, the Board was reconstituted to consist of 30 states, members of the UN or of the specialized agencies. In 1982, the Assembly increased the membership to 41.[2] In October 1991, a joint memorandum from the Nordic countries of Denmark, Finland, Norway and Sweden, was sent to the Secretary-General of the UN for submission to the General Assembly.[3] As major contributors to UN operational activities, noting clear tendencies of a marginalization of the UN, they had set up the Nordic UN project in 1988. Part of its findings identified weaknesses in the system of governance of UN development activities:

> The sessions of many governing bodies have become huge gatherings simultaneously dealing with a wide spectrum of matters at different levels of governance, from overall political issues to micro-management. New, small, governing bodies that would meet more frequently, are needed to improve the effectiveness and efficiency of the system.

The Nordic countries proposed the establishment of a small executive body for each of the UN funds and programmes including UNICEF, with the key function of providing a link between the member states and the management of each organization. These bodies would primarily exercise operational governance, which includes:

- Monitoring the performance of the funds and programmes;
- Assuming that the mandates, policies, priorities and strategies set by higher-level governing bodies are carried out, and in a transparent manner;
- Deciding on plans and budgets;
- Encouraging and examining new programme initiatives.

The size of the new bodies would be limited to 15–20 members, appointed for three years, with a possible representation of 50 per cent from recipient countries and 50 per cent from donor countries. They would make decisions by consensus. In cases of disagreement, decisions could be taken by 'double majority', i.e. majority among the recipient constituency and majority among the donor constituency.

In December 1993, the General Assembly decided that the current governing bodies of UNDP, UNFPA and UNICEF would be transformed into Executive Boards, composed of 36 members, subject to the authority of ECOSOC. Developing countries were not willing to accept the limitation to 20 members proposed by the Nordic countries, on the grounds of 'democratic representation'.[4]

As from 1994, the composition of the UNICEF Executive Board was therefore reduced from 41 to 36. ECOSOC elects states to sit on the Board from state members of the UN or of the specialized agencies or of the International Atomic Energy Agency. The seats are allocated to 8 African states, 7 Asian states, 4 Eastern European states, 5 Latin American and Caribbean states and 12 Western European and other states including Japan.

At its first regular session in 1994, the Board decided to abolish two committees of the whole, previously responsible for programme and administrative and financial matters, and to establish ad hoc groups on specific issues as required. The size of the Bureau was reduced to consist of a president and four vice-presidents, representing five regional groups.[5]

The role of the Executive Board of UNICEF is shown in Figure 3.1.

The Board holds an annual session, as well as regular sessions between the annual sessions. All sessions are held at UN headquarters in New York.

The Secretariat

The UNICEF secretariat comprised 5594 posts in 1998, down from an apex of 7600 in 1995. The decrease appears to be due in part to a policy decision by the Executive Director of making the agency leaner and more effective

---

The Executive Board, as the governing body of UNICEF, is responsible for providing intergovernmental support to and supervision of the activities of UNICEF, in accordance with the overall policy guidance of the General Assembly and of the Economic and Social Council of the United Nations.
  Its role is, subject to the authority of the Council, to:

1. Implement the policies formulated by the Assembly and the coordination and guidance received from the Council;
2. Receive information from and give guidance to the Executive Director on the work of UNICEF;
3. Ensure that the activities and operational strategies of UNICEF are consistent with the overall policy guidance set forth by the General Assembly and the Council;
4. Monitor the performance of UNICEF;
5. Approve programmes, including country programmes;
6. Decide on administrative and financial plans and budgets;
7. Recommend new initiatives to the Council and, through the Council, to the Assembly as necessary;
8. Encourage and examine new programme initiatives; and
9. Submit annual reports to the Council in its substantive session, which could include recommendations, where appropriate, for improvement of field-level coordination.

Source: UNICEF Worldwide, http://www.unicef.org/uwwide/exboard.htm, 23 March 1999.

Figure 3.1   The role of the Executive Board of UNICEF

through restructuring and downsizing, and, in part, to budgetary constraints.

In 1998, 14 per cent of its staff were assigned to its headquarters in New York, and 86 per cent in the field, i.e. in 8 regional offices and 125 country offices worldwide. UNICEF also has a research centre in Florence, Italy, a supply operation in Copenhagen and offices in Tokyo and Brussels.

In 1997, staff consisted of 161 nationalities, 82 per cent of whom were from developing countries. Women occupied 38 per cent of professional staff and 27 per cent of director posts. Forty-seven per cent of all professional staff were National Professional Officers NPOs, who work in their own countries and are chosen for their special knowledge of local situations, languages and cultures. NPOs are mainly employed by UNICEF and UNDP. They are paid local rates of pay from 10 to 30 per cent above the maximum of the general service salary scales approved by the UN for a specific area, but, in general, below UN professional salary rates .[6]

Except for NPOs, UNICEF staff have the same status as UN staff: they are international civil servants entitled to the guarantees provided by the 1946 Convention on the Privileges and Immunities of the United Nations. They are subject to the same Staff Regulations and Rules, they have the right to appeal to the UN Joint Advisory Boards and to submit a complaint to the UN Administrative Tribunal.

As one exception, shared with UNDP, UNHCR, WFP, UNITAR and the International Court of Justice, UNICEF is exempt from the nationality quota system applicable in the UN system under the geographical distribution formula. The reasons for this limitation in the words of the Secretary-General were that such organs

> are designed exclusively for the purpose of giving assistance ... it is imperative that the quality and cost of service provided as well as the explicit requirements of the recipient countries should not be prejudiced by any rigid formula of geographical distribution in the appointment of the staff.[7]

This was a wise decision, meant to avoid the frequent conflicts between competence and nationality caused by rigid nationality quotas for the appointment or promotion of staff in many UN organizations. Furthermore, it is difficult to envisage how to apply the UN geographical distribution system, based mainly on budgetary contributions of member states to the UN budget according to a fixed scale of assessments, to an organization like UNICEF which has no member states and whose budget is only financed by voluntary contributions.

The secretariat is headed by the Executive Director, appointed by the UN Secretary-General in consultation with the Executive Board. As noted in Chapter 2, the appointment of the last two Executive Directors was marred by a political rivalry between the US and European governments. In the last appointment, the Executive Board was not 'consulted' but it was 'convinced' to accept the US fiat of a single US candidate, through the good offices of Secretary-General Boutros-Ghali. Urquhart and Childers[8] have criticized the tradition of a major contributor, the US, having a permanent monopoly of the leadership of certain UN funds and programmes including UNICEF, as having 'ceased to have any even pragmatic justification'. Secondly, appointments are made without reference to a set of specific required qualifications for the post. Urquhart and Childers have proposed to rationalize (depoliticize) the appointment process of heads of funds and programmes and, by the same token, to lighten the Secretary-General's and Executive Board's burden. A statement of criteria for the post should first be approved. The Secretary-General should then appoint a small group of highly experienced governmental advisers, representatives of industrialized and developing countries and experts in the fund's field of work. This panel would review the candidates' merits, seek more information on them, search out others if necessary, and present to the Secretary-General a shortlist of the best available candidates. The Secretary-General could then choose and present a candidate to the Executive Board on the basis of independent expert advice and enquiry. Alternatively, the Executive Board should play a review and screening role before the Secretary-General selects a candidate. In 1996, WHO adopted criteria which a candidate for the post of director-general must fulfil and gave its executive Board a detailed role in screening and interviewing candidates and deciding on a shortlist, followed by the election of one candidate.[9] What is good for WHO should be good for UNICEF.

The strength of UNICEF and at least one of the keys to its success is that it has decentralized its structure to give a large degree of autonomy to its country offices in contrast to WHO, where decentralization has concerned regional offices without affecting country representatives. UNICEF stresses the 'centrality' of the country programme and country office with a focus on building local capacity. In 1996, under the Management Excellence Programme, UNICEF has transferred several headquarters functions to regional and country offices and delegated increased authority to the field in areas such as programme planning and management. Major operational decisions are left to the discretion of country representatives, and they also direct all UNICEF operations at field level, answering directly to the Executive Director.[10]

In a recent interview,[11] a long-serving UNICEF field representative confirmed the policy:

> The UNICEF representative in a country has enormous responsibility and authority delegated to him, and enormous flexibility to decide what to do and what not to do. There is very little bureaucracy and red tape. It is an opportunity to use your own creativity in finding non-conventional solutions to the pervasive, persistent problems of children ... we deal not only with supplying goods to help children's programmes, we also help in the conceptualization and design of the programmes and their monitoring – the evaluation and documentation of successes and failures.

The extended family

National Committees

National Committees are not part of UNICEF's formal structure, but have become close and essential partners, with formal links with the Executive Board and the agency itself. They expand UNICEF's renown and influence among the populations of the rich countries, whose governments, foundations, NGOs, private businesses and individuals provide most of UNICEF's resources.

In the UN family, UNESCO's Constitution is alone among specialized agencies in providing for National Commissions set up by member states to act in an advisory capacity to their respective delegations to the General Conference and to function as liaison agencies (Art. VII). The 180 Commissions, composed of members of intellectual and scientific communities, are linked with UNESCO, implement activities on behalf of UNESCO and disseminate information about the organization. They also participate in the elaboration, execution and evaluation of UNESCO's programme. The main difference with UNICEF National Committees is that UNESCO Commissions do not engage in fundraising: UNESCO's regular budget is financed by Member States through contributions while UNICEF's budget is entirely dependent on voluntary contributions, hence the necessity for constant and active fund-raising. Set up in industrialized countries only, UNICEF National Committees are national NGOs that support the goals and work of UNICEF, an IGO. Through legal agreements with UNICEF, the Committees agree to operate within the policies set by UNICEF and to undertake advocacy, education and fund-raising programmes for the agency.[12]

The Committees have evolved from small beginnings as volunteer groups rallying seasonally to sell greetings cards and other products into highly professional groups. The first National Committee was established in 1946 in Yugoslavia to assist the UNICEF postwar programme for that country. Following the example of the US and Belgium which had formed Committees in 1947, the Executive Director, Maurice Pate, promoted the creation of similar committees in other countries. More National Committees were formed in the Federal Republic of Germany (1952), and in Denmark, Norway and Sweden (1954). By 1984, 26 Committees had been established in Europe and 33 worldwide. In 2000, there were 37, supported by more than 100 000 volunteers. Most Committees are established on the combined initiatives of UNICEF supporters, and/or of UNICEF itself, in consultation with the governments of the countries concerned: the latter's consent to the creation of a Committee is required.

National Committees have first to be recognized by UNICEF on the basis of a Cooperation Agreement, which may be varied to take account of the laws of a particular country or the mandate and structure of a particular Committee. Only one UNICEF National Committee may be established in a country, a policy also applied by the Movement of the Red Cross for the setting up of National Red Cross or Red Crescent Societies. Simultaneously, National Committees for UNICEF have to be recognized by government authorities as a legitimate national NGO.

National Committees should have a broadly based composition of persons sympathetic to UNICEF and its goals, representing a cross-section of society. The governing body of a National Committee should be a group of volunteers, preferably influential people or experts in any relevant activity, representing national and local organizations. The Committees' day-to-day work is carried out by a secretariat of paid employees. Most Committees have honorary chairmen including distinguished personalities. Following the practice of many other NGOs, Committees have recently engaged professional public information and fund-raising officers.

Relationships between Committees and the UNICEF secretariat and between the Committees and national NGOs have, at times, been difficult. The value of the Committees' work in advocacy and fund-raising was underestimated by the secretariat for a number of years. Disagreements occurred over the use of funds collected by the Committees. European Committees complained that the information material prepared in New York was not adapted to a European audience. In spite of urging by the UNICEF secretariat, some Committees were reluctant to have a close relationship with national NGOs, for reasons of autonomy and concern that the name of UNICEF might be used more to further the ends of NGOs than those of the agency.[13]

National Committee representatives have the right to attend the UNICEF Executive Board meetings as observers. They may circulate statements and, with the agreement of the Chairperson, make oral statements. They may also give advice and suggestions in the field of national and international fund-raising campaigns, public information and greeting cards. In 1983, the Executive Board recognized the Committees as full-fledged partners of the agency.

National Committees provide UNICEF with annual workplans based on their long-term planning and yearly budgets. Committees may solicit, receive and acknowledge donations, gifts and bequests on behalf of UNICEF. Committees act as UNICEF's sales and distribution agents within the country for the marketing, distribution and sale of UNICEF greeting cards and other products. Organizing fund-raising campaigns for UNICEF programmes of cooperation, including the sale of UNICEF products, forms an important part of Committees' work.

Current guidelines define the following percentages which National Committees may normally retain from the revenue sources shown below:[14]

- interest on funds due UNICEF   100% of interest income
- grants received from governmental authorities or private individuals and which are clearly earmarked for supporting the National Committee   100% of gross revenue
- fund-raising appeals on in-house direct mail lists   25% of gross revenue
- fund-raising appeals on donor acquisition   25% of net revenue
- other fund-raising activities   25% of net revenue
- greeting card and other UNICEF product sales   25% of gross revenue
- donations unrelated to Committee activities   10% of gross revenue
- unsolicited funds-in-trust given to UNICEF for specific UNICEF-assisted Projects through the Committee   0% of gross revenue

Committees' accounts are audited annually by certified external auditors and submitted to UNICEF.

National Committees are the main voice of UNICEF in the countries which provide most of the agency's income: they have an essential role of advocacy and education, by raising awareness in the population of those countries, including children, about the situation facing children in countries assisted by UNICEF, about the rights of children everywhere and about UNICEF's programmes. They maintain contact with the media, organize seminars and support education for development in schools. They work with political, judicial, health and educational institutions on the development issues prioritized by UNICEF.

A number of National Committees have supported the process leading to the adoption of the Convention on the Rights of the Child, then promoted its ratification by their government, and are now involved in the formal process of required governmental reporting on progress in implementing the Convention. Some of them have promoted the adoption by the UN General Assembly on 25 May 2000 of the two

Protocols to the Convention, one on the sale of children, child prostitution and child pornography, and the other on the involvement of children in armed conflict. They also provide advocacy and awareness campaigns on such issues as child labour, anti-personnel mines and children affected by HIV/AIDS.

In addition to and closely connected with advocacy, fund-raising is a major and essential activity of the Committees. They contributed about 30 per cent ($331 million) of UNICEF's income in 1995, up from 20 per cent in 1989, which rose to 36 per cent ($346.5 million) of UNICEF's income in 1998.[15]

The UK Committee was established in 1956. Its annual income has grown from under £0.5 million in 1976 to over £10 million in 1998. Of this income, $6.8 million was for programmes to benefit children and their families, 86 per cent for UNICEF's international programmes and 14 per cent for the Committee's own programmes of advocacy in the UK. Administration costs amounted to just over 5 per cent of total income. Fund-raising expenditure amounted to 26 per cent: £3.65 was raised for every pound spent on fundraising. In November 1994, the UK Committee launched the UK Baby-Friendly Hospital Initiative after two years of preparatory work with 40 NGOs, medical professional associations and the Department of Health. It included the 'Charter for Mothers', which outlines breastfeeding rights.[16]

In 1996, the Swedish Committee helped organize the World Congress against Commercial Sexual Exploitation of Children, held in Stockholm in August 1996. Also in 1996, European National Committees and UNICEF's Regional Office for Europe in Geneva cooperated with the Council of Europe in developing the European Strategy for Children, which the European Parliament adopted in 1996. The Strategy calls for full implementation of the Convention on the Rights of the Child by the Parliament's 40 member states.[17]

The Canadian Committee, founded in 1955, enjoys the support of about 45 000 regular volunteers to implement fund-raising, information and advocacy, while more than 2 million school children collect coins for UNICEF every year. The Committee supports UNICEF projects in over 150 developing countries, with the financial support of the Canadian International Development Agency and of some provincial governments. About 11 per cent of the Committee's revenue is spent on administration costs.[18]

Since 1996, the UNICEF Regional Office for Europe, in Geneva, has become the focal point for management of relations with National Committees. The Annual Meeting of National Committees is the highest organizational body of cooperation between Committees and UNICEF.

The Meeting, composed of delegations of all National Committees, organizes debates on major policy issues and planning.

Non-governmental organizations

The action of a growing number of NGOs in humanitarian emergencies and in development, and their influence in the promotion of human rights, has been amply documented and recognized. Article 71 of the UN Charter has allowed ECOSOC to make arrangements for consultation with both national and international NGOs. In 1999, 1707 NGOs were granted consultative status with ECOSOC. NGOs have been associated with the work of most UN specialized agencies, also by giving them consultative status, with appropriate responsibilities and privileges.

As for National Committees, UNICEF has formalized its relationship with NGOs by establishing links with both its secretariat and its Executive Board and by setting up an NGO Committee on UNICEF.[19]

When UNICEF was created in 1946, the UN General Assembly requested the new agency, in part, to appeal to all voluntary relief agencies to continue and intensify their activities and to take the necessary measures in order to cooperate with these agencies. The 1950 resolution extending the Fund decided, in part, that its administration obtain from inter-governmental and non-governmental organizations having a special interest in child and family welfare the advice and technical assistance which it may require for the implementation of its programmes.[20] NGOs have shown their capacity to mobilize people and communities for self-reliant and sustained development. Through their advocacy efforts, they have raised awareness about the needs of children and influenced public opinion to address those needs. They have worked with governments and UNICEF to shape national policy and legislation affecting children. They have worked as grass-roots partners in the implementation of UNICEF-assisted country programmes. They have helped UNICEF provide the food, supplies and medicine vital to emergency operations. Through additional funding, NGOs have contributed to building more primary schools, training more health workers, increasing the outreach of safe water and sanitation programmes, and immunizing more children.

In 1979, the International Year of the Child would not have taken place without the initiatives of NGOs. NGOs were actively involved in the drafting process and in the adoption of the Convention on the Rights of the Child in 1989. NGOs participated in the drafting of the World Declaration and Plan of Action of the World Summit for Children, held in 1990.

In addition to the more traditional NGOs, several prominent organizations of business and professional people in the private sector assist UNICEF in specific programmes. Among them, Rotary International is a key partner, together with UNICEF, WHO, the US Agency for International Development and the US Centers for Disease Control and Prevention, in the global programme to eradicate polio. From 1987 to 1998, Rotary provided approximately $140 million to UNICEF for polio campaigns and has been active in mobilizing funds and vaccine donations from other agencies. Through its Worldwide Service Project, Kiwanis International is a major partner in the international campaign to eliminate iodine deficiency disorders. From 1994 to 1998, Kiwanis channelled more than $18 million to UNICEF-assisted projects in more than 60 countries. The Lions Clubs adopted the issue of children living or working on the streets as their focus for 1997 and 1998. As part of its worldwide campaign to eradicate violence against girls and women, Zonta International provided $225 000 in 1997 to support the UNICEF-assisted Girls Education Project in South Africa.[21]

NGOs with consultative status have been represented at UNICEF Executive Board meetings and Programme Committee sessions since 1951. They may circulate statements, or, if the Board's chairperson agrees, make oral statements to the Board on relevant topics.

The NGO Committee on UNICEF, created in 1949 on the initiative of NGOs, is composed of 126 international NGOs in consultative status with UNICEF. The Committee acts as the liaison with NGOs around the world. It provides an important source of information, documentation and advice, and exchange of experience. It organizes numerous consultations, symposia and regional and international meetings. The Committee works through an elected board of eight NGOs and develops most of its activities through specialized working groups focused on health and nutrition, education, child rights, youth participation and other issues. The Committee has developed links to regional NGO networks for children. Members of the Committee include, among others, Defence of Children International, Human Rights Watch, the International Federation of Red Cross and Red Crescent Societies, the International Save the Children Alliance, religious organizations, health-care NGOs, the World Organization of the Scout Movement, etc. In 1979, the Committee's site, originally based in New York, was changed to a dual New York/Geneva basis.

In 1991, the Committee held its first regional conference in Africa (Zimbabwe) followed in 1993 by a conference for Central America, Belize, Panama and Mexico held in Guatemala. A consultation was also held in 1993 in Central Europe (Poland). The NGO Committee was represented at

The Mission of the NGO Committee on UNICEF in the new Millennium is to involve the membership in initiatives for child development, to participate with UNICEF on leadership for children and to be advocates for the children of the world.

Terms of reference:

1. To facilitate a two-way exchange of information and experience between UNICEF and NGOs at international, regional and national levels, recognizing the assistance and support which each can give to the other.
2. To encourage consultation and cooperative efforts among NGOs and between NGOs and UNICEF on child-related matters.
3. To build on past achievements and existing strengths of the NGO Committee.
4. To develop strategic planning for policy and advocacy on child-related issues at national, regional and international levels.
5. To bring such strategic planning to the attention of UNICEF and of other agencies, bodies and groups working for children.
6. To provide a forum for the substantive discussion of UNICEF policies and programmes and of issues related to children generally.

Source: UNICEF Document: http://www.unicef.org/mission.htm

Figure 3.2 Mission and Terms of Reference of the NGO Committee on UNICEF

all major UN conferences and summits during the 1990s, through children caucuses, seminars and other activities, including the 1995 Fourth World Conference on Women. Its current project, started in 1996, concerns Unregistered Children in South-East Asia. It has been extended into South Asia.

The Mission and Terms of Reference of the NGO Committee on UNICEF are listed in Figure 3.2.

Goodwill Ambassadors and celebrities

UNICEF is the first UN body to gain the support of internationally known personalities to carry its message on behalf of children, to broaden its own image, particularly among young people, and to raise funds. As mentioned in Chapter 2, Danny Kaye, the comedian, was recruited by Maurice Pate as the first UNICEF Ambassador from 1953 until his death in 1987. Audrey Hepburn served as a deeply sensitive Goodwill Ambassador from 1988: she was always a caring participant, not a detached observer. After a mission to Ethiopia, Somalia or the Sudan, she would say: 'I am returning from hell. What I saw is unthinkable: children who die, women who have nothing to eat. It's not possible.' A first donation of $100 000 was made to UNICEF shortly after her death in 1993, through the Audrey Hepburn Memorial Fund. Peter Ustinov has served for almost 30 years in countless television and personal appearances. Other celebrities who give generously of their time and talents include Harry Belafonte, Liv Ullmann, Julio Iglesias and many other well-known artists and high-level sports performers. For instance, Goodwill Ambassador Tetsuko Kuro-yanagi, Japanese actress and television performer, has brought in more than $20 million for the UNICEF programmes she has visited since 1984. Roger Moore, UNICEF Special Representative for the Film Arts, is also Honorary Chairman of Kiwanis International's campaign to raise $75 million to eliminate iodine deficiency disorders. Moore has been involved with UNICEF since the early 1980s. Galas and concerts by performers of popular or classical music also produce additional funds.[22]

By 1998, UNICEF partnership had grown to include 18 Goodwill Ambassadors, Spokespersons and Special Representatives who promote the agency internationally, as well as 161 celebrities worldwide who support UNICEF's work at the national level.

Impressed by the success of UNICEF in this approach, the UN has recently enlisted the French pop singer Enrico Macias, the opera singer Luciano Pavarotti, the Nobel Peace Prize recipient Elie Wiesel, the basketball player Magic Johnson and the movie actor Michael Douglas as 'Messengers of Peace', to promote the work of the UN in world affairs. A few other celebrities are supporting UNFPA and UNESCO as Goodwill Ambassadors.[23] These organizations may benefit from a more open exposure to the general public, although their different aims and achievements cannot compete with the popularity of the children's cause promoted by UNICEF. Furthermore, neither the UN nor UNESCO could expect substantial additional funding from this initiative – both are mainly financed by obligatory contributions, unlike UNFPA which is wholly financed by voluntary contributions.

Funding the Fund

UNICEF is wholly financed by voluntary contributions, hence its need for a constant, active promotion of its programmes and achievements and calls for financial support.[24]

Income

Contributions come from two main sources: governments and IGOs, and non-governmental/private sector groups and individuals.

Total income for 1998 was $966 million, of which 62 per cent was provided by governments and IGOs, and 33 per cent by non-

Table 3.1   UNICEF total income 1991–98 (US $m)

1991	807
1992	938
1993	866
1994	1006
1995	1011
1996	944
1997	902
1998	966

Source: UNICEF Annual Reports.

governmental sources – another 5 per cent came from other sources. As a comparison, the UN regular budget for 1998–1999 was $2.5 billion, while the WHO budget for 1998/9 was $1.8 billion, including a regular budget of $842 million and estimated voluntary contributions of $956 million.[25] Total UNICEF income for 1988 was $709 million, of which 70 per cent came from governments and IGOs, and 30 per cent from non-governmental sources.

The slow evolution of less governmental contributions and more non-governmental contributions may be attributed to the decline in support of industrialized countries to international development organizations, and their belief that more support should come from the private sector.

The evolution of total income for the period 1991–98 is shown in Table 3.1. It shows a low level in 1991, a high level in 1995, again a lower level in 1997 and a higher level in 1998.

The United States has been the largest government donor to UNICEF since its creation and remained so in 1998 with a contribution of $162 million. However, it was in fifteenth place on the basis of contributions to UNICEF vs. GNP with a 0.69 per cent per capita contribution. The next four highest contributors, in 1998, were Sweden ($75 million), Norway ($71.4 million), the Netherlands ($44.7 million) and Japan ($38.7 million). On the other hand, the first five highest per capita contributions to UNICEF in 1998 were Norway (16.55), Sweden (8.72), Denmark (7.52), Luxembourg (6.71) and the Netherlands (5.54). Among the IGOs, the highest contribution, $16 million, came from the European Union.

The first five Committees for UNICEF having made the largest contributions were, for 1998, Japan ($76.5 million), Germany ($47.3 million), the Netherlands ($41 million), France ($30.6 million) and Spain ($22.6 million).

The other largest non-governmental contributions were from the United Nations Foundation, Inc. created by R. E. (Ted) Turner ($3 million),

Rotary International ($4.5 million) and Tetsuko Kuroyanagi, Japan ($2.5 million).

In the same year, $182 million were generated by the private sector, which includes the greeting card and related operations.[26]

Under its medium-term plan for 1998–2001, UNICEF established for the first time a funding target of $1.5 billion for 2005, implying an ambitious annual growth rate in income of 7 per cent.[27]

Partnership with the private sector

In addition to the donations made by foundations or individuals to UNICEF in 1998, the US Committee for UNICEF received in November 1999 a $26 million grant from the Bill and Melinda Gates Foundation. The grant is to be used in the fight to eliminate maternal and neonatal tetanus (MNT) by 2005. In December 1999, WHO, Rotary International and UNICEF announced that the same Foundation would provide $50 million along with $28 million from Turner's United Nations Foundation in a partnership to support the accelerated efforts to eradicate polio by the end of the year 2000.[28]

The UN Secretary-General, in his report *Renewing the United Nations: A Programme for Reform*[29] stressed the particular importance of the relationship of the UN and the organizations of the UN system with the business community. This innovative approach, which broke away from decades of UN hostility towards the 'evil' multinational corporations, has been adopted with caution by UNICEF. In a speech given to the Harvard International Development Conference on 16 April 1999, Carol Bellamy rejected the patronizing view that the private sector could provide only money but that it should be seen as a source of knowledge and expertise for multilateralism. She also made clear that business and industry are driven by the profit motive, while the work of the UN is driven by a set of ethical principles. While UNICEF has the most extensive corporate involvement of any single UN agency, this is subject to 'due diligence'. For instance, UNICEF attaches ethical strings to its supply contracts, favouring companies that pledge to avoid links with such activities as landmine production and exploitative child labour. UNICEF does not deal with cigarette companies or accept contributions from manufacturers of infant formula. Under these conditions, Warner Brothers, Turner Network Television and others are key supporters of the 'Trick or Treat for UNICEF' campaign, while companies like British Airways, the Sheraton and Westin hotel chains and American Express are involved in UNICEF marketing efforts linked to specific fund-raising activities.[30]

Table 3.2   Percentage of programme expenditures by sector

	1985 %	1989 %	1994 %	1998 %
Child health	30	40	33	32
Water and environmental sanitation	21	15	15	11
Child nutrition	6	6	8	6
Community development, women's programmes	5	7	11	13
Education and early childhood development	11	7	13	14
Planning, advocacy and cross-sectoral support	14	15	20	24
Emergency relief	13	10	(a)	(a)

Note (a): Emergency relief percentage is not shown on the 1994 and 1998 data.

Source: *UNICEF Annual Reports*, 1990, 1999.

Expenditures

In 1998, total expenditures amounted to $878 million, the 1989 total expenditure being $501 million. Total programme cooperation ($784 million) amounted to 89 per cent of the total expenditure. Management and administration of the agency were an additional 9 per cent, and write-offs and other charges amounted to 2 per cent.

Table 3.2 shows the percentage of programme expenditures by sector in 1985, 1989, 1994 and 1998.

The UNICEF programme budget in each country is allocated according to three criteria: under-five mortality rate (the probability of a child dying between birth and five years of age, expressed per 1000 births); income level (GNP per capita); and the size of the child population. In 1998, Sub-Saharan Africa continued to receive the greatest share of UNICEF resources, followed by the Asian region.

The total programme expenditure for 1998 ($784 million) represented a decline of around 9 per cent compared to 1997, mainly due to a range of country-specific situations.

Conclusion

While Carol Bellamy is serving her second five-year term, UN member states should be asking for a review of the modalities for the selection of the Executive Director. The UNICEF Executive Board should also be given a substantial role in screening candidates, well beyond its present passive right to be consulted. Fears of upsetting the US and of reducing US moral and financial support to UNICEF should a non-US candidate be selected in the future are no longer to be taken too seriously, in view of the broad geographical and financial support given to the agency. The merits of past and present US incumbents of the post of Executive Director are not at issue: they have all made a substantial contribution to UNICEF's success. However, candidates of other nationalities could also have made their contribution. The main point is to satisfy the General Assembly's often repeated resolution that 'no post should be considered the exclusive preserve of any Member State or group of States' and to trust that the Secretary-General should respect this principle when appointing staff members, including at the highest level.[31]

Decentralization is indeed one key to UNICEF's success, an example that other UN organizations would be well advised to study and possibly adapt to their own status and structure. It is, however, only one key among several: the main key is the relevance and effectiveness of an organization's programmes.

The absolute necessity to obtain voluntary funding for the survival and development of the agency and the innovative spirit of its leaders have led to the creation of an extended family of UNICEF supporters, beyond the classical structure of the Executive Board and secretariat. The dynamism of National Committees in 'rich' countries – a realistic proposition in the UN realm of 'equal countries' – with their 100 000 volunteers, has made UNICEF very popular in terms of its work with a direct impact on its funding. The sale of greeting cards, Trick-or-Treat and Change-for-Good collections are all clever means of enticing generosity for a good cause. The parallel role of NGOs as another circle of UNICEF friends and collaborators is another source of programme and financial support. As for National Committees, formal relationships have been established with both the Executive Board and the secretariat, in order to maintain a necessary unity of purpose.

As a pioneer in the UN system, UNICEF has innovated by enlisting celebrities as public relations relays for UNICEF's programmes, particularly among young people, and has again, expanded its fund-raising base.

The increase in UNICEF's income – from $113 million in 1976 to $966 in 1998 – is evidence of the effectiveness of its work and of its fund-raising policy. It is indeed striking that its 1998 income, made up only of voluntary contributions, is approximately the same as that of WHO, which consists of both obligatory and voluntary contributions.

UNICEF's new funding target of $1.5 billion for 2005 sounds unrealistic, but it may be an effective basis for fund-raising.

4
Children's Health: the Main Programme

One of the reasons for the establishment of UNICEF, in 1946, was that the Fund's resources be used, in part, 'for child health purposes generally'.[1]

UNICEF's expenditures on child health have consistently been the highest of all programmes: 33 per cent for the period 1947–85, 30 per cent in 1985, 40 per cent in 1989, 33 per cent in 1994 and 32 per cent in 1998.[2]

As shown in Chapter 1, the specialized agencies, including WHO, and a few governments fought against the creation of UNICEF and later against its extension, or agreed to an extension only on the condition that UNICEF be firmly inserted within the UN secretariat and its activities strictly controlled by the specialized agencies. During the debates in the Third Committee of the UN General Assembly in 1950, the delegate from South Africa recalled the warnings of specialized agencies, especially the FAO and WHO, against the establishment of a special agency for young people, as such an organization would give rise to much overlapping between the Fund and those specialized agencies.[3]

The issue was particularly important for WHO, an organization which is 'to act as the directing and co-ordinating authority on international health work', as prescribed by Article 2 of its Constitution. Among other functions, WHO is to promote maternal and child health and welfare, to strengthen governments' health services, to furnish technical assistance and aid in emergencies, to stimulate and advance work in the eradication of epidemic, endemic and other diseases, to promote and conduct research in the field of health, and to provide information, counsel and assistance in the same field. For Dr Brock Chisholm, the first Director-General of WHO, the suggestion that another organ should operate in the field of health without the approval of WHO would denounce the agreement set between WHO and the UN. Bringing up an argument which was often raised later, he said that it was WHO's responsibility to see that UN activities did not disrupt the orderly development of national health services, an effect which might easily be produced if money, supplies and services were to be poured in for a short period of time without a planned effort to build up a country's national services, so that the work could be carried on after outside aid had stopped. He stated that the World Health Organization was the only agency which was in a position to consider all factors. WHO and UNICEF should not find themselves competing for the favour of governments. 'It was the right and duty of WHO to approve UNICEF programmes relating to health as it was the right and duty of other agencies to approve programmes which came within their province.'[4]

In the event, the First World Health Assembly took an even more drastic position in a resolution adopted in July 1948: as UNICEF's health projects fall within the competence of WHO, WHO was ready and willing to handle these projects as soon as suitable arrangements could be made. The Assembly recommended the creation of the Joint Committee on Health Policy of UNICEF/WHO as a temporary body to operate only until all the health activities of UNICEF had been taken over by WHO or had been terminated. An exception was made for the programme of BCG vaccination, established by agreements between the Danish, Norwegian and Swedish Red Cross, governments and UNICEF.[5]

The Joint Committee was created but UNICEF health activities were not taken over by WHO. These activities expanded over the years, as UNICEF found its niche and affirmed its autonomy as a successful operational agency, first in emergencies, then in development.

UNICEF's creation, survival and expansion in the public health field were, and still are, an obvious challenge to WHO. While institutional cooperation was formally established between the two organizations, there were periods of hidden or open tension when UNICEF took initiatives which seemed to deviate from WHO's approved policies.

Institutional cooperation between UNICEF and WHO

The First World Health Assembly recommended, in July 1948, that the Joint Committee on Health Policy of UNICEF/WHO should 'regulate' all health programmes and projects of UNICEF already initiated or to be initiated in the future. The Committee would act as the advisory medical body whose advice would be followed by UNICEF in accordance with its general policy, including advice on public health, medical and sanitary administration. All medical programmes and projects would be approved only on the recommendation of the Committee and their implementation would be in accordance with expert advice given by WHO. At its third meeting in April 1949, the Committee approved the following principles, emphasizing the directing and supervisory role of WHO over UNICEF health programmes: international health experts required for assisting governments in drawing up plans of operation for UNICEF health programmes would be provided by WHO; these plans for operations would be approved by the Director-General of WHO; UNICEF's role in health programmes would be limited to furnishing supplies and services. In spite of the agreements reached, the WHO members of the Committee expressed some concern over the expansion of technical staff and health activities within UNICEF.[6] In the health field, UNICEF was therefore to be closely supervised by WHO and all its programmes were to be approved by WHO. In May 1951, the World Health Assembly approved its Executive Board's recommendation for the uninterrupted continuation of the Joint Committee.[7]

The Joint Committee had been originally conceived by WHO as a strict controlling device over UNICEF's health programmes. UNICEF resented this control as a 'corset' handicapping its work and development. Over the years, an evolution took place: the Committee stopped approving individual programmes and limited its role to health policy guidance. UNICEF started employing its own medical advisers and staff.

Following the 1953 decision of the General Assembly to make UNICEF permanent, WHO's attitude became more positive toward UNICEF. With the appointment of a new WHO Director-General, Dr M. G. Candau (Brazil), a friendly cooperation between (almost) equals, was established with the Executive Director of UNICEF, H. R. Labouisse.

The World Health Assembly gave recognition to UNICEF's work in a resolution of May 1954.[8] Considering that the projects carried out by WHO jointly with UNICEF were among the most important activities of WHO and had contributed greatly to the improvement of maternal and child health on a wide basis, the Assembly believed that the cooperative relationship which had proved so effective should be maintained and strengthened. However, the different systems of financing and budgeting in the two agencies created disturbing uncertainties in planning. In January 1960, the WHO Executive Board approved the new terms of reference of the Joint Committee.[9] In part, the Committee was to review from time to time the overall needs of mothers and children in the health field and to recommend to the UNICEF Executive Board the types of health programmes, having as their objectives the improvement of the health of mothers and children, which could appropriately receive UNICEF support. In the 1950s and 1960s, UNICEF assistance to WHO activities included support for maternal and child health projects, the malaria eradication and smallpox eradication programmes, grants-in-aid to selected schools of medicine and public health, and nutrition.

The original membership of the Committee comprised four representatives from each institution. This was increased to five in 1951 and six in 1968. Its membership is thus made up of six WHO Executive Board members and six UNICEF Executive Board members, one of whom is the President of that Board, as ex officio member. WHO's Executive Board appoints one representative and an alternative from each WHO region. In practice, it appears that the UNICEF representation, with the strong support of its own secretariat, has generally showed more stability and consistency than the WHO delegation, whose membership changes often. This reinforces the influence of UNICEF in the Committee.

The Committee met every second year until the World Summit for Children in 1990, meeting from then on annually.[10] The Committee's secretariat is located in the Office of the Director-General of WHO.

Relationships between UNICEF and WHO again came to a low in the 1970s and 1980s as a result of the many initiatives of UNICEF's Executive Director J. P. Grant, which angered H. Mahler, appointed Director-General of WHO in 1973. Mahler felt that some of these new schemes were in breach of the jointly agreed Health for All strategy and resented the fact that Grant did not always consult with WHO before launching a new Initiative.

In 1990, the World Summit for Children adopted 27 goals, of which 21 were concerned with health. The Joint Committee monitored progress in achieving these health goals on an annual basis. The Committee also contributed to promoting vigorous immunization campaigns. Carol Bellamy, Executive Director of UNICEF said that, for the previous 49 years, the Committee had been instrumental in guiding the collective efforts of WHO and UNICEF to improve the lives of children and women. Continued cooperation between UNICEF and WHO was indispensable.[11]

In May 1997, at the thirty-first session of the Joint Committee, both Dr Nakajima, the then Director-General of WHO, and Carol Bellamy, Executive Director of UNICEF, lavished praise on the Committee's work and usefulness. The former said that in 1978, the Committee had been an important facilitator for the Conference on Primary Health Care held at Alma-Ata jointly sponsored by the two organizations, and had helped to stimulate the productive participation of NGOs. The Committee had been very much involved in the implementation of the primary health care strategy, helping to develop country-specific activities and community involvement in primary health care activities.

The UNICEF/WHO Joint Committee's composition was extended to include UNFPA in 1998 at the latter's request. A high-level inter-secretariat committee had been established in February 1996 in order to strengthen cooperation between the three agencies at the country level. In September 1996, the Executive Director of UNFPA presented to the Executive Board of UNDP/UNFPA the argument that it should take part in JCHP discussions since they included such matters as those relating to follow-up to the International Conference on Population and Development: the Board approved this proposal. In October 1996, the executive heads of both WHO and UNICEF accepted this new partner. WHO acknowledged that UNFPA makes an important contribution to the worldwide effort to improve the health of women, adolescents and children. However, WHO recalled its own unique leadership role in health among the organizations active in the health field, under the guidance of policy defined by the WHO Executive Board and the World Health Assembly.

The secretariat of the new WHO/UNICEF/UNFPA Coordinating Committee on Health (CCH) is provided by WHO. It is composed of 16 members selected by the Executive Boards of the three organizations, one from each region of the organization concerned (five each from UNICEF and UNFPA, six from WHO). The first meeting, held in July 1998, adopted recommendations relating to three main programme areas of collaboration: safe motherhood, vitamin A, and adolescent health and development.[12] The new Committee's terms of reference are listed in Figure 4.1.

The JCHP was not a decision-making body, although it formulated recommendations. One of its main functions was to produce joint reports and statements on areas of common interest to WHO and UNICEF. The new CCH and its recent counterpart, the Joint Consultative Group on Policy (JCGP), attended by UNDP, UNFPA, UNICEF, WFP and IFAD, are seen as offering a potentially effective mechanism for coordination within the UN system if substantive issues are addressed.

UNICEF is also a member of the Inter-Agency Standing Committee, which is composed of all the key UN and non-UN humanitarian agencies, including WHO. Under the chairmanship of the UN Emergency Relief Coordinator, the Committee attempts to coordinate humanitarian assistance activities.[13]

Comprehensive or selective primary health care?

UNICEF, together with WHO, took an active part in planning for the International Conference on Primary Health Care held in Alma-Ata in

1. The WHO/UNICEF/UNFPA Coordinating Committee on Health (CCH) shall meet biennially, or in special session if required, normally in Geneva. The Committee shall be chaired in rotation by a member of the Executive Board of each Organization; WHO, as the lead agency in international health, will chair the first session.

2. The role of the Committee will be:
   - to facilitate the coordination of health policies and programmes of the three organizations;
   - to review the overall needs for strategic, operational and technical coordination in the fields of maternal, child, adolescent and women's health, with a prioritized focus on disease and health ramifications based on WHO mortality and morbidity statistics, and reproductive health, including family planning and sexual health, to ensure regular exchange of information in these areas and to make recommendations to the respective Executive Boards for follow-up action by the secretariats, as appropriate, with due regard for the respective mandates of the organizations involved;
   - to promote consistency in implementation strategies and activities among the three organizations and with other partners, for the maximum benefit of Member States, especially at the country level within the context of the Resident Coordinator system and, in this context, to ensure that these are guided by the overall policy framework for health development as defined by the Health Assembly;
   - to receive and review progress and assessment reports presented by the Director-General of the World Health Organization, the Executive Director of UNICEF or the Executive Director of UNFPA, on activities pertaining to the health of children, young people and women . . .;
   - to consider matters of common concern to WHO, UNICEF and UNFPA which the Executive Boards or the secretariats of the respective organizations may refer to this Committee;
   - to report to the WHO, UNICEF and UNFPA Executive Boards on the foregoing matters.

Source: WHO Executive Board Res. EB103.R17, January 1999.

Figure 4.1   WHO/UNICEF/UNFPA Coordinating Committee on Health Terms of Reference (excerpts)

1978, and in endorsing the Declaration of Alma-Ata based on primary health care (PHC). WHO's approach has been to formally emphasize the 'comprehensive' PHC approach, i.e. the 'horizontal' integration of all health programmes and activities into national policies, strategies and plans of action (see Chapter 2).

In 1979, Walsh and Warren introduced the 'selective' model of PHC which questioned the Alma-Ata concept as being unattainable because of the cost and personnel required. The selective approach would institute health care directed at preventing, controlling, eradicating or treating the few diseases responsible for the greatest mortality and morbidity in

According to Walsh and Warren (1979), until comprehensive PHC can be made available to all, services aimed at the most important diseases may be the most effective means of improving the health of the greatest number of people. Selective PHC is the most cost-effective type of medical intervention. On the basis of high morbidity and mortality and of the feasibility of controlling them, a circumscribed number of diseases are selected for prevention in a clearly defined population. The principal recipients of care are children up to three years old and women in the childbearing years. The care provided is made up of measles and diphtheria-pertussis-tetanus (DPT) vaccination for children over six months old, tetanus toxoid for all women of childbearing age, encouragement of long-term breast feeding, provision of chloroquine for episodes of fever in children under three years old in areas where malaria is prevalent and, finally, oral rehydration tablets and instruction. These services are provided by fixed units or mobile units. The cost of fixed units is similar to that of basic PHC, although efficiency should be much greater. Whether the system is fixed or mobile, flexibility is necessary. The care package can be modified at any time according to the patterns of mortality and morbidity in the area served. It is important, however, for the service to concentrate on a minimum number of severe problems that affect large numbers of people and for which interventions of established efficacy can be provided at low cost.

Source: M. Koivusalo and E. Ollila, *Making a Healthy World* (Helsinki: Stakes; London and New York: Zed Books, 1997), Box 8.3, p. 115 – by permission.

Figure 4.2 Selective primary health care (PHC)

developing countries and for which there are means of control in terms of the efficacy and cost of interventions. The elements of selective primary health care are described in Figure 4.2.[14]

Grant's 'Child survival and development revolution' launched in 1982 was clearly based on selective PHC: from the eight elements of PHC, four techniques had been included in a package called GOBI, along the lines of Walsh and Warren's concept: growth monitoring, oral rehydration, breastfeeding and immunization.

Grant's enthusiasm, although supported by many heads of state and the World Bank, met with the open hostility of the equally ebullient Director-General of WHO, Dr. Halfdan Mahler. As noted by Walt,[15] in some countries, the way the UNICEF programmes were implemented seemed contradictory to the integrated approach of PHC. They were often run as separate projects. Even if they were incorporated into ministry of health programmes they were run like vertical programmes with their own staff, vehicles, logos and accounting systems.

Mahler objected strongly to what he perceived as selective (not comprehensive), top-down (without community involvement), vertical (not horizontally integrated) programmes. He also resented what he felt was a sort of duplicity on the part of Grant following a jointly agreed policy, under the technical direction of WHO, the lead organization of health.

In his address to the World Health Assembly in May 1983, he attacked UNICEF – without naming it – as showing 'little patience' and imposing 'fragmented action from above':

> I am referring to such initiatives as the selection by people outside the developing countries of a few isolated elements of primary health care for implementation in these countries; or the parachuting of foreign agents into these countries to immunize them from above; or the concentration on only one aspect of diarrhoeal disease control without thoughts for the others. Initiatives such as these are red herrings that can only divert us from the track that will lead us to our goal. They belong to the distant past of international meddling with national health affairs ... Such meddling failed then and it will fail now ...

Mahler added that he had no doubt whatsoever about the good intentions of these 'would-be benefactors', making it all the more difficult to reject their overtures. He suggested that governments carry out all 'the component parts of the strategy of Health for All in their entirety at the same time ...'.

Mahler deplored in 1986 the attacks against Health for All, considered as:

> ... an empty slogan, an unrealistic ideal based on romantic ethics, primary health care a too unwieldy vehicle to reach this ideal; ... that it will take a whole generation to modify the attitude of the medical profession, and that non-professional health workers do not inspire the confidence of people; ... and that governments are only pretending to be faithful to the principles of the Alma-Ata declaration, while in reality they are setting up PHC projects as small additions to existing ministries of health structures in order not to rock the ministerial boat.
>
> The alternatives being proposed? There are as many as there are health theorists and pushers of vested interest, often jumping on the same PHC bandwagon that they seem so intent on derailing. So governments of developing countries are being confronted with all sorts of remotely concocted proposals to pursue other kinds of health activities – often presented with seductive promises in neat self-contained packets.[16]

On UNICEF's side, there was a feeling of misunderstanding and of an unnecessary and unfounded public condemnation. Grant justified his proposed 'revolution' by the impact of the global recession in the early 1980s. Most governments began to restrict their investments in education and health. The Child Survival Revolution was designed to highlight the presence of a new capacity for social organization to make dramatic progress in health for all, through social mobilization.[17] As noted by Black,[18] selective PHC meant setting priorities and concentrating on problems which were known to cause illness and death, especially among the poor, and for which cost-effective remedies were available. GOBI was not meant to be a substitute for PHC, but to boost the movement by delivering tangible and measurable results.

It was also observed that WHO had run vertical programmes at both headquarters and country level: the completed Smallpox Eradication Programme, the Expanded Immunization Programme, the Control of Diarrhoeal Diseases Programme, the Onchocerciasis Control Programme in West Africa. These could be criticized as examples of selective PHC.

In spite of the conceptual superiority of integrating all elements of PHC at national and local levels, as jointly agreed by WHO and UNICEF at the Alma-Ata Conference, UNICEF has openly diverged from the WHO-supported comprehensive PHC approach, to WHO's chagrin. On the other hand, UNICEF's GOBI approach has been appreciated and supported by donors, the World Bank and many governments, because of its clear, quantified, low-cost and well-focused objectives. WHO should also recognize that it has itself launched a number of vertical programmes, even though they are supposed to be integrated within national health programmes.

In the final analysis, the distinctions between comprehensive and selective PHC may be considered marginal in the overall public health context. It seems that the heated confrontation of the 1980s between WHO and UNICEF on this issue has now subsided. An important step has been taken by both agencies in the direction of comprehensive PHC with their new joint strategy of Integrated Management of Childhood Illness, which started in 1992 (see below).

The promotion of breastfeeding

Promoting breastfeeding is an area where cooperation between WHO and UNICEF could be taken for granted. Indeed, most of the initiatives taken in this area were initiated by both agencies. The Meeting on Infant Malnutrition held in Bogota in 1970 and the Meeting on Infant and

Young Child Feeding in Geneva in 1979 were at the origin of the joint preparation by both agencies and final adoption by the World Health Assembly of the International Code of Marketing of Breast-milk Substitutes in 1981 (see also Chapter 2).

The Code, reaffirmed on numerous occasions by the World Health Assembly, was developed to protect mothers and health workers from commercial pressures by manufacturers of breast milk substitutes. It prohibits the provision of samples to mothers or health facilities (except for professional research) because of the negative impact on breastfeeding. It also prohibits inducements to health workers leading them to promote a particular product and to abstain from promoting breastfeeding.

According to WHO, breastfeeding is one of the most effective, low-cost interventions for neonatal health. WHO recommends that infants should be fed exclusively on breast milk from birth to four to six months of age; that is, they should be given no other liquids or solids than breast milk, not even water, during this period. For WHO, given the worldwide variation in growth velocity, an age range is an essential element of this feeding recommendation.

After this initial four-to-six month period of exclusive breastfeeding, children should continue to be breastfed up to two years of age or beyond, while receiving nutritionally adequate and safe complementary foods. Starting complementary food too early or too late are both undesirable. Ideally, the decision when precisely to begin will be made by a mother, in consultation with her health worker, based on her infant's specific growth and development needs.

This recommendation was based initially on the technical review and discussion undertaken in 1979 at the joint WHO/UNICEF meeting. The meeting's statement and recommendations were subsequently endorsed by the World Health Assembly. Important additional scientific evidence, including that most recently in 1995 from the WHO Expert Committee on the use and interpretation of anthropometry, underscores the reliability of the earlier review.[19]

Since 1993, key UNICEF publications have recommended exclusive breastfeeding 'for about the first six months of life', thus deviating from the official policy statement issued by WHO considered by UNICEF as 'outdated terminology'. UNICEF's position is based on knowledge about the damaging effects of early complementary feeding upon both breast milk intake and infant morbidity.[20] Four to six months, or for about the first six months of life, with or without an age range? UNICEF may have its own views, but a debate on the appropriate public health recommendation should be carried out between the two institutions, under the authority of the relevant WHO Expert Committee, in order to reach a common, public position. There would be a clear advantage in the two organizations speaking publicly with only one voice on such an important issue in order to avoid confusion among professionals and mothers.

UNICEF's divergent view is another sign that the Fund is, at times, loath to accept WHO's scientific and technical authority on public health issues in order to affirm its own identity and autonomy, at the risk of creating an open conflict which can only damage the name of the two UN agencies.

Is the Code applied? From its adoption up to 1998, 160 member states (84 per cent of WHO member states) have reported to WHO on action taken by them to give effect, in whole or in part, to its principles and aim. Such activities include mainly the following:

- adoption of new legislation and regulations;
- review, amendment and updating of existing legislation and regulations;
- preparation and updating of guidelines for health workers, manufacturers, distributors and retail outlets;
- negotiation and updating of agreements with health workers and infant-formula manufacturers;
- prohibiting the distribution of product samples to the general public and mothers;
- establishment of committees responsible for monitoring and evaluating the implementation of national measures adopted to give effect to the Code.

WHO estimated, in 1998, that globally, exclusive breastfeeding rates remained low. An estimated 35 per cent of infants were fed only breast milk at some point between birth and four months of age. In April 1998, the *British Medical Journal* produced compelling evidence that the Code was widely violated, based on a large, systematic and random survey of mothers and health professionals in Bangladesh, Poland, Thailand and South Africa. One tenth of all mothers interviewed and a quarter of all facilities visited had received free samples of milk, bottles or teats – none of them for research purposes. Violating information had been received by 30 per cent of health facilities, and 11 per cent of health workers surveyed had received gifts, three-quarters of which bore a company brand name.

These findings were confirmed by a survey carried out in 31 Asian, African, European and Latin American countries between January and

September 1997 by the International Baby Food Action Network (IBFAN). The survey results showed that in nearly every participating country, the main producers of infant formula and other breast milk substitutes do not comply with the requirements of the Code. Mothers, health workers and hospitals still receive free samples and supplies from numerous companies, but headed by the four major ones: Abbott Ross, Mead Johnson, Nestlé and Wyeth. The companies' underlying messages are that, although 'breast is best', breast milk needs to be supplemented. According to the report, very few companies dare to advertise infant formula directly to the public. The focus has now shifted to the promotion of follow-up formulas, complementary foods, milk for one-year-olds and toddlers, and formula milks for mothers.[21]

One of the most effective ways to promote and protect breastfeeding and to counter or decrease the companies' interference is the Baby-Friendly Hospital Initiative launched jointly by UNICEF and WHO in 1992 – 'baby-friendly' being another expression or slogan coined by Jim Grant. With the support of local and international NGOs, 171 countries have adopted the Initiative. The number of 'baby-friendly' hospitals rose from about 4300 in 1995 to more than 12 000 by the end of 1997, and to more than 16 000 by the end of 1999.

To qualify, a hospital must demonstrate to a team of assessors that all hospital practices are in line with the 'Ten Steps to Successful Breastfeeding', guidelines on maternity practices also jointly developed by UNICEF and WHO. They require that every maternity facility has a written breastfeeding policy in which all health workers are trained. Mothers should be informed of the advantage of breast over bottle, and helped to establish and maintain lactation. Mothers and babies should be allowed to remain together through rooming-in. Newborn infants should receive no food other than breast milk unless medically indicated. Hospitals must not accept free or lowcost supplies of breast milk substitutes, feeding bottles or pacifiers.[22]

The promotion of breastfeeding has met a new, lethal obstacle. Research has confirmed that infants whose mothers are HIV positive run a risk, currently estimated to be at least 1 in 7, of contracting the virus through breastfeeding. To assist policy-makers and health workers in addressing this risk, UNICEF has joined with WHO and the Joint UN Programme on HIV/AIDS (UNAIDS) to issue guidelines on infant feeding. These guidelines warn of the potential harm in mixing breastfeeding and artificial feeding: feeding infants solids or fluids in addition to mother's milk in the first few months of life may injure the baby's gut and allow the HIV virus to enter body tissues. The guidelines also usefully call for access to voluntary and confidential HIV counselling and testing for women and men, enabling them to make informed infant feeding decisions.

In spite of this advice, these are difficult or even impossible decisions. The Chief of Obstetrics and Gynecology at Makerere University Medical School in Kampala, Uganda made the dilemma clear: 'Twenty-seven per cent of babies born to infected mothers become infected from breast-feeding. In rural areas, 85 per cent of babies will die from dirty water used in formula.' Furthermore, using formula has a cost: a year's supply of artificial milk for infants will cost a Vietnamese family more than the country's per capita GDP, and comparable data can be found in other developing countries.

A recent trial concluded in Thailand has shown that a short course of antiretroviral pills given to pregnant women during the last weeks prior to and during labour successfully cut the rate of vertical transmission during pregnancy and delivery by half. Because the Thai women were also given safe alternatives to breast milk and did not breastfeed, the short course of treatment was able to cut overall mother-to-child transmission in the study population to 9 per cent, compared with a norm in developing countries of up to 35 per cent.[23]

The Safe Motherhood Initiative

In October 1999, WHO, UNFPA, UNICEF and the World Bank issued a joint statement on priority actions aimed at reducing the number of women who die during pregnancy and childbirth.[24] Each year, close to 600 000 women die from complications related to pregnancy and childbirth. In addition, these complications contribute to more than three million infant deaths within their first week of life and another three million stillbirths.

Maternal mortality shows a stark gap between industrialized and developing countries, with 98 per cent of all maternal deaths occurring in the latter. In developed countries, there are approximately 27 maternal deaths per 100 000 live births each year. In developing countries the average is 18 times higher, at 480 deaths per 100 000 live births.

The joint statement noted that the low social status of women in developing countries is an important factor underlying maternal mortality. Low social status limits women's access to economic resources and basic education, impeding their ability to make informed decisions on childbearing, health and nutrition. Poor nutrition before and during pregnancy contributes to poor health, obstetric problems and poor pregnancy outcomes for both women and their newborns.

Some 80 per cent of all maternal deaths worldwide are the direct result of complications arising during pregnancy, delivery or the first six weeks after birth. Four of the five main causes of maternal deaths are infections, high blood pressure, obstructed labour and unsafe abortion. The remaining 20 per cent of maternal deaths are the result of pre-existing health conditions and include anaemia, malaria, heart disease and HIV/AIDS, conditions that are exacerbated by pregnancy or its management.

The statement defined three key areas for action:

- Safe motherhood can be advanced through respecting existing human rights, through empowering women to make choices in their reproductive lives with the support of their families and communities.
- The access to and quality of maternal health services need to be improved. All deliveries should be overseen by skilled attendants and essential care should be available when obstetric complications arise.
- Women need to be able to choose if and when to become pregnant, through ensured access to voluntary family planning information and services.

The statement underlined that a ready supply of health providers with essential midwifery skills, backed up by referral services for complications, was critical in preventing maternal deaths. Furthermore, prevention of unwanted pregnancies is one of the key strategies for reducing maternal mortality. Thus, in addition to midwifery and referral services, there is also a need to provide client-centred family planning services with safe and effective contraceptive methods and counselling.

The Safe Motherhood Initiative was first promoted by WHO, following an International Conference on Safe Motherhood held in Nairobi in February 1987, co-sponsored by WHO, the World Bank and UNFPA, and supported by UNDP.[25] Was UNICEF not invited, or was the agency not interested? According to Black,[26] UNICEF's support for safe motherhood was initially lukewarm. Could this attitude stem from UNICEF's reluctance to be drawn into the family planning area, which includes contraception among other measures?

In 1990, the World Summit for Children set as one of the major national and international goals the reduction of maternal mortality rates by half of 1990 levels to be achieved in the year 2000. Its Plan of Action[27] included an eloquent plea for family planning. It stressed

the importance of responsible planning of family size and the many advantages of child spacing to avoid pregnancies which are too early, too late, too many or too frequent. Pre-natal care, clean delivery, access to referral facilities in complicated cases, tetanus toxoid vaccination and prevention of anaemia and other nutritional deficiencies during pregnancy are other important interventions to ensure safe motherhood and a healthy start in life for the newborn.

In 1993, the UNICEF Executive Board finally endorsed a policy on family planning promoting, in part, safe motherhood and breastfeeding, and the provision of 'appropriate' support for family planning services.

UNICEF's initial contribution to the Safe Motherhood Initiative was mainly in the training of traditional birth attendants and children's immunization. In the mid-1990s, the agency adopted a broad approach to safe motherhood to incorporate human rights, communication, education and gender programmes, with a special focus on the rights and needs of adolescents, without neglecting specific projects on the accessibility and improvement of obstetric services.

For example, in 1995, UNICEF-supported programmes in Bangladesh emphasized the decentralization of essential obstetric services, the development of clinical protocols and community mobilization. Eleven district hospitals were linked with the obstetric and gynaecology departments of 11 teaching hospitals for training and guidance in this process. In 1996, the Ministry of Health of Yemen launched a five-year plan to upgrade the skills of 4000 community midwives and strengthen local health services for women, with funding and technical support from UNICEF and other organizations. Yemen had one of the highest maternal death rates in the world (1400 per 100 000 births).[28]

Maine and Rosenfield[29] have recently argued that the global Safe Motherhood Initiative has been ineffective and that the main reason for a disappointing record is the lack of a clear, concise, feasible strategy. According to the authors:

> One common misconception is that maternal mortality can be reduced through general socioeconomic development (i.e. improvements in women's nutrition, education, and social status). Evidence from a variety of settings has shown that this is not true. In fact, maternal mortality, unusual among public health problems, is primarily affected by institutionally-based medical interventions.

They recommend focusing efforts on improving the quality of, access to and utilization of emergency obstetric care services, which means upgrading services that people can reach, such as district hospitals and health centres.

The joint statement of the four UN agencies has recognized the need to improve the access to and quality of maternal health services, but family planning is also crucial in preventing unwanted pregnancies.

The Bamako Initiative

The Bamako Initiative was another specific public health scheme conceived and launched by Jim Grant in 1987. Although the WHO Regional Office for Africa was, with UNICEF, party to the meeting of African Ministers of Health during which the Initiative was announced, it appears that the headquarters of WHO, responsible for world health policies, was not consulted beforehand on the policy content of the Initiative and on its implications for WHO's essential drugs policy. In spite of its intrinsic but debatable merits, the Initiative became another issue straining the relationship between WHO and UNICEF. It also strained the relationship between WHO headquarters and its Regional Office for Africa. WHO's Drug Action Programme, like other headquarters-run programmes, had by-passed Regional Offices to a large extent. The Regional Office for Africa wanted to proceed with the Initiative in spite of WHO headquarters' reservations.[30]

The original Initiative proposed that UNICEF, working with WHO, the World Bank and the African Development Bank as well as bilateral agencies, would provide funds to the least developed countries in sub-Saharan Africa for the following: initial funding of development costs for basic equipment required for primary level health services; a limited number of basic drugs and support costs during the period of the programme. The provision of drugs would be dependent on the levying of drug charges in amounts sufficient to cover operational costs, including salaries and the replenishment of drugs and supplies for the UNICEF Maternal and Child Health/ Primary Health Care programme (see also Chapter 2).

While the Initiative was endorsed by the UNICEF Executive Board at its 1988 session,[31] there was no World Health Assembly resolution to formally adopt it as a distinct WHO policy. Also in 1988, the WHO Regional Office for Africa and UNICEF adopted eight fundamental principles as operational guidelines for the Initiative, linking it to primary health care (PHC) and essential drug policies:

(a)   National commitment to accelerating the provision of universally accessible PHC services;

(b)   Substantial decentralization to the district level of the health ministry's decision-making for the management of PHC;

(c)   Decentralized management of community resources, thus allowing the funds collected at local facilities to remain under community control;

(d)   The application of consistent principles governing community financing for health care services throughout the different levels of the health system, making it inappropriate to provide free service at urban hospitals while requiring payment for community-based services;

(e)   Substantial government financial support for primary health care (PHC), to ensure that the health budget is maintained at least at its current level of support to district and local services;

(f)   Essential drug policies that are compatible with, and complementary to, the rational development of PHC;

(g)   Measures for ensuring that the poorest people have access to PHC services;

(h)   The clear definition of intermediate health system and management objectives and the establishment of indicators to measure them.[32]

Some of WHO's reservations about the Initiative were expressed during a meeting of the UNICEF/WHO Joint Committee on Health Policy held in January 1991. Participants stressed that a 'meeting of minds between UNICEF and WHO is essential': the Bamako Initiative differs from the WHO essential drugs programme in that the latter takes a comprehensive approach to the accessibility of essential drugs and their rational use, including secondary and tertiary levels, whereas the Initiative is concerned mainly with the first level of primary health care. It was, however, suggested that the two approaches could be complementary. 'The Bamako Initiative is a simple programme which, if used properly, could enhance PHC development, particularly at village level.' However, responsibility for health care cannot be wholly delegated to the community: the government must continue its general, normative functions and finance the health care system. Economic and financial reasons alone (funding drugs) are not enough to determine strategy. A related concern, on the part of WHO, was the increasing prominence of the World Bank in African health development.[33]

According to the UNICEF Annual Report for 1994, experience in the first six years of the Initiative had confirmed that even in low-income countries, people are prepared to pay a reasonable fee for the use of local facilities if the quality of services improves, if the resources generated are reinvested in the community, and if users have a say in the way their health facilities are managed. One of the benefits of the Initiative was improved immunization coverage and protection against diarrhoeal diseases and malaria. The 1995 Report showed the positive results obtained in the two earliest participants in the Initiative, Benin and Guinea: immunization coverage was raised in Benin from 14 per cent in 1985 to 73 per cent in 1993. In both countries, a number of community-managed health services generated sufficient resources to cover essential drug costs and recurrent local expenditures, as well as saving for future health investments. The Initiative was attracting substantial financial resources to UNICEF from the World Bank, USAID and other agencies. In 1996–97, UNICEF supported a major evaluation of the Initiative in eight countries, which highlighted several problems: delays in salary payments, too little emphasis on preventing illnesses, the inability of the poorest families to pay nominal fees for essential drugs, irregular supplies of these drugs and a need for greater community participation, particularly from women. On the other hand, preventive health care was promoted in several African countries, as UNICEF helped supply Bamako centres with vitamin A and iron-folate supplements for children and women. To help these same countries to prevent malaria, UNICEF supplied the centres with bed nets impregnated with mosquito repellents. Even in poor communities, health centres were able to sell enough nets to recover costs.[34] In Senegal, the modest financial contributions of health service clients to PHC, based on a strategy inspired by the Bamako Initiative, made these services financially autonomous. In effect, the public health sector was now co-financed by the state, local communities and the patients. WHO reported in 1998 that in Africa, access to drugs was still inequitable, even though it had been improved by introducing cost recovery as part of the Bamako Initiative and other similar initiatives.[35]

In a statement given in Bamako, Mali in March 1999, Carol Bellamy attributed the success of the Bamako Initiative, in part, to its flexibility. She recalled that some 35 countries had implemented the eight basic principles of the Initiative for use in nationwide programmes, involving such major components as immunization, vitamin A supplementation, safe motherhood, guinea-worm eradication and community participation activities. In Africa alone, the Initiative had helped ensure access to affordable and sustainable primary health services for more than 60 million people through the revitalization of 6000 health centres – managed and partially funded by local communities or districts in countries including Cameroon, Gambia, Mali, Mauritania, Niger,

Nigeria and Togo. At the same time, she did not hide some of the Initiative's potential problems: decentralization may affect the implementation of a coherent national health policy because of conflicting local interests, and preventive care may suffer because curative and hospital-based care is more visible and often reaps more financial and political benefits.[36]

The immunization of all the world's children

As recalled in Chapter 2, in September 1978, the International Conference convened jointly by UNICEF and WHO adopted the Alma-Ata Declaration. The Declaration included immunization against the major infectious diseases as one of the eight elements required, so that, by the year 2000, all mankind could benefit from primary health care.

In the 1960s, training programmes for the management of vaccination programmes had not yet been initiated, there was no systematic notification of vaccination coverage rates or vaccine quality, in particular in developing countries, and, finally, vaccination programmes were rarely included in the activities of national health services.

In 1974, the World Health Assembly created the Expanded Programme on Immunization (EPI) and recommended that WHO member states develop or maintain immunization and surveillance programmes against some or all of the following diseases: diphtheria, pertussis, tetanus, measles, poliomyelitis, tuberculosis, smallpox and others, where applicable, according to the epidemiological situation in their respective countries. In 1978, the Assembly included immunization as a component of primary health care and maternal and child health and such initiatives as the International Year of the Child. The WHO Director-General was requested to give high priority to the programme so that the goal of providing immunization for all children of the world by 1990 could be achieved.

In May 1976, the Assembly recorded its appreciation of the important role played by UNICEF, jointly with WHO, in supporting national immunization programmes.[37] Within the GOBI package launched by UNICEF in 1982, 'I' stood for immunization against the six vaccine-preventable childhood diseases, tuberculosis, diphtheria, whooping cough, tetanus, poliomyelitis and measles.

In 1974, coverage for children under one year of age in developing countries was well below 5 per cent. In 1987, for the first time in history, coverage exceeded 50 per cent for all vaccines except measles (at 46 per cent).

By 1991, WHO and UNICEF reported that the goal of immunizing 80 per cent of the world's children had been achieved. This had resulted in more than three million deaths from the six EPI diseases being averted each year.

In a WHO report, the 1993 Global Advisory Group concluded that the success of the global EPI represented 'one of the most important public health triumphs of this century and [is] a major contribution towards the global target of Health for All'. The Group was, however, concerned by the failure to move beyond the 80 per cent coverage target achieved in 1990 and the reductions in coverage in some countries on every continent. The problem of 'reaching the unreached' was particularly important in Africa. The World Development Report 1993 *Investing in Health* issued by the World Bank had identified immunization as one of the most cost-effective public health interventions.[38]

UNICEF supported EPI – albeit giving it a UNICEF name 'Universal Children's Immunization' (UCI) – by providing cold chain (ensuring that vaccines remain effective), sterilization and injection equipment, funds for the training of workers, monitoring and evaluation, and – most significantly – high quality, low-cost vaccines. In 1982, UNICEF's Supply Division in Copenhagen purchased 130 million doses of the six major vaccines (against polio, measles, tuberculosis, diphtheria, pertussis and tetanus). During the 1990s, UNICEF procured a total of 4.4 billion doses, shipped to about 100 countries. The agency is the world's largest purchaser of vaccines, spending over $100 million per year on vaccines and safe injection equipment.

It also played a prominent role, together with NGOs, in mobilizing political, religious and community leaders, and the media, to ensure that all children were immunized. Total investment in immunization activities by UNICEF for the period 1983–92 exceeded $600 million.[39]

Large-scale campaigns were carried out by declaring national vaccination days in specific countries with the support of political leaders, generally prompted by UNICEF and other partners. The Colombia campaign – three days of vaccinations, one month apart, in mid-1984 – led by President Belisario Betancur and his Health Ministry saw almost one million children vaccinated: it served as a model for other national campaigns. In 1985, three 'days of tranquillity' allowed 250 000 children to be vaccinated during a truce negotiated between the El Salvador government and the Farabundo Marti National Liberation Front. This model, supported by UNICEF and WHO, was also repeated in the midst of civil wars in Uganda, Lebanon, the Sudan, Angola, the Former Yugoslavia and Afghanistan.[40]

The eradication of poliomyelitis

In 1985, the Pan American Health Organization (PAHO) passed a resolution to eradicate polio from the Americas by 1990. By 1991, the last clinical case of polio was reported from the region, and the Americas were certified polio-free in 1994.

Following the pioneering role of PAHO, in 1988, the World Health Assembly established the goal of eradicating polio by the year 2000. The resolution thanked especially UNICEF for its overall efforts and Rotary International for its 'Polio Plus' Initiative. Other major partners are the US Centers for Disease Control and Prevention, and the governments of Australia, Belgium, Canada, Denmark, Finland, Germany, Italy, Japan, the United Kingdom and the United States. The US-based Task Force for Child Survival and Development, sponsored by WHO, UNICEF, the World Bank, UNDP and the Rockefeller Foundation, is another member of the polio network, which is also supported by NGOs and volunteers. Private foundations – e.g. the UN (Ted Turner) Foundation and the Bill and Melinda Gates Foundation – and corporate partners including De Beers and Pasteur Mérieux Connaught also support the Initiative.

The eradication goal was endorsed in 1990 by the UNICEF-initiated World Summit for Children. The last case in China was found in 1994 and eradication was achieved in the Western Pacific region in 1995.

The following strategies have been adopted:

- conducting national mass immunization days in all polio-endemic countries, while strengthening routine immunization services, to achieve high levels of coverage against the disease;
- improving disease surveillance systems, including laboratories, to enable prompt detection and investigation of every case of polio;
- implementing local, rapid 'outbreak response' or mass immunization when a suspected polio case is detected;
- targeting a country's remaining high-risk areas for 'mop-up' or mass immunization as polio declines in that country.

WHO and UNICEF have also recommended that in all countries with high under-five mortality and where vitamin A deficiency is a public health problem, vitamin A supplements should be provided at the same time as the polio vaccine. The campaign is considered as a 'booster shot' for health care delivery. It should strengthen primary health care by expanding immunization and other preventive services, providing better access to care, improving disease surveillance and increasing public awareness of services available. The strategies and infrastructure developed for the campaign should pave the way for better control of diphtheria, measles, neonatal tetanus and other diseases of public health importance.

As with the smallpox eradication campaign, the long-term benefits will far outweigh the short term-costs. More than $500 million are spent annually on routine polio immunization, whereas approximately $100 million are needed annually over the five years from the year 2000 to achieve the goal. After eradication, as much as $3 billion are expected to be saved annually by the year 2015, including costs for hospitalization and rehabilitation. Savings may then be transferred to other priority health activities. In human terms, when the goal is achieved, no child will be paralysed or killed by the disease even after immunization stops.

In January 2000, WHO and UNICEF urged leaders of countries where the final battle to eradicate polio by the end of year 2000 was being waged to give their full cooperation.[41] The WHO Director-General and Carol Bellamy noted significant achievements since the launch of the campaign in 1998:

- The number of polio cases had fallen from an estimated 350 000 in 1988 to some 5200 reported cases in 1998;
- The proportion of the world's children living in polio-infected areas had dropped from 90 per cent to less than 50 per cent;
- Polio had been eradicated from the Americas, Europe, the countries of the Western Pacific and much of the Middle East, and it had disappeared from most of northern and southern Africa.

Rotary International announced its Polio Plus programme in 1985. The programme raised funds from Rotarians, other individuals, firms and foundations and obtained government funds. With the political and technical endorsement of WHO and the collaboration of WHO and UNICEF, the programme mobilized tens of thousands of volunteers to assist in mass immunization campaigns around the world. In January 2000, Rotary International's President reiterated the support of 1.2 million Rotarians worldwide to the eradication effort. In India alone, Rotary mobilized 150 000 volunteers for national immunization days.[42]

Among other donors, in 1999, Pasteur Mérieux Connaught made a donation of 50 million doses of polio vaccine for National Immunization Days in five war-torn countries: Angola, Liberia, Sierra Leone, Somalia and South Sudan. $28 million were donated by the UN Foundation (Ted Turner) and $50 million by the Bill and Melinda Gates Foundation.[43]

The Children's Vaccine Initiative and its successor

This Initiative was launched at the World Summit for Children in New York in 1990 by five sponsoring agencies, UNICEF, WHO, UNDP, the World Bank and the Rockefeller Foundation. It involved governments, NGOs, industry and research groups. Its motivation was that the global progress of children's immunization was hampered by various problems with the available vaccines: the vaccines were not totally effective, they were often given too late to be potent, they often lacked the ability to tolerate tropical heat and they required multiple shots that necessitated complex delivery systems.

The original promoter of this new Initiative was, again, UNICEF's James Grant, under the influence of Dr D.A. Henderson, Dean of the School of Public Health, Johns Hopkins University (the former senior WHO official who had directed the successful smallpox eradication campaign), of William Foege of the Task Force for Child Survival and of the Rockefeller Foundation. At its April 1990 meeting, Grant recommended to the UNICEF Executive Board the allocation of $15 million for a programme 'expected to facilitate the eventual creation of a single-dose, multiantigen vaccine that can be administered very early in life'.[44] As related by Muraskin,[45] the Board rejected this proposal on the grounds that UNICEF should not be involved in support of biomedical research: it should remain a field-oriented organization supporting programmes at the country level to provide direct and immediate benefits to children and mothers. It should be concerned with the purchase and delivery of vaccines, not their research and development. The UNICEF lead also aroused new problems with WHO: while both agencies had collaborated reasonably well on the implementation of EPI/UCI, WHO did not appreciate the proposed intrusion of UNICEF into vaccine research, one of its own constitutional responsibilities, and insisted on having a central role in any proposed programme. In turn, the WHO vaccine-oriented programmes were being criticized for a lack of focus on vaccine development and their inability to raise sufficient funds to have a real influence on research. Furthermore, critics felt that WHO, under the Nakajima administration, lacked the technical and managerial ability to assume the leadership of the new programme.

The Declaration of New York, signed by the participants of the World Summit for Children on 10 September 1990, called on the world to use current science to make new and better vaccines. The vaccines should be one or two doses, given early in life, combined in unusual ways so as to reduce the number of injections, to be more heat stable, to be useful against a wide variety of diseases and to be affordable. In addition, investments should be made to simplify production and quality control methods, support field trials, speed licensing and help production in developing countries. The Declaration called on world leaders to 'commit themselves to a children's vaccine initiative that aims to produce and deliver "ideal" children's vaccines'. To WHO's satisfaction, it requested that this organization take the lead in establishing an International Task Force for Vaccine Development, along with UNICEF, UNDP, the World Bank and other interested international and national groups.[46]

In 1991, it was decided that CVI would take the form of an independent entity sited in Geneva, while WHO would not lead the initiative.

CVI was not a new institution, but a network and a global think-tank for vaccines and immunization. It aimed at improving the global supply and quality of existing vaccines, facilitating a dialogue between the public and private sectors on the research and development of new vaccines and developing strategies to ensure that these vaccines would be affordable for use in the developing countries. CVI was to build a global forum to include developing agencies, governments, donors, public sector and commercial vaccine manufacturers, vaccine researchers and national immunization programme managers. The intent was that, through establishing a dialogue between all key players in the global vaccine system – from research, testing, licensing and production to quality control, vaccine procurement and delivery – CVI would be able to identify weaknesses and potential bottlenecks in the system and seek workable solutions.

In 1992, UNICEF noted that the prices it paid for vaccines had increased by an average of 23 per cent. In 2000, the trend was for decreasing costs for traditional vaccines and higher costs for newer vaccines.

UNICEF and WHO were helping developing countries which produce large amounts of vaccine to improve the quality of their products and become self-sufficient. They also tried to persuade vaccine suppliers to moderate their price increases. In addition, under the CVI-run Vaccine Independence Initiative, countries were required to rigorously plan for their vaccine needs and corresponding vaccine budget over a two- and five-year period. The Initiative was to assist developing countries to procure vaccines through the UNICEF system and to pay for the vaccines either in local or hard currencies. High-quality but low-cost vaccines are provided through the UNICEF warehouse in Copenhagen, which accepts non-convertible currencies. It also includes a revolving fund to pre-finance vaccine procurement. UNICEF uses local currencies for in-country expenses and reimburses the revolving fund in dollars.The establishment in 1994 of the WHO Global Programme for Vaccines and Immunization

(GPV) was a reflection of the new priorities identified by CVI. The new programme integrated two operational units: EPI and the Vaccine Research and Development Unit and created a third, the Vaccine Supply and Quality Unit.

In 1997, CVI received a renewed vote of confidence from its co-sponsoring agencies in a meeting endorsing its new strategic plan. CVI was instrumental in the creation of the International Vaccine Institute in Seoul, Korea, uniquely dedicated to research, development and capacity building in the field of vaccines.[47]

In spite of recurring public statements of self-appreciation, CVI was disbanded and replaced, in 2000, by a new entity, called the Global Alliance for Vaccines and Immunization (GAVI).

The decision was taken during a meeting in Bellagio, in March 1999, during which the CVI Director stated that 'it became quickly obvious that WHO ... was in total disagreement with the way chosen by the majority of the working group' – a group convened by the World Bank – i.e the proposed strengthening of CVI. Participants then opted for the setting up of a new, smaller body without a mandate in matters of policy, fund-raising or priority-setting. In early April 1999, the Chief Executive Officers of Pasteur Mérieux Connaught, Merck Vaccines, Wyeth Vaccines and SmithKline Beecham Biologicals wrote to WHO, the World Bank and UNICEF to express their disappointment as to the failure of discussions held in the previous 12 months with a view to finding ways to improve children's immunization in the poorest countries.[48]

The official justification for the creation of GAVI was based on a one-year review of immunization-related activities undertaken by the major interested parties of CVI, which identified the following major gaps:

- stagnant immunization programmes with a decline in the basic EPI coverage for certain diseases as well as marked regional discrepancies;
- delay in the introduction of newly developed, highly efficacious vaccines against major killers such as Hepatitis B, haemophilus influenza b and yellow fever into the poorest countries;
- limited investment into vaccine research for diseases with high burden in developing countries in preference to diseases in developed countries with lesser global importance but higher financial value.

GAVI is a new partnership including UNICEF, WHO, the World Bank, the Bill and Melinda Gates Children's Vaccine Program, the Rockefeller Foundation, the vaccine industry, bilateral agencies and others. Its strategic objectives are as follows:

- to improve access to sustainable immunization services;
- to expand the use of all existing cost-effective vaccines;
- to accelerate the development and introduction of new vaccines;
- to accelerate research and development efforts for vaccines and related products especially needed by developing countries;
- to make immunization coverage an integral part of the design and assessment of health and international development efforts.

A Global Fund for Children's Vaccines was created. It will promote the financing of underutilized and new vaccines, vaccine access and infrastructure, and research and development of priority vaccines for poor populations and countries. It received a grant from the Bill and Melinda Gates Foundation of $150 million a year for five years. The Clinton Administration announced, early in 2000, a commitment to securing $50 million for the GAVI Vaccine Fund, to increased funding for research critical to the development of vaccines for malaria, tuberculosis and HIV/AIDS and to working with the World Bank and developing nations to improve health care structure.

The WHO Director-General chairs the Board of the Alliance for the first two years. The Executive Director of UNICEF will serve as Chair for the subsequent two years. The secretariat of GAVI is sited in the UNICEF Office for Europe in Geneva.

In February 2000, WHO and the Joint United Nations Programme on HIV/AIDS (UNAIDS) announced the creation of a new Initiative, separate from GAVI, to promote the development of an AIDS vaccine. UNICEF was not a partner in this new Initiative.[49]

Fighting the AIDS epidemic

According to a report issued in November 1999 by WHO and the Joint United Nations Programme on HIV/AIDS (UNAIDS), since the beginning of the AIDS epidemic, 50 million individuals worldwide have been infected with HIV, of whom over 16 million have died. In 1999, AIDS deaths reached a record 2.6 million, while an estimated 5.6 million adults and children worldwide became infected with HIV. So far, the disease has left 8 million children without a mother or both parents, the vast majority of them in sub-Saharan Africa. The total was expected to reach 13 million in 2000, of whom 10.4 million would be under the age of 15. In Uganda, 11 per cent of children are orphans because of AIDS. These orphans are often socially isolated because of the stigma of the disease, they are less likely to be immunized, and more likely to be malnourished and illiterate and more vulnerable to abuse and exploitation.[50] WHO was the first UN agency to take up AIDS as a critical issue in 1986. WHO's Special – then Global – Programme on AIDS (GPA) was created in 1987, stimulating programmes in over 100 countries in the first 18 months of its existence. In 1988, WHO and UNDP formed an Alliance to Combat AIDS. The Global AIDS Strategy was built upon three broad objectives: prevention of HIV infection, reduction of the personal and social impact of HIV infection, and unifying national and international efforts against AIDS. In the absence of a vaccine or cure for AIDS, the promotion of public information and education measures about personal habits was an essential element of the WHO Strategy in order to prevent the spread of the disease. These measures have included the promotion of safe sexual behaviour, in particular through the use of condoms, the provision of counselling and other forms of health and social services. In 1992–93, approximately 60 million condoms were provided to national programmes.

UNICEF was originally reluctant to engage in the global battle to combat AIDS. The philosophy quietly adopted by many rich countries and development agencies was: 'don't create demand' – don't create expectations that cannot be met on medical and financial grounds. It was reported that 'at UNICEF, the health division fought a bitter rear-guard battle from 1992 to 1994 to avoid involvement in AIDS'. J. Sherry, Director of Programme Development for UNAIDS, then senior health administrator at UNICEF, used his post to expand UNICEF's traditional mission to include teenagers contracting the sexually transmitted disease.[51]

Once these initial objections were overcome, UNICEF focused essentially on AIDS prevention through health education. At headquarters, UNICEF worked closely with the WHO GPA and was a member of all major AIDS coordinating committees. At field level, UNICEF offices supported the development of posters, pamphlets, videos, radio announcements and other information materials, AIDS-prevention training for health workers, use of schools, churches, women's groups, etc., to deliver AIDS messages, monitoring of the sterilization of immunization equipment against the possible transmission of HIV and other infections, and approval and supply of disposable syringes and needles only after close scrutiny of plans for disposal.[52]

However, UNICEF's prevention action is still limited by its reticent position regarding contraceptive devices. Although AIDS prevention includes individual and mutual protection through the use of condoms, UNICEF's policy on family planning has precluded its public support for, or participation in, the provision of condoms, as promoted by the WHO GPA. In 1967 it was agreed in the UNICEF/WHO Joint Committee on Health Policy that UNICEF assistance would be given for the development of maternal and child health services, but that this assistance would exclude the provision of contraceptives. A UNICEF representative said in 1996 that the agency's position on family planning had 'not changed over many years'. UNICEF 'has no policy on contraception or abortion' and it 'doesn't make its resources available to any agencies working in these areas'.

The reason for UNICEF's position is the fear of losing supporters and financial contributions – particularly in the US – by opposing the dogma of the Vatican, which forbids the use of condoms for both reproductive and illness-protection purposes, as well as the views of other religious, traditionalist and political groups and lobbies in this sensitive area. UNICEF is therefore following the Catholic Church's prescriptions to promote abstinence or one partner only as the only acceptable prevention measures. However, UNICEF has not tried to prevent other UN agencies and other partners from 'safe-sex' promotion through condoms and it has been willing to purchase condoms for other agencies on a reimbursable basis when other sources of supply could not be found.[53]

The Joint United Nations Programme on HIV/AIDS (UNAIDS) was established in January 1996 in Geneva, as a co-sponsored programme bringing together UNICEF, UNDP, UNFPA, UNESCO, WHO and the World Bank. This creation was a response to criticisms expressed by a number of governments and other donors regarding the lack of coordination of actions carried out in the field by these organizations, occasional duplication of efforts and unnecessary rivalry. As the main advocate for global action on HIV/AIDS, the programme's mission is to lead, strengthen and support an expanded response aimed at preventing the transmission of HIV, providing care and support, reducing the vulnerability of individuals and communities to HIV/AIDS and alleviating the impact of the epidemic. A small organization – 162 posts with an annual budget of $60 million – UNAIDS is the AIDS programme of the six co-sponsors together with its own activities. Its co-sponsors integrate UNAIDS policies and strategies into their ongoing work. UNICEF has not objected to UNAIDS' widely accepted affirmation, in a recent report, that young women 'need to protect themselves from pregnancy, sexually-transmitted diseases (STDs) and HIV', nor to the message that 'condom use means safer sex' and that drug users and their sex partners should have, as part of a package, access to condoms. A report issued in 1999 by the Johns Hopkins School of Public Health has recommended that condom use must substantially increase to help stop the spread of HIV/ AIDS and other STDs: 'narrowing the gap between condom need and use is a major public health challenge.'[54]

In the late 1990s, UNICEF maintained its prevention and care approach. Life skills programmes for children and youths were introduced in schools and community settings, and youth-friendly services were incorporated into health care centres to help prevent and treat sexually transmitted diseases among the young. UNICEF supported programmes that strengthen the capacity of families and communities to care for orphans and other children affected by AIDS.

In July 2000, Carol Bellamy recalled in an article that HIV/AIDS was the gravest crisis facing humanity today: 'The epidemic is a tyranny as intolerable and ruthless as any kind in history.' She stressed that the core of the prevention campaign can be summed up in two words: safe sex. However, she still refrained from saying that safe sex is essentially based on the use of condoms.[55]

A renewed WHO/UNICEF partnership

Since 1992, WHO and UNICEF have joined forces in a strategy for reducing the mortality and morbidity associated with the major causes of childhood illness, the Integrated Management of Childhood Illness (IMCI). IMCI is not a vertical programme; it is an integrated strategy which demands an active collaboration between all existing programmes such as oral rehydration therapy, acute respiratory infections, immunization, malaria control, nutrition, and essential drugs.[56] The strategy initially focused on improving care at the first level of health facilities, where children arrive sick every day, most of them with one or more of the major causes of illness and death. The need for integration at health facilities to rationalize the task of health workers became evident. A set of generic clinical guidelines for managing childhood illness was completed in 1996: it was used as the basis for introducing this component of IMCI in countries, subject to adaptation to national conditions.

In the year 2000, the focus was on improving the quality of care of children at first-level health facilities – centres and outpatient services – in both rural and urban areas through the use of standardized procedures in an integrated approach to health care. The curative component of IMCI addresses the most common life-threatening conditions for children, adapted to each country, focusing on diarrhoea, pneumonia, measles and malaria (where applicable), as well as the management of severe malnutrition and nutrition counselling. IMCI integrates simple life-saving technologies promoted by UNICEF and WHO, such as oral rehydration therapy, into a more comprehensive approach which addresses not only individual diseases but the sick child as a whole. As IMCI expands in countries, it is anticipated that single disease programmes focused on childhood diarrhoea (CDD) and acute respiratory infections (ARI) will be phased out. IMCI also has health promoting and preventive counselling, vitamin A and iron supplementation and treatment of helminth infestations: all children, not only sick children, should be targeted with these preventive and promotive interventions. IMCI pays particular attention to improving the communication and counselling skills of health workers.

By 2000, more than 35 countries had expressed interest in IMCI, ten of which had adapted guidelines on the management of childhood illness, including six which had carried out the first round of training at district level.

The World Bank has recognized IMCI as one of the most cost-effective components of a package of essential clinical and public health services. IMCI receives the financial support of a number of governments through their development assistance agencies, both for global activities and in individual countries. At country level, partnerships in support of the WHO/UNICEF strategy have been established with government departments, development agencies, universities, NGOs and community-based organizations.

Conclusion

WHO and UNICEF have similar objectives in the area of health, although UNICEF's mandate is limited to children and mothers: for WHO, the objective is the attainment by 'all peoples' of the highest possible level of health including persons of all ages – UNICEF seeks the improvement of the health of children through the reduction of infant, child and maternal morbidity and mortality.

Formally, UNICEF affirms that WHO is a 'vital partner' in the development of its health strategy and that it relies on WHO for authoritative technical guidance, as well as in operational programme design, monitoring and evaluation.[57]

The reality of the first fifty years shows alternating cooperation, competition and conflict. WHO initially opposed the creation of UNICEF and then tried to limit its activities by placing it within the UN secretariat under close supervision of the UN specialized agencies. When these attempts failed, WHO has constantly insisted on its leadership in public health policies.

The creators of UNICEF, its Executive Board and its executive directors set up and managed a semi-autonomous institution, with valuable and visible programmes. While they formally acknowledged the technical authority of WHO, they often affirmed the Fund's separate identity by creating separate programmes, by launching innovative initiatives, without always adhering to WHO-approved policies or without prior consultation with WHO.

The first reason for these recurrent problems is that envisaged by those who opposed UNICEF's creation: creating an agency concerned with children's health (and other areas) raised a risk of overlapping and therefore competition and conflict, with the mandate of the specialized agency charged, in part, with the promotion of maternal and child health and welfare.

Some of the conflicts have emanated from the dynamism, conviction and activism of such executive heads as WHO's Mahler and UNICEF's Grant and his periodic initiatives.

The structure and management of the two organizations are different. While WHO has decentralized regional offices, its headquarters plays a key role in defining worldwide policies. Both WHO headquarters and regional offices are known for their bureaucratic style of management. WHO country offices have limited autonomy and few resources.

In contrast, UNICEF has a strong country-level presence, with relatively autonomous country representatives and a practice of responding to country needs in innovative ways. UNICEF is widely seen as an effective operational and supply institution, with a capacity to mobilize support by effective public relations. Its programmes and initiatives are perceived as clear, achievable at low cost, with a strong political appeal. While WHO's normal channel is through ministries of health, UNICEF may approach directly heads of government in view of the broad scope of its programmes, an approach often used by Jim Grant to 'sell' his programmes. Finally its 'children first' concern has universal appeal.

Stereotypes reflect the long-time rivalry and antagonism. As described in the 'Potantico Retreat' report of 1996:

UNICEF saw WHO as ponderous, bureaucratic and ineffective at the country level. WHO saw UNICEF's advocacy work at country level turning into public relations exercises and its support going to establish parallel systems instead of building capacity in the public health sector. Doubts were expressed about the sustainability of UNICEF's operations in many countries. Against this, UNICEF was often admired for its employment of nationals, its long term commitment in many countries, its communications skills, its ability to respond quickly and to attract multiple partners.[58]

To these points, one may add that the WHO leadership and staff may resent UNICEF's better visibility in both industrialized and developing countries and its appeal to many constituencies.

The 'change of the guard' in WHO with the appointment of Gro Harlem Brundtland as a very dynamic Director-General in 1998, and her insistence on a 'difference' (with the prior management) and WHO's participation in a number of joint programmes and initiatives, may have opened the way to a more constructive relationship between UNICEF and WHO. The joint WHO/UNICEF 'Integrated Management of Childhood Illness' Initiative is an encouraging sign of renewed partnership. However, joint programmes do not reduce the natural urge of each agency to prove its worth, independently, in the same domain, for reasons of prestige and fund-raising. WHO has been particularly active recently in UNICEF's domain by launching several new initiatives and in creating in 1998 a new department for Child and Adolescent Health and Development.[59]

A reasonable balance between the assertion of autonomy and the necessity of joint programmes has to be found. The synergy of WHO's knowledge and UNICEF's operational performance and advocacy would benefit the health of the world's children as well as enhance the image of both agencies.

A continuous effort in this direction depends mainly on the political will of the WHO Director-General and of the UNICEF Executive Director and of their Executive Boards, with the support of like-minded governments.

5
Nutrition, Education, Sanitation

Among UNICEF's many other programmes, this chapter has selected three that are important: food aid and nutrition, education, and water supply and sanitation. In the same way as UNICEF is playing in the same public health field as WHO, these programmes involve UNICEF and other organizations to varying degrees. The main issue is to identify and assess the role of UNICEF in relation to that of other organizations in the same field.

Food aid and nutrition

According to the 'Plan of Action for Implementing the World Declaration on the Survival, Protection and Development of Children in the 1990s',[1] hunger and malnutrition contribute to about half of the deaths of young children. In 1990, it was estimated that more than 20 million children suffered from severe malnutrition, 150 million were underweight and 350 million women suffered from nutritional anaemia. According to the 1998 World Health Report,[2] one-fifth of the population of developing countries did not have access to enough food to meet basic needs. Low-income countries with a food deficit continued to face declining food production and complex emergencies that have displaced massive numbers of people. The prevalence of protein-energy malnutrition in children under five in developing countries declined from at least 42 per cent in 1975 to over 31 per cent in 1996, indicating that in general dietary protein had become widely available. Anaemia, mostly due to iron deficiency, was the most common nutritional deficiency worldwide in the 1970s and has remained so. Over the past 20 years there has been some decrease in the prevalence of iodine deficiency disorders, particularly in years following near-universal salt iodization by 1995 in most countries affected. Vitamin A deficiency was decreasing worldwide, but severe forms were still common in parts of sub-Saharan Africa.

UNICEF's expenditures on child nutrition have been relatively limited: 9 per cent of its budget for the period 1947–85, 6 per cent in 1985, 1989 and 1998, 8 per cent in 1994.[3]

Food aid

In its early years, UNICEF's focus was on feeding hungry children in war-ravaged countries. At the peak of its operations in Europe, six million children received each day a balanced supplementary meal with dried milk and other protective foods provided by UNICEF, and locally produced grains, potatoes and vegetables. As needs in Europe decreased, supplementary feeding shifted to the Middle East for mothers and children among the Arab and Jewish refugees, and for refugees in India and Pakistan. Child feeding programmes were then initiated in some countries in Asia and Latin America, mainly to teach the value of milk and other protective foods, along with better use of a country's own supplies of fruits and vegetables. In order to increase the local supply of good milk, UNICEF also helped European countries to develop their own milk conservation plant.[4]

Famines have recurred in many countries for economic and sometimes political reasons, and in natural or man-made emergencies, and the need for emergency feeding has not subsided. Although UNICEF has continued to provide foods in emergencies, the bulk of food aid has been provided by the World Food Programme (WFP) since 1963. In 1998, WFP delivered 2.8 million metric tonnes of food aid to nearly 75 million people in emergencies and long-term refugee operations and development projects. WFP focuses on the most vulnerable: women, children and the elderly. Its expenditures for 1998 were $1.348 billion, more than UNICEF's total income for the same year ($968 million), of which approximately $58 million were earmarked for nutrition.[5]

Nutrition

As previously noted, in 1960, UNICEF commissioned a special survey into the needs of children: the FAO participated with a report on the nutritional needs of children. The 1979 WHO/UNICEF conference on infant and young child feeding stimulated action to promote breastfeeding. In 1982, Italy funded the WHO/UNICEF Joint Nutrition Support Programme ($85.3 million) which followed the primary health care approach. Projects contained elements of oral rehydration therapy, breastfeeding, the eradication of goitre, food production and women's activities. In 1984, UNICEF equipped nutrition centres and demonstration areas, community and school orchards and gardens, and fish and poultry hatcheries in 27 200 villages. The agency also provided stipends to train 27 700 village-level nutrition workers.[6]

The GOBI formulation launched as part of the 1982 'child survival and development revolution' addressed nutrition concerns. 'G', which stands for child growth monitoring, is meant to identify signs of undernutrition in small children. 'B' stands for breastfeeding. One of the three 'Fs' attached to GOBI stands for food supplements.

The 1990 World Summit for Children found that improved nutrition requires (a) adequate household food security, (b) a healthy environment and control of infections and (c) adequate maternal and child care. Its plan of action identified the following most essential needs for the young child and pregnant woman: the provision of adequate food during pregnancy and lactation; the promotion, protection and support of breastfeeding and complementary feeding practices; growth monitoring; and nutritional surveillance. However, the Plan recognized that meeting these needs requires employment and income-generating opportunities, the dissemination of knowledge, and supporting services to increase food production and distribution . In other words, as for public health, a sound economy is a necessary foundation to combat hunger and malnutrition – to which one should add other factors such as good governance, and external and civil peace.

In 1991, WHO and UNICEF convened an international conference in Montreal entitled 'Ending hidden hunger: a policy conference on micronutrient malnutrition'. The conference was co-sponsored by the FAO, UNDP, the World Bank, the United States Agency for International Development (USAID) and the Canadian International Development Agency (CIDA), and was attended by ministerial-level delegations from 55 countries, as well as by representatives of many international, governmental, bilateral and non-governmental scientific organizations. Its main objective was the strengthening of international commitment to eliminating or reducing substantially iodine, vitamin A and iron deficiency.

In view of the rapidly growing body of evidence that vitamin A deficiency and supplementation significantly influence infant and child mortality in deprived populations, WHO, in collaboration with UNICEF, USAID and the National Institutes of Health, USA, organized a series of technical consultations which established a new scientific consensus on supplementation standards for iodine and vitamin A, as well as on mortality factors related to vitamin A.[7]

In 1992, the World Declaration and Plan of Action for Nutrition was adopted by the International Conference on Nutrition organized by the FAO and WHO. UNICEF was not invited as a full sponsoring partner, although it was involved in the preparation of the conference and in conference follow-up meetings at regional and subregional levels. The FAO organized a World Food Summit in Rome in November 1996. The Rome Declaration on World Food Security reaffirmed the right of everyone to have access to safe and nutritious food, consistent with the right to adequate food and the fundamental right of everyone to be free from hunger. Government representatives pledged their political will and common commitment to reduce the number of undernourished people to half their present level by no later than 2015. The summit was supported by a number of governments, IFAD, UNDP and the World Bank, foundations and private sector corporations. UNICEF was not listed as one of its supporters.[8]

The role of WHO and FAO in nutrition

Both organizations have a mandate in the field of nutrition, which includes child nutrition: only UNICEF has a specific mandate for child health which includes nutrition.

Following the 1992 WHO/FAO International Conference on Nutrition, the role of WHO was to develop strategies in the following areas:

- preventing and managing protein-energy malnutrition;
- overcoming micronutrient malnutrition;
- promoting maternal, infant and young-child nutrition;
- preventing diet-related noncommunicable diseases;
- preventing foodborne diseases;
- preparedness for and management of nutrition emergencies;
- promoting research and training in nutrition.

WHO provides guidance – standards, norms, training material – in the area of newborn health to address other issues such as the management of sick newborn and the care of moderately pre-term/low-birth-rate infants. WHO initially promoted worldwide awareness of protein-energy malnutrition through publications, cooperation with countries in national nutrition surveys, training of personnel and research. WHO/FAO expert groups have elaborated guidelines for nutritional assessment, nutritional requirements, the role of nutrition units, and national nutrition policies and strategies.

By 1997, over 160 countries had received technical and/or financial support from WHO for developing and implementing their national food and nutrition policies and plans. The WHO global database on national nutrition policies and programmes provides information on the progress of countries. The WHO global database on malnutrition and child growth covers 80 per cent of the world's under-five children, and the database on breastfeeding covers 65 countries (over 60 per cent of the world's population).

WHO strategies to prevent malnutrition in children in the early twenty-first century include supporting countries in eliminating iodine deficiency and its associated brain damage, vitamin A deficiency and its associated blindness and death, and iron deficiency anaemia with its associated mortality and morbidity; improving infant and young child feeding through the promotion of breastfeeding and proper complementary feeding; and more effectively addressing the nutritional needs of the ever-growing emergency-affected populations.[9]

The FAO's constitution mandates the organization, in part, to raise levels of nutrition of the peoples and to contribute towards an expanding world economy ensuring humanity's freedom from hunger. Nutrition is one of its concerns, together with land and water development, plant and animal production, fisheries, forestry, agriculture and world food security. Its Food and Nutrition Division assesses and monitors nutritional situations and requirements and provides advice and assistance to FAO member states aimed at improving the nutritional status of all, particularly the poor and most vulnerable groups in developing countries. The FAO undertakes and publishes studies, including Nutrition Country Profiles and nutrition education materials. While it does not focus specifically on children, the FAO provides dietary guidelines and nutrition education materials for use at the community level as well as expert scientific advice to policy-makers and programme designers to ensure that the nutrient requirements of women are met throughout their life cycle.

UNICEF is not a party to such bodies as the Joint FAO/WHO Expert Committee on Food Additives, or the Codex Alimentarius Commission, the ruling body of the Joint FAO/WHO Food Standards Programme.[10]

UNICEF's own programmes in food aid and nutrition

Even though UNICEF cannot compete with the WFP on food aid, and with WHO and the FAO on nutrition policies and scientific studies, it generally follows policies set by these organizations, and joins them in specific activities. UNICEF has maintained its profile as an effective operational agency for children's and women's welfare in this field, within the limits of scarce resources. As a catalyst, UNICEF has been at the forefront of several well-publicized initiatives with the support of WHO – which were reviewed in Chapters 2 and 4.

In 1990, the UNICEF Executive Board approved a strategy for improved nutrition of children and women in developing countries for the year 2000. The Board identified three types of action:

1. Actions that address the manifestations and immediate causes of malnutrition, such as the promotion of breastfeeding, nutrition rehabilitation, the provision of certain essential drugs, the promotion of oral rehydration therapy, direct feeding programmes and the distribution of micronutrients.
2. Actions that address the underlying causes of malnutrition, such as immunization, the expansion and improvement of the primary health care delivery system, health and nutrition education and communication, family planning, household food security, improved feeding practices, maternal and child care, environmental sanitation and water supply, and literacy and education.
3. Actions that address the basic causes of malnutrition, such as improved situation analysis, policy dialogue, technology assessment and development and advocacy.

The broad scope of these actions exposes the number of factors which affect malnutrition and the need for considerable resources to address its symptoms and, even more, its causes.[11]

A few examples of UNICEF's varied programmes and activities over the years follow. The creation in 1983 of UNIMIX, a high-calorie, high-protein food mixture, by an innovative UNICEF representative and his Oxfam colleague in Sudan is related in Figure 5.1.

In the area of household food security, in 1989, UNICEF provided direct support for household food production in several African countries. In Tanzania, communities received UNICEF assistance to plant 100 000 acres of food crops. In Nigeria, improved seeds and planting materials were distributed to farmers. In the same year, UNICEF gave support to vitamin A deficiency control programmes by the distribution of 105 million high-dose capsules, mainly in Bangladesh and Indonesia. According to a 1999 WHO report, iodine deficiency disorder (IDD) is a significant public health problem in 130 countries, affecting a total of 740 million people. In spite of measurable progress being made through universal salt iodization, there are nearly 50 million people who are estimated to still be affected by some degree of IDD-related brain damage. IDD constitutes the single

In 1983, while serving in the Sudan as UNICEF Representative, Mr. S.S. Basta launched a series of nutrition surveys which showed that famine and diarrhoeal diseases were on the increase. Together with the Oxfam representative, N. Weiner, also a nutrition scientist, they envisaged the creation of a high-calorie, high-protein food mixture targeted to children. They mixed sugar and sorghum (local products) with milk powder. The expected benefits of the mixture were: (a) the high sugar content could protect the milk powder from bacterial contamination, or at least lessen it; (b) such a food could be transported and stored in hot climates, with minimal rancidity since fat content was low; (c) the low moisture content ensured that it was light to transport and that fungal or bacterial contamination was minimal; (d) it would not require heat or water. The resulting mixture met recommended requirements for calorie, protein, calcium and other minerals, using standard FAO/WHO food composition tables. Its composition was also approved by the Sudanese Nutrition Institute in the Ministry of Health. Basta called the mixture UNIMIX (short for UNICEF mixture). Once production, packaging and storage problems were solved (a Sudanese industrialist agreed to produce and package the mixture in his factory for free), demand for the product rose rapidly: tons of UNIMIX were distributed to feeding centres, clinics and rural hospitals, and displaced persons' camps.

In 1985, UNICEF's Regional Office in Nairobi began producing the mixture for use in Southern Sudan. Nairobi had created a logistical base in Northern Kenya for Operation Lifeline Sudan. Then UNIMIX was sent from Kenya to other emergencies in Somalia, Rwanda, Burundi and Congo.

UNIMIX is still being produced in various countries in Africa, Asia and Europe. It is not produced by UNICEF but by local manufacturers, although the agency sometimes provides the vitamin and mineral premix for the production. Initially, UNICEF and/or the World Bank built the production facilities in some countries. UNIMIX is not produced under a UNICEF patent, but according to UNICEF specifications.

Source: Information provided by S.S. Basta in 1999 complemented by information received in July 2000 from the UNICEF Supply Division in Copenhagen.

Figure 5.1 How UNIMIX was created

greatest cause of preventable brain damage in the foetus and the infant, and retarded psychomotor development in young children. The deficiency, stemming from a lack of iodine in the diet, often results in goitre, an enlargement of the thyroid gland. In severe cases, IDD can lead to mental retardation, stunted growth, paralysis and death. Iodine-deficient women are more prone to miscarriages and stillbirths. If born, their child may die in infancy or suffer from mental and physical disorders.

A UNICEF survey found in 1993 that Laos had one of the worst rates of iodine deficiency disorder in the world. Iodizing the salt supply in Laos and other developing countries is an inexpensive and simple solution to this health problem. In 1998, UNICEF helped the Russian Federation identify and address its iodized salt needs. UNICEF supported information campaigns and provided iodizing equipment and employee training for salt factories.

Although UNICEF has been a pioneer in supporting IDD control since the 1960s, WHO assumed leadership in this area in 1999. Under the direction of its activist Director-General, Dr Gro Harlem Brundtland, WHO announced its plans to eradicate IDD within the first decade of the new century, through an intense programme of salt iodization and iodine delivery. WHO would still continue to collaborate with UNICEF and the International Council for Control of Iodine Deficiency Disorders, two major WHO international partners in this area.[12]

According to a 1999 UNICEF report, the impact of vitamin A supplementation on reducing child mortality is comparable – if not greater than – that of any single immunization against a childhood disease. Long known as a cause of blindness, vitamin A deficiency (VAD) had increasingly been recognized in the 1990s as significantly heightening a child's risk of dying from measles and diarrhoea. In countries where VAD is a problem, ensuring that children receive adequate vitamin A can reduce mortality by 23 per cent. WHO and UNICEF recommend that vitamin A supplementation be included in routine immunization activities and such events as National Immunization Days in all countries where the under-five mortality rate is greater than or equal to 70 per 1000. In 1998, many countries dispensed vitamin A during polio campaigns and other immunization programmes.

In March 1999, UNICEF, WHO, donor governments and private sector groups, including USAID, CIDA and the Ottawa-based Micronutrient Initiative, met to give impetus to a Global Vitamin A Partnership. The Partnership aims at saving millions of young lives, either by fortifying foods with vitamin A or providing an efficient twice-a-year capsule costing two cents to produce. During the meeting in Washington, DC, Carol Bellamy commended countries like Zambia and the Philippines, where vitamin A fortification and supplementation have been highly successful. She noted that in Bangladesh some 700 000 volunteers gave their time to ensure that children receive twice-a-year vitamin A capsules.[13]

Education

According to a UNICEF report published in 1999,[14] an estimated 855 million people were functionally illiterate. Over 130 million children of school age in developing countries were growing up without access to basic education, while millions of others were in substandard learning situations. Girls represent nearly two out of every three children in the developing world who do not receive primary education (approximately 73 million of the 130 million out-of-school children).

In sub-Saharan Africa, the primary enrolment rate is close to 60 per cent: over 40 million primary school age children are not in school. In South Asia, primary enrolment has climbed from under 60 per cent in 1970 to nearly 70 per cent: 50 million primary school age children are not in school. Nearly two-thirds of women in the region are illiterate, compared with about one-third of men. About 40 per cent of children entering primary school drop out before reaching grade five, the highest regional rate. In a few Eastern European countries and countries of the Commonwealth of Independent States, the quality of schooling has dropped. For UNICEF, the portrait is not just one of general decay but of re-emerging inequality, with poor families less able to pay for their children's education, and children in rural areas and from ethnic minorities disproportionately affected.

On the other hand, in Latin America and the Caribbean, primary enrolment has expanded at an annual rate of 4.4 per cent between 1960 and 1980, and became virtually universal with regional enrolment over 90 per cent. Primary enrolment in the industrialized countries stands at close to 100 per cent. There is parity in boys' and girls' enrolment rates at the primary and secondary levels.

There is a correlation between the level of education and mortality and fertility rates, although political, economic and other factors are also at work. A 10 percentage point increase in girls' primary education enrolment can be expected to decrease infant mortality by 4.1 deaths per 1000, and a similar rise in girls' secondary enrolment by another 5.6 deaths per 1000. Additional education may also reduce fertility rates and maternal deaths in childbirth. In Brazil, illiterate women have an average of 6.5 children, whereas those with secondary education have 2.5 children. Infant mortality rates in Nicaragua tend to fall as a result of female education among poor households, according to a study published in 1999 in the *American Journal of Public Health*.[15] UNICEF's expenditures on formal and informal education are higher than those for food aid and nutrition: 15 per cent for the period 1947–85, 13 per cent and 14 per cent in 1994 and 1998, with lower rates – 11 and 7 per cent – in 1989 and 1994.[16]

UNICEF's growing interest in education

The mandate of UNICEF did not include education per se. The agency was initially only concerned with providing knowledge on health and nutrition. UNICEF's interests expanded progressively to all aspects of education, including formal and informal education, with a focus on primary education and on the education of girls, with the support of a number of human rights legal instruments.

Education is the major activity of UNESCO. Its priorities are to achieve basic education for all adapted to today's needs, and to develop higher education. It helps train teachers, educational planners and administrators, and encourages local building and equipping of schools. Cooperation between UNESCO and UNICEF was therefore required and practised: it did not seem to arouse the types of conflicts which arose between UNICEF and WHO in the field of health.

The right to education was affirmed in the 1948 Universal Declaration of Human Rights. Its Article 26 also prescribed that 'Education shall be free, at least in the elementary and fundamental stages'. The right of everyone to education was confirmed in Article 13 of the 1966 International Covenant on Economic, Social and Cultural Rights. Principle 7 of the 1959 Declaration of the Rights of the Child stated that 'The child is entitled to receive education, which shall be free and compulsory'. Between 1960 and 1966, UNESCO held four World Regional Conferences on Education which helped establish time-bound regional goals to provide free and compulsory primary education for all children. The meetings were held in Karachi (1960), Addis Ababa (1961), Santiago (1962) and Tripoli (1966).

As previously noted, the Survey on the Needs of Children commissioned by UNICEF in 1960 included a UNESCO contribution on children's educational needs. The UNICEF Executive Board then agreed to extend the agency's assistance to elementary education, agricultural education and vocational training. UNICEF's interest in informal education based on alternative pedagogy stemmed from reports presented by the International Council for Education Development in 1973 and 1974 to UNICEF's Executive Board. However, UNICEF correctly maintained that informal education schemes should not be a substitute for the mainstream educational systems. An innovative approach to health education known as Child-to-Child was launched in 1979 and is used by more than eighty countries. This participatory programme advocates children being seen as active promoters and not just receivers of health. In 1991, the Child-to-Child Trust won UNICEF's annual award, given in the name of Maurice Pate, for what was described as a 'new, effective and revolutionary idea' in working with children for better health.[17]

In 1979, the International Convention on the Elimination of Discrimination Against Women was opened for signature. It entered into force in 1981. The Convention calls, *inter alia*, for equal rights in education.

According to Black,[18] early in 1982, Grant made a determined but vain attempt to persuade UNESCO to collaborate on a major initiative to promote 'primary education for all' – no doubt, on the 'Health for All' model. One of the two 'Fs' attached to the GOBI formulation of 1982 stands for 'female education', a modest compensation for UNESCO's rejection of a broader scheme.

Cooperation improved with a change of leadership in UNESCO.[19] A Joint Committee on Education consisting of representatives of the Executive Boards of UNESCO and UNICEF was set up in 1989 to promote collaboration between the two organizations. Ten years later, in February 1999, UNESCO and UNICEF finally signed a memorandum of understanding outlining areas of common interest and future collaboration.

The Convention on the Rights of the Child was adopted by the UN General Assembly on 20 November 1989. Confirming and expanding on the earlier Declaration, the Convention reaffirmed the right of the child to education. States parties were to make primary education compulsory and available free for all, encourage the development of different forms of secondary education, make higher education accessible to all, make educational and vocational information and guidance available and accessible to all children, and take measures to encourage regular attendance at school and reduce drop-out rates (Art. 28). The Convention entered into force in September 1990.

In March 1990, the World Conference on Education for All, sponsored by UNDP, UNESCO, UNICEF and the World Bank – later joined by UNFPA – was held in Jomtien, Thailand. Giving belated satisfaction to Grant's earlier initiative, it played the same role for education as the International Conference on Primary Health Care had played for health. It called for universal quality education, with a particular focus on the world's poorest citizens. Jomtien marked the emergence of an international consensus that education is the single most vital element in combating poverty, empowering women, promoting human rights and democracy, protecting the environment and controlling population growth.

In September 1990, the World Declaration on the Survival, Protection and Development of Children agreed to at the World Summit for Children recognized that the provision of basic education and literacy for all was among the most important contributions that can be made to the development of the world's children. Participants committed themselves, in part, to work for programmes that:

reduce illiteracy and provide educational opportunities for all children, irrespective of their background and gender; that prepare children for productive employment and lifelong learning opportunities, i.e. through vocational training; and that enable children to grow to adulthood within a supportive and nurturing cultural and social context.

In the Plan of Action for implementing the Declaration, participants adopted the following measure, among others:

Universal access to basic education, including completion of primary education or equivalent learning achievement by at least 80 per cent of the relevant school age children with emphasis on reducing the current disparities between boys and girls.[20]

UNICEF's *State of the World's Children 1999* launched an 'Education Revolution' integrating a number of well-established principles: learning for life; accessibility, quality and flexibility; gender sensitivity and girls' education; the state as key partner; and care for the young child. The aim is not only to give children basic numeracy and literacy skills but also to equip them to appreciate their own rights, respect the rights of others, and take control of their own lives.

In a report of 1999 to its Executive Board, the UNICEF secretariat emphasized the need for programming within a rights perspective. This required more explicit attempts to find children not in school and to get them enrolled. Among the unreached, girls must continue to be the highest priority. Building more schools does not necessarily lead to higher enrolment. The essential core of a basic education must include, but go beyond, literacy and numeracy. Africa has been and must remain a regional priority for education.

UNICEF's strategies and areas of action for the new century include the following:

1. Early childhood care for survival, growth and development: getting young children ready for school and for life.
2. Equity of access and completion: getting all children into school and keeping them there.
3. Increased quality: ensuring that children learn what they need to learn.
4. Adolescent education, participation and development: helping adolescents get educated and involved.
5. Planning, financing and managing education: empowering families and communities.

6. HIV/AIDS prevention and control.
7. Programming in situations of instability and emergency.

An Education For All Forum Secretariat, based at UNESCO, is coordinating an end-of-decade assessment of progress. Technical input is provided to the Forum by a Technical Advisory Group consisting of representatives of the five partner agencies, UNESCO, UNDP, UNFPA, UNICEF and the World Bank. General trends are disappointing. In spite of a slight growth in formal pre-school enrolments, the growth in enrolment of school-age children in some regions has barely kept pace with population growth, and some countries show an actual decline in enrolment rates. Many of the studies show low levels of learning achievement.[21]

Development education

While the essential part of UNICEF's education programmes concern developing countries, i.e an orientation towards the 'South', another programme, called development education, is addressed to Northern countries[22]. It has been defined as a process of sensitization of citizens in industrialized countries to the socio-economic development problems of the 'South', to increase understanding of those problems and to promote action or support towards their solution. This process is also intended to promote UNICEF's role and programmes in Northern countries, and to give support to its funding by governments, foundations, business firms, NGOs and private citizens.

UNICEF became actively involved in development education in 1975 and was the 'lead' agency for the UN system in this field from 1979 to 1984. The stimulus for this programme came from its national committees, especially those in the Nordic countries and in the USA. UNICEF's concern was to link the concept to the situation of children in the developing countries, and its target groups were identified as teacher-training colleges, teachers and parents of the primary and secondary schools, publishers of children's books, and youth and NGO groups in the industrialized countries. Women's groups, religious organizations, trade unions, parliamentarians and local authorities, librarians and others were later included. The programme was undertaken in close cooperation with national committees and NGO allies in industrialized countries. The programme has included the publication of development education kits, 'Papers, News and Notes', the organization of study trips, workshops and seminars.

For instance, each year, the French Ministry of Education sends a letter to all university 'recteurs', academic inspectors, directors of department services of the national education ministry, and heads of secondary, primary and elementary schools, calling their attention to the importance of the role played by UNICEF. The letter briefly explains the role of the agency and suggests that students should be made aware of the dramatic situation in which many children live, that they become conscious of the interdependence of different regions of the world, that they develop a sense of social justice and that they understand the effect of violence in relations between states and individuals. Educational documentation and support is provided by the French National Committee for UNICEF.[23]

Recent education programmes

The UNICEF-assisted Community Schools Project in Egypt, begun in 1992, has brought education to 4000 girls in about 150 small villages in remote rural areas of the Upper Nile region. Girls' enrolment had been low in the region, where a third of the population lives in hamlets at least five kilometres from the nearest government schools. Many parents were reluctant to send their daughters to faraway schools. The free, multigrade schools in the project offer flexible schedules to suit local needs. Communities provide a simple building for the classes and participate in managing their own schools. The government covers salaries, books and training of teachers. UNICEF provides training for project teams, curriculum development and some educational material. In 1997, the Ministry of Education announced its intention to expand the scheme nationally, with major financial support forthcoming from the Canadian International Development Agency and the Netherlands, to be later joined by USAID.

Reaching girls in rural areas is also a priority for Yemen, where the UNICEF-assisted Hamlet Schools programme started in 1993 has reached 7000 children in Yemen's remote provinces. Each village donates labour and land for the creation of a primary school.

In 1998, the UNICEF Girls' Education Programme, with major support from Canada and Norway, continued to promote the development of gender-sensitive classrooms in 52 countries through activities such as teacher-training and the creation of new textbooks and curricula. In West and Central Africa, the African Girls' Education Initiative supported 4200 schools and literacy centres, more than double the number supported in 1997.

Alternative active learning methods have been introduced in Bangladesh through a UNICEF-assisted government programme, Intensive District Approach to Education for All (IDEAL). By the end of 1998, the programme had been implemented in grades one and two of more than

11 000 schools in one quarter of the country's districts. UNICEF helped start the Pratham Mumbai Education Initiative in India in 1993 by bringing together municipal officials with 150 representatives from various communities, including those most marginalized. The purpose of the Initiative is to make school accessible to disadvantaged children, and help them enrol in school and stay there. It received financial support from a local credit institution and from British Airways. UNICEF has provided initial financing support and training. By 1997, the Initiative served 38 000 children in 1600 pre-schools at minimal cost to families. The partnership also introduced 'Joyful Learning' – a programme which features 'learning by doing' and the use of educational games – to 1256 municipal primary schools serving 400 000 children.[24]

Water supply and environmental sanitation

Lack of clean water, inadequate sanitation and poor hygiene practices are among the underlying causes of child deaths and illness from disease and malnutrition. According to WHO estimates, 1.2 billion people in the world have no access to safe drinking water, while 2.9 billion people do not have access to proper sanitation systems. Every year, more than five million individuals die from illnesses linked to unsafe drinking water, unclean domestic environments and improper excreta disposal. Women and girls, who are assigned the task of fetching water in most cultures, often have to walk long distances for water which is often unsafe. The poor in many non-serviced urban areas pay as much as 20 to 30 per cent of their income for small quantities of water of poor quality. A UNICEF report notes that high costs and low efficiency and reliability have characterized public utility services across much of the developing world. Privatization may further marginalize the poor.[25]

UNICEF involvement

UNICEF's support for rural water supply and sanitation started in 1953, initially on a pilot- or demonstration-project scale, then in the late 1960s as a response to drought emergencies. Since then UNICEF has supported government programmes for the provision of a minimum level of water supply and sanitation for those most in need. This involved primarily the rapid drilling and installation of boreholes with handpumps in rural areas. In the late 1960s and 1970s, UNICEF and donor assistance diversified into relatively large-scale national water programmes, including the provision of sophisticated drilling rigs and equipment, gravity-fed systems, protected springs and wells, and upgrading of traditional water sources in rural areas.

UNICEF's intervention in providing hardware in the technological area of sanitary engineering may appear as an unnecessary and costly extension of its mandate, in an indirect peripheral approach to basic children's welfare. During Maurice Pate's terms of office, some Executive Board members doubted that water supply was a field into which UNICEF should enter because of potentially high costs; others thought aid in this field was largely outside of UNICEF's mandate. In 1953, the Board agreed that UNICEF could help 'demonstration' projects for safe water and excreta disposal in rural areas.[26]

However, these initial doubts were later cleared and limitations lifted. The second Executive Director, Henry R. Labouisse, justified UNICEF's support in that young children are particularly vulnerable to diarrhoea and other diseases due to lack of sanitation, which also contributes to child malnutrition.

> Thus, the provision of safe water is one of the most effective and economical ways to help child health within the framework of primary health care ... An accessible water supply is a great convenience: lessens the drudgery of mothers, makes possible their use of more time for other activities and encourages self-help community efforts.[27]

Labouisse felt that improvements in children's health are incompletely achieved without improvements in water supply and the disposal of waste water. Also involved are personal hygiene, appropriate disposal of excreta, household cleanliness, food storage and handling, disposal of solid wastes (garbage) and the environment around the house. UNICEF therefore also supports environmental sanitation measures, especially disposal of waste water and human waste (e.g. by provision of water-seal pans and slabs for latrines). UNICEF's assistance has been limited to rural and peri-urban areas – where wells and latrines can be used – because the agency does not have sufficient resources to cooperate in the construction of large-scale urban water supply or sanitation systems.

To encourage support for these measures, UNICEF's programmes in the 1980s stressed health and sanitation education, the orientation and increased participation of community-level workers, and the diffusion of information through women's organizations.

Funding

UNICEF's expenditures on water and environmental sanitation decreased from 18 per cent in the period 1947–85, to 15 per cent in 1989 and 1994, to 11 per cent in 1998.[28]

According to a 1995 UNICEF report, of approximately $3.5 billion per year spent in rural areas of developing countries in the last decade, the UNICEF contribution, primarily in low-cost rural systems, averaged $65 million per year (excluding emergencies), which was less than 2 per cent of the total investment. This shows UNICEF as a 'small player' in this field, but its limited financial resources – $81 million in 1994 for water and environmental sanitation programmes – are somewhat offset by its advocacy and catalytic role. With an emphasis on low-cost approaches, UNICEF contributed directly to the provision of water supply to an estimated 165 million people and of sanitation to 28 million people during the period 1990–94.

UNICEF partners and international support

As in other areas, UNICEF is not alone in this field. First, the agency works with governments and NGOs. Second, it is associated with a large number of UN agencies in specific domains: with the well-endowed World Bank in rural, peri-urban and slum areas; with the UNDP/World Bank Water Supply and Sanitation Programme; with UNDP and the UN Department for Development Support and Management Services on water resources policy development; with the UN Environment Programme on the environmental impact of water-related activities; with WHO on sanitation and hygiene; with the World Meteorological Organization on hydrological surveys; with UNESCO on the assessment of water resources and training, education programmes, fresh water issues and research and development; with FAO on rural water resources management for agricultural purposes; with the International Atomic Energy Agency on nuclear and isotope technology in hydrological studies; with the UN Industrial Development Organization on industrial water resources needs and pollution control; with the International Water and Sanitation Centre on information and communication issues; with UN regional commissions and with regional development banks; and with other donors on environmental health, communication, hygiene education, sanitation, gender issues and technology development and transfer.[29]

These agencies and bodies were associated in the follow-up to the recommendations of the United Nations Water Conference held in Mar del Plata, Argentina in March 1977. The Conference endorsed the goal that all nations should seek to provide adequate drinking water and sanitation facilities for all people by the year 1990. This plan was approved by the UN General Assembly in December 1977. Member states and

18 UN organizations, including UNICEF, were urged to intensify their actions to carry out the agreements of the conference.

The 1989 Convention on the Rights of the Child urges countries, in part, to provide children with clean drinking water and to assure parents and children of the advantages of hygiene and environmental sanitation (Article 24.2(c) and (e)). At the World Summit for Children in 1990, goals were set to achieve safe water and sanitation for all by the year 2000.

According to a 1996 WHO report, during the International Drinking Water Supply and Sanitation Decade (1981–90), some 1.6 billion were served with safe water and about 750 million with adequate excreta disposal facilities. However, because of population growth of 800 million people in developing countries, by 1990 there remained a total of 1.015 billion people without safe water and 1.764 billion without adequate sanitation. Overall progress in reaching the unserved has been poor since 1990.

WHO, UNICEF's frequent partner, has been involved in environmental sanitation since its creation. The First World Health Assembly decided to include environmental sanitation in the 'top category' in the organization's programme of work. The Twelfth World Assembly in 1959 sanctioned a programme for the improvement of community water supplies. The programme was designed to help developing countries in assessing their needs, in formulating policies and programmes for meeting those needs, and in creating national and regional organizations for planning, financing, constructing, managing and operating community water supplies. The programme grew rapidly, and in 1967 it included WHO-assisted projects in 83 countries, involving the services of 121 full-time WHO sanitary engineers.[30]

No undue rivalry between WHO, the leader in health policy, and UNICEF, the operational agency, has been noted in this area, but it was only in May 1997 that both organizations adopted, for the first time, a common operational strategy, in a meeting of the Joint Committee on Health Policy. The Committee agreed that 'WHO and UNICEF should emphasize sanitation and hygiene as an essential element of human development and as the fundamental basis for health in their joint efforts in the area of water supply and environmental sanitation'. However, the Committee noted that specific future plans and activities still needed to be elaborated.[31]

The pumps of India

Around 70 per cent of India is separated from the water table by a deep rock shield, and many Indian villages that rely on underground water are extremely vulnerable to drought.[32] In the 1950s, the Indian government had identified 153 000 villages as 'water-scarce', most of them in hard-rock areas. In the 1960s, there was a series of droughts and in 1967 the situation became critical in Bihar and Uttar Pradesh when many of the existing wells dried up. Some 250 villages were faced with evacuation to refugee camps. UNICEF flew in 11 pneumatic drilling rigs capable of boring through 150 feet of rock in about eight hours. As the water table continued to recede, the government asked UNICEF for more drilling equipment. Between 1970 and 1974, UNICEF shipped in 125 hammer rigs, along with trucks and spare parts. Each of these rigs could drill about 100 boreholes a year, theoretically supplying water to 12 000 villages and about 9 million people. But boreholes need efficient pumps and those available were poor quality cast-iron replicas of European and American models, which broke down frequently.

Following the recommendations of a 1975 workshop sponsored by UNICEF, WHO and the government of India, UNICEF water supply staff found locally a pump, the Sholapur pump, that had originally been designed by a self-educated Indian mechanic. They modified this for easier mass production and maintenance, renamed it the India Mark II and field-tested it in 1976 and 1977. Mass-production of the India Mark II started in 1977–78, with 600 units a month. By 1984, 36 manufacturers were producing 100 000 pumps a year. By 1987, annual production had reached 200 000. A 1984 survey, commissioned by UNICEF, found that in six states in India, 80 per cent of the pumps were operational at any one time. Every year about 50 000 new pumps (the new user-friendly model is India Mark III) are installed in India and an equal number is exported to other countries in Asia, Africa and Latin America.

Poisoned wells in Bangladesh

In November 1998, a press report announced that 'A Safe-Water Plan turns Poisonous in Bangladesh – High Arsenic Levels in Tube-Well System Are Bringing Slow Death to the Population'. UNICEF was then blamed for the unexpected public health disaster arising from its long-standing, acclaimed and successful water supply programme.[33]

Until the 1970s, most villagers drank highly polluted water from hand-dug wells or natural ponds often shared with bathing cows and water buffaloes. Children were dying at high rates from cholera, dysentery, typhoid, and hepatitis caused by unsafe water.

UNICEF's first major assistance to the country's water supply network came in response to a devastating cyclone that hit Bangladesh in 1970 and some 10 000 damaged tubewells were repaired. UNICEF together with the World Bank and other aid agencies assisted the government and local organizations in installing nearly 900 000 tubewells. Tubewells are cylinders sunk into the ground, some with wide diameters for irrigation, others narrower for pumping clean drinking water from the aquifers.

UNICEF was the main proponent of these wells, creating its own designs and providing the material to the Bangladesh government which, in turn, paid the drilling costs.

The tubewell programme saved millions of lives. As tubewell use grew together with the spread of oral rehydration therapy – which prevents and treats diarrhoeal dehydration – infant mortality declined by 40 per cent from 1980 to 1990. Deaths of children under five from diarrhoeal dehydration declined from 150 000 in 1983 to 110 000 in 1996.

Contamination of the groundwater by arsenic was discovered in 1994 by the Dhaka Community Hospital in the western areas of Bangladesh. Arsenic poisoning may lead to ulcers, skin lesions, gangrene, nerve damage and various forms of cancer. Millions of people in Bangladesh are believed to be at risk. There is no treatment for the poisoning, though if a person stops drinking the arsenic-infected water at an early stage, the effects of diseases may stop. It is generally agreed that the arsenic contamination of groundwater in Bangladesh is of geological origin. The arsenic derives from the geological strata underlying the country.

In August 1998, the World Bank approved a $32.4 million credit to Bangladesh to help tackle the water contamination crisis. So far, many initiatives have focused on water quality testing and control with a view to supplying arsenic-free drinking water, thereby reducing the risk of further arsenic-related disease. According to a WHO report of February 1999, only a few reliable options are available: shallow hand pump for zones where arsenic is undetected; arsenic-free water from deeper aquifers; rain water harvesting; pond-sand filtration; bucket-type household treatment; and piped water from safe or treated sources.

UNICEF and the other organizations concerned – WHO, UNESCO, IAEA, UNIDO, the FAO and the World Bank – launched a joint initiative in 1998 to face this major public health issue on an emergency basis. Joint studies with local institutes have been carried out to test household arsenic removal techniques and the quality of alternative drinking water sources. Urgent requirements include simple, reliable, low-cost field testing equipment and robust technologies for arsenic removal at wells and in households. UNICEF has assisted the government of Bangladesh in testing over 25 000 tubewells across the country. Additionally, any new deep tubewell sunk with UNICEF assistance will be tested for arsenic before use. UNICEF will also test every six months wells financed by the Fund.

Cases of arsenic in drinking water have also been reported in Argentina, Bangladesh, Chile, China, Ghana, Hungary, India, Mexico, Thailand and the USA. At the global level, delayed effects from arsenic poisoning, the lack of common definitions and poor reporting and local awareness in affected areas are major problems in determining the extent of the problem and developing adequate solutions. As recognized by UNICEF, the arsenic problem in Bangladesh is a long-term emergency, with no easy solutions.

Should UNICEF continue to install tubewells, subject to proper arsenic testing, and continue to promote their use? Or, as a major reversal of public policy and a painful acknowledgement of public health failure, should they preach a return to the use of surface waters subject to filtration? Or should UNICEF stop all its water supply programmes, not because of the poisoned wells, but because this activity appears to go beyond its mandate, while maintaining its role in the field of environmental sanitation and education?

Conclusion

Food aid and nutrition are natural concerns for UNICEF. Child survival and development require adequate food for expectant mothers, infants and children. However, these concerns are shared with other organizations. The WFP has taken over most of the international food aid for emergencies as well as for development. Nutrition is part of the FAO's mandate. One of WHO's mandated strategies is to promote maternal, infant and young-child nutrition – a strategy shared by UNICEF. The promotion of breastfeeding is a cause common to both WHO and the Fund. WHO assumed leadership in iodine deficiency disorder control in 1999.

The World Summit goal in this area was to reduce by one half the 1990 levels of severe and moderate malnutrition among children under five. A very honest UNICEF report stated in 1999 that there had been some improvement in reducing child malnutrition worldwide, but the rate of improvement had been slow, and, moreover, it had decreased substantially in the 1990s.[34] The report rightly showed that malnutrition is not simply a consequence of disease and inadequate diet, but that it has many more elements: social, political, economic and cultural. Factors also involve discrimination against women, lack of access to education and correct information, economic resources, household access to food, child and maternal care, and access to basic social services, safe water and sanitation. Progress was, however, made in addressing vitamin A deficiency, iodine deficiency and anaemia.

UNICEF has a well-based interest in education, particularly in health education. Its studies and experience have led the Fund to properly focus on primary education and girls' education. In 1999, in her first report, K. Tomasevski (Croatia), the UN Special Rapporteur on the Right to Education, confirmed UNICEF's approach by arguing that rights-based development and human rights criteria should be applied to education. In her inaugural report, she gave considerable attention to the denial of primary school education to girls and to gender-specific aspects of the right to education. She stated to the UN Commission on Human Rights: 'It may well be that women's rights shall lead the way for the mainstreaming of human rights in development, and education may represent the catalyst.'[35]

UNICEF's main 'rival', or rather 'partner', in this field is UNESCO, while WHO is involved in health education.

One of the World Summit's goals was to achieve universal education and completion of primary education by at least 80 per cent of primary school-age children by the year 2000. The reduction of gender disparities was also part of the goal. Although some advances have taken place, due in part to UNICEF's initiatives and support, it is unlikely that this ambitious goal was reached for well-known reasons: poor national governance with low priority on social targets, armed conflicts, child-soldiers, the economy, child labour, culture, religion and tradition biased against the education of girls, etc.

In water and sanitation, the World Summit goal was to achieve universal access to safe drinking water and to sanitary means of excreta disposal by the year 2000. Estimates for 1999 suggested that this was far from being achieved owing to many factors: the vastness of the task, with nearly six billion people to be covered; the increasing difficulties of obtaining water; conflicts which have disrupted systems and sources; more limited resources, including the decrease of official development aid; and the fact that sanitation has very limited impact on disease reduction unless accompanied by often complex measures to promote behavioural change based upon increased awareness and understanding of hygiene issues.[36]

The number of UN agencies involved in water resources raises serious questions as to the risk of overlapping and waste of resources. UNICEF has so far escaped such suspicions because of its mainly operational and supply role in rural areas of developing countries. However, the Fund's role in this area has decreased, in part because of the increasing action of the World Bank with its large financial resources.[37] UNICEF should probably focus more on environmental sanitation and education, and leave water supply to other organizations, governments and the private sector.

Whatever the obstacles, problems and disappointments in all these fields, there is a need for the continuation of UNICEF's presence, advocacy and action within its statutory mandate, provided that the focus of its programmes is regularly evaluated and that real cooperation prevents overlapping with other organizations.

6
Natural and Man-Made Emergencies

According to a UN report issued in 1999, the world experienced three times as many natural emergencies in the 1990s as in the 1960s. The year 1998 was the worst on record for weather-related natural disasters. In the Caribbean, hurricanes Georges and Mitch killed more than 13 000 people; a June cyclone in India caused an estimated 10 000 deaths. Major floods hit Bangladesh, India, Nepal and much of East Asia, with thousands killed. Two-thirds of Bangladesh was inundated for months, making millions homeless. More than 3000 died in China's Yangtze flood, millions were displaced and the financial cost was estimated at $30 billion. Fires ravaged tens of thousands of square kilometres of forest in Brazil, Indonesia and Siberia, with devastating consequences for human health and local economies. In Afghanistan, earthquakes killed more than 9000 people. In August 1999, Turkey suffered one of the most devastating earthquakes in recent history.[1]

There was a significant increase in the number of wars in 1998, mostly internal wars. Besides the wars between Ethiopia and Eritrea and between India and Pakistan over Kashmir, civil wars started, continued or resumed in Afghanistan, Angola, Burundi, the Democratic Republic of the Congo, the Former Yugoslavia (Kosovo), Guinea-Bissau, the Republic of the Congo, Rwanda, Somalia and Sudan. Violence erupted in East Timor preceding and following the territory's vote for independence from Indonesia.

Natural emergencies affect populations and put children at risk. Children are major victims in external and internal conflicts. In addressing the needs of children in conflict, UNICEF presses for commitments from governments and military bodies to protect children. It has negotiated ceasefire agreements to allow the provision of food or immunization to children and mothers. It has urged an end to the use of child soldiers and the universal adoption of the global ban on anti-personnel landmines.

The humanitarian role of UNICEF

UNICEF was created as a humanitarian organization which dealt, initially, with emergencies affecting the survival and development of children in the aftermath of the Second World War. In the 1970s, the Fund was recognized as a development institution but it always retained significant emergency activities. There was, and there is, therefore, a constant need to combine humanitarian relief with long-term development objectives, which Carol Bellamy called in 1999 a holistic approach.[2]

In 1964, the UNICEF Executive Board adopted an explicit policy on the Fund's involvement in emergencies. It provided that UNICEF should be involved in the immediate post-disaster relief phase only in exceptional circumstances, where such assistance was not available from other sources. The main role of UNICEF was to be in the diversion of supplies for immediate needs and in special aid for the rehabilitation phase. In a statement to the Executive Board in 1972, Executive Director Labouisse said that this policy was still valid as a general guide to the Fund's participation in emergency situations, although, in his view, the main emphasis of UNICEF should continue to be on long-term programmes. Labouisse also emphasized two points which remain valid today: first, response should vary according to each individual case; second, in cases of internal conflicts, assistance should be provided to both sides.[3]

In 1992, the Executive Board reaffirmed that UNICEF should 'continue providing emergency assistance to refugee and displaced women and children, particularly those living in areas affected by armed conflict and natural disasters', in accordance with the Fund's mandate and 'in collaboration with other UN agencies and the international community'.[4]

In 1996, the Executive Board urged UNICEF to respond to all kinds of emergencies, including 'silent' and 'forgotten' emergencies, i.e. the impact of common childhood ailments and poverty in developing countries. The Board endorsed measures to strengthen preventive actions, including stand-by arrangements and emphasis on sustainable development strategies. The Board supported the developmental approach taken by UNICEF in dealing with emergencies since, in its view, sustainable development was essential in preventing emergencies. The Board further recommended a strong linkage between relief and development, as well as the need to continue working in post-conflict reconstruction and recovery. The Board endorsed a four-pronged approach including prevention, preparedness, emergency assistance and rehabilitation, and recovery assistance.[5]

UNICEF's current mandate

Its Mission Statement (see Figure 2.1) commits UNICEF to ensure 'special protection for the most disadvantaged children – victims of war, disasters, extreme poverty, all forms of violence and exploitation and those with disabilities'. It 'responds in emergencies to protect the rights of children. In coordination with United Nations partners and humanitarian agencies, UNICEF makes its unique facilities for rapid response available to its partners to relieve the suffering of children and those who provide their care'.

UNICEF defines an emergency as a situation which threatens the lives and well-being of large numbers of a population and in which extraordinary action is required to ensure their survival, care and protection. Such emergencies may be created by natural or technological disasters, epidemics or conflicts. Victims of emergencies, women and children in particular, require immediate care, including shelter, food, health protection and clean water. In UN terminology, a complex emergency is a humanitarian crisis in a country, region or society where there is significant or total breakdown of authority resulting from internal or external conflict and which requires an international response that extends beyond the mandate or capacity of any single agency. In such emergencies, populations may also need legal and physical protection to prevent harm and ensure their access to humanitarian assistance.

According to a report issued by UNICEF in 1996,[6] the principal goals of UNICEF's emergency-related cooperation with international and national partners are:

1. To prevent the exposure of children to risks by addressing the root causes of conflicts.
2. To ensure the survival of the most vulnerable children and women – including those displaced within their own countries – and their protection against malnutrition and disease during the dangerous and chaotic early days of acute emergencies through access to essential life-saving and life-sustaining services.
3. To assure protection against intentional violence, exploitation, abuse, rape and recruitment into armed forces.
4. To support the rehabilitation and recovery of people and communities through developmental actions to restore psychosocial health, mater-

nal and child health care, schools and water supply and sanitation systems.

5. To promote long-lasting solutions through the creation and strengthening of self-help capacities at family and community levels and in particular through support for the participation of women in the development and management of such solutions.

UNICEF's specific role is to advocate and act for children. As a humanitarian actor, its function is to ensure that the needs and rights of the child are always given priority on the humanitarian agenda and are analysed in a systematic and comprehensive manner.

Like other organizations, it attempts to bring a developmental orientation to its emergency action. UNICEF also provides non-food relief items if required. Since the creation of the UN Department of Humanitarian Affairs (DHA) in 1991, UNICEF has supported its efforts to improve coordination of the international response to complex emergencies, a difficult and thankless task in view of the large number of autonomous organizations in the field. It supports an active role for the Inter-Agency Standing Committee in advising the UN Emergency Relief Coordinator on the strategic approach, coordination arrangements and division of responsibilites to be adopted in each complex emergency.

UNICEF complements the mandates of sector-oriented partners, including UN agencies and NGOs. UNICEF's main emergency partners are the UNHCR, the WFP (which also has a dual mandate of providing both food relief and development), UNDP (in preventive development, post-crisis capacity development, rehabilitation and recovery of national social infrastructures), WHO, UNESCO, the International Committee of the Red Cross (ICRC) and the Save the Children Alliance.

UNICEF concluded a Memorandum of Understanding with UNHCR on 14 March 1996 which assigns responsibility to the two organizations for advocacy, promotion and strategy formulation, and for operational activities for both refugees in host countries and returnees or displaced populations in their countries of origin. The Memorandum underlines that UNICEF's particular strength and contribution arises from its long-term country presence and perspective. As one example of cooperation in the health field, UNHCR is to advise UNICEF immediately of a new refugee situation where measles vaccination is a priority need. UNICEF will then provide measles vaccine together with related equipment and supplies, including cold chain equipment, vaccination cards and vitamin A supplements. UNHCR and UNICEF have also signed Field Level Memoranda of Understanding in specific countries.[7]

UNICEF has also concluded a series of global stand-by agreements with organizations, networks or centres of excellence for the provision of technical expertise in a number of fields. Such agreements exist or are being negotiated with the Norwegian Refugee Council, the Disaster Relief Agency (Netherlands), the Centers for Disease Control and Prevention (US), the Danish Refugee Council, the Swiss Disaster Relief, the Swedish Rescue Services Board, the Agency for Personnel Service Overseas (Ireland), the Overseas Development Administration (UK) and the International Executive Service Corps. Externally available expertise covers such fields as radio communications, vehicle and equipment maintenance, warehousing and logistics, health, education, water supply, psychosocial health and trauma recovery, care of unaccompanied children, child rights, conflict resolution and mediation. UNICEF representatives have also concluded activity-specific agreements at country level with such NGOs as Save the Children (UK) and (US), and Italian NGOs.[8]

UNICEF has created its own Rapid Response Teams (RRTs), on stand-by for immediate deployment to crisis locations to enhance or establish an effective UNICEF presence. The designated staff – 36 in 1996 – are experienced in emergency programming; material management, supply and logistics; and management, administration and finance. The agency has developed stand-by stockpiles in Copenhagen of communications, transportation and warehousing equipment, as well as office equipment stocks and survival packs for its RRT personnel.

In 1988, 8 per cent ($32 million) of UNICEF programme resources were expended in emergencies. In the 1990s, emergency expenditures rose year after year: $49 million in 26 countries in 1990, $111 million in 50 countries in 1991, $167 million in 54 countries in 1992, $223 million in 64 countries in 1993.[9] The proportion of emergency expenditures in relation to total expenditures increased to a peak of 28 per cent ($223 million) in 1993, followed by a gradual decrease. UNICEF estimates that future emergency expenditures will average 15–20 per cent of total annual programme expenditures.

The proportion of emergency expenditures for the period 1993–95 – $642 million – by sector was:

- 34 per cent on health;
- 18 per cent on education;
- 16 per cent on planning/advocacy/programme support;
- 13 per cent on nutrition/household food security;
- 11 per cent on CEDC/women/communities;

- 6 per cent on water/sanitation;
- 2 per cent on general emergency relief (shelter, materials, blankets, cooking utensils).

Emergency programmes are almost entirely funded through voluntary contributions, primarily through consolidated inter-agency appeals. UNICEF participated in 16 such appeals in 1996.

Humanitarian dilemmas

Humanitarian interventions are normally initiated only at the request of or with the consent of national authorities. However, the absence of such authorities in 'failed states' prevents the possibility of obtaining such agreements. In cases of internal wars, consent has to be obtained from both governmental authorities and armed rebels. For UNICEF, as well as for other humanitarian organizations dealing with emergencies, this raises a series of legal, political, moral and programmatic dilemmas. They include the debate over sovereignty and humanitarian intervention, the charge of interference within the domestic jurisdiction of a state under a humanitarian pretence, the relevance of neutrality and impartiality in the face of genocide and ethnic cleansing, and the need to give help to victims on 'both sides'.

The 'both sides' aid policy was applied early by UNICEF, notwithstanding major political hurdles. Non-partisan relief started with Pate and continued with his successors (see Chapter 2). Following emergency programmes in the late 1940s in former 'enemy countries' in Europe, UNICEF was involved on both sides in the Chinese civil war (1946–47), in the Nigerian civil war (1967–70), in Kampuchea (1979–81), and more recently in Mozambique, Angola, Uganda, Afghanistan, Cambodia, Sri Lanka, Lebanon and El Salvador.

UNICEF's non-political stance was an important element in the Secretary-General's decision to appoint the Fund as lead agency in delivering relief to the Vietnam-dominated government in Kampuchea (1979–81). Along with the ICRC, UNICEF coordinated most non-communist, governmental assistance, while Oxfam administered the international NGO consortium.[10] In selecting Grant to head Operation Lifeline Sudan (1989), the Secretary-General availed himself of UNICEF's recognized competence in such circumstances and of Grant's own prestige. In each situation, UNICEF provided humanitarian assistance to civilians without conveying diplomatic recognition of the insurgency, or in the case of Kampuchea, without diplomatic recognition of the

Vietnamese-supported Kampuchean government which had succeeded the genocidal Khmer Rouge.

However, UNICEF carried out these tasks with discretion as a de facto mandate without trying to create a doctrine of 'right and duty of humanitarian intervention'. UNICEF is an intergovernmental body which depends mainly on governments for its work. Contrary to an often-expressed view, the General Assembly Resolution 57 (I) which established the Fund did not grant it powers of intervention in internal wars. Its position and role are thus different from that of NGOs such as Médecins Sans Frontières (MSF) which claim and practise an autonomous right of humanitarian intervention without the consent of national authorities or against their will.[11] Other issues, which concern UNICEF and other organizations, include the interference of conflict in natural emergencies, the uneven media exposure of some emergencies causing uneven funding and assistance, the possibility of preventing emergencies, and the difficult transition of emergency work into development.

Recent humanitarian operations

UNICEF is involved in both natural and man-made emergencies. However, this distinction may be moot when conflicts add to the damage caused by natural emergencies. A few examples of recent UNICEF interventions follow.

Natural emergencies

In January 2000, an earthquake in Western Colombia measuring 6.0 on the Richter scale destroyed cities and villages, leaving more than 150 000 people homeless, including an estimated 60 per cent of children and women. UNICEF staff, together with representatives of the Colombian Red Cross, first carried out a rapid assessment of the most urgent needs of children and women in the area. UNICEF staff also evaluated the effect of the quake's damage on health, nutrition and education projects in the region. The agency's response to the emergency was to include: distribution to families of Basic Survival Kits which contain tents, blankets, kitchen utensils, water tanks, lamps and first-aid items; distribution of education kits, school materials, notebooks and pencils to children whose education had been disrupted by the emergency. In cooperation with the Colombian Red Cross and the National Emergency Organization, UNICEF was also preparing a radio, TV and information campaign focusing on the needs of children during the emergency. Finally, 150 volunteers from the Colombian

Movement of Children for Peace were deployed to help children overcome the trauma of the quake.

Early in February 2000, several floods caused by cyclones hit Southern Africa. Cyclone Eline and torrential rains caused rivers to overflow their banks in Mozambique, a country trying to recover from a long civil war: over 100 000 had been made homeless including some 22 000 children under five. In Zimbabwe, in the midst of a severe economic crisis, some 250 000 persons were rendered homeless by floods. In Botswana, at least 10 000 dwellings were destroyed and at least 90 000 were affected. In Madagascar, in the wake of flooding caused by Cyclone Gloria, preliminary.reports indicated that some 560 000 people were affected, with 10 000 left homeless and another 12 000 out of reach.

As seen on TV reports, thousands had remained stranded and in need of rescue, in spite of the assistance provided by the South African military and other western countries. Malaria and diarrhoea were threatening. In addition to the destruction of houses, bridges and roads had been washed away. There was urgent need for shelter, basic survival supplies and health assistance.

UNICEF concentrated on getting medicines in place before outbreaks of diseases occurred, and on ensuring access to safe water, health services and sanitation facilities. UNICEF was developing shelters, feeding stations and distribution points. Many other agencies were involved in the immediate relief work and preparing for the long process of reinstallation of shattered populations and the reconstruction of destroyed infrastructures.[12]

Ethiopia: famine and war

From early 1999, a serious drought developed across Eastern Africa, placing millions of people in danger of starvation. The failure of rains seriously affected the nutrition, health and general welfare of approximately 16 million people in a dozen countries, including millions of children. Throughout 1999 and early 2000, the UN system issued early warnings about the gravity of the food situation threatening populations in Ethiopia, Eritrea, Somalia, Sudan, Kenya, Djibouti, Uganda, Burundi, Rwanda and Tanzania. Persistent drought and poor rainfall, together with the effects of conflict and insecurity, have devastated crops and livestock, and eroded food stocks in the region, which also hosts thousands of refugees and internally displaced persons.

In Ethiopia alone, UNICEF estimated in April 2000 that about 8 million people, out of a total population of 55 to 60 million, were in danger, including about 1.4 million children under the age of five.[13] In some of

Ethiopia's most traditionally food deficient areas, high population density combined with extensive soil depletion and decreased arability had created chronic nutrition needs. Ethiopia has one of the world's highest levels of stunting among children due to malnutrition (66 per cent of children are undernourished). In Southern Ethiopia, a nutrition survey indicated that over 24 per cent of children are acutely malnourished, weighing below 80 per cent of the standard weight for height measurement. Ethiopia also has very low primary school enrolment (24.9 per cent), poor access to safe drinking water (under 20 per cent) and poor health care services. With an under-five mortality rate of 173 per 1000, an estimated 1300 children will die each day. With the second-highest population in Africa, it is one of the poorest countries, ranked 172 out of 174 in 1999 in its overall level of development.

UNICEF reported that 'some 300 000 people have been forced away from their homes [in Eritrea] by a border dispute with neighboring Ethiopia – the population of Eritrea is about 3 million. The challenges of being displaced from their homes – away from employment, food sources, health care and education – are multiplied by the drought conditions'.[14]

On 7 April 2000, UNICEF complained of 'poor donor response to Ethiopian emergency'. While this may have been due in part to general donor fatigue, it is likely that the main reason was the bloody and costly war carried out by Ethiopia and Eritrea since May 1998 for the ownership of over 300 square kilometres of desert land and its effects on the populations of both countries. Both governments called for massive and urgent food relief while losing thousands of soldiers in battles recalling those of the First World War, and spending millions of dollars on armaments. The International Institute for Strategic Studies in London estimated that Ethiopia spent $467 million on its armed forces in 1999, up from $140 million before the war. Both countries have bought tanks, helicopters, anti-tank missiles and fighter jets. The president of Eritrea, Issaias Afwerki, claimed that, by early 2000, the fighting had taken a total of 70 000 lives. The Ethiopian president, Meles Zenawi, refused the passage of food through the Eritrean ports of Assab and Massaoua and rejected truce offers.

A number of diplomats and humanitarian officials believed that the two countries were victims more of the war than of the drought. Others agree that the famine has been caused by the drought, but add that it is compounded by the wasteful, lasting and cruel border war.

The 1984–85 Ethiopian famine, which caused the death of more than a million people from lack of water and food, also had strong political overtones. Its major cause had been the collectivization programme initiated by the Marxist military junta led by Colonel Haile Mariam Mengistu, which disrupted Ethiopian agriculture. Mengistu prevented distribution of food to areas that supported rebel forces. Relief came late, as throughout 1983 and 1984 many donor countries' representatives tended to ignore the urgent pleas of Ethiopia's Relief and Rehabilitation Commission concerning the impending crisis, in part due to hostility to the regime. Warnings of a famine from Save the Children (SCF) were initially mistrusted, as British officials in Addis Ababa and World Food Programme representatives felt that the SCF had a 'vested interest' in 'promoting disasters'.[15] Western public opinion was finally aroused by the pictures of dying children and women conveyed by the media, and by the Band Aid campaign organized by Bob Geldof.

The dilemma faced by donor governments and humanitarian organizations during the 1984–85 famine was either to provide relief to a communist government in war against its own people, or to abstain from relief at the risk of hurting the ailing populations. The French NGO Médecins Sans Frontières (MSF) found that the western aid to Ethiopia was used in part to deport massively some of its rural population out of areas held by rebels into areas controlled by the government. Refusing to be an alibi, MSF publicly denounced this policy and was then expelled from Ethiopia by Mengistu. French medical teams later returned surreptitiously.[16] Donor governments and humanitarian organizations face a similar dilemma: food relief may support the armed forces and prolong the war. Western governments have adopted a dual approach: give assistance and encourage mediation efforts for an end to the conflict.

An organization like UNICEF has no peacemaking mandate and cannot but direct its resources towards humanitarian relief to the children and mothers, victims of the drought and war.

By April 2000, UNICEF had dispatched 86 tons of BP-5 high protein biscuits (donated by the governments of Norway and the US), which do not require preparation, water or cooking. Millions of sachets of oral rehydration salts (ORS) were delivered to the affected countries in the region, as well as essential drugs for malnourished and sick children. UNICEF has supported measles and vitamin A campaigns. UNICEF activities also included water tankering, the construction of shallow wells and repair of hand pumps, the rehabilitation of non-functioning water schemes as well as borehole drilling. Community water tanks and individual family water jugs were shipped to help people gain, store and use water supplies.

A UNICEF representative recalled recently that there are well-known solutions to famine prevention by breaking 'the vicious grip' of the drought cycle.[17] It requires an effective early warning system and preparedness for shortages, irrigation and land conservation, changes in crop patterns, diversification of economic activities and the relocation of some people. However, these technical solutions require good governance and the achievement of civil peace.

Angola's civil war

In August 1999, Carol Bellamy told the UN Security Council that three decades of war had left Angola's children without the most basic guarantees of human security and without the essential services all children need to survive, grow and develop.[18] According to 1997 assessments, under-five mortality was at 292 per 1000 live births and 42 per cent of Angola's children were moderately or severely underweight for their age. Only 50 per cent of school-age children were enrolled in classes, with a high drop-out rate after the first grade, especially for girls. The resumption of the war in December 1998 led to further deterioration. More than 1.6 million people had been displaced from their homes and thousands of children had been recruited as fighters in the conflict. In 2000, UNICEF's Child Risk Measure ranked Angola as the country whose children were at the greatest risk of death, malnutrition, abuse and development failure. Carol Bellamy told the Council that 'Our analysis points to the conflict in Angola as the greatest determinant of this sad reality'.

A survey carried out in 1995 found that 66 per cent of children in Angola had seen people being murdered, 91 per cent had seen dead bodies, and 67 per cent had seen people being tortured, beaten or hurt. In all, more than two-thirds of children had lived through events in which they had defied death.

The conflict in Angola between the Popular Movement for the Liberation of Angola (MPLA), whose members later formed the Angolan government, and the National Union for the Total Independence of Angola (UNITA), predates Angola's independence. When the Portuguese left Angola in 1975, the conflict degenerated into a civil war between the MPLA led by José Eduardo dos Santos, supported by Cuban troops, themselves backed by the USSR, and UNITA, led by Jonas Savimbi, with the support of the South African army, backed by the US. The end of the Cold War led to the withdrawal of the Cuban troops, the independence of Namibia and the end to South African support for UNITA. However, the conflict continued, leaving hundreds of thousands dead and tens of thousands disabled. UN-monitored elections held in September 1992 were won by dos Santos: its results were rejected by Savimbi who resumed the fighting. A ceasefire took effect in November 1994, following the signing of the Lusaka Protocol by the two parties. The conflict started again in December 1998.

On 23 December 1998, in a Presidential Statement, the UN Security Council called for an immediate cessation of hostilities and, again, said that the primary responsibility for the failure to achieve peace in Angola lay with the leadership of UNITA. The Council also expressed concern at the plight of those most vulnerable groups, such as children, women, the elderly and internally displaced persons. In April 2000, the Council voted to tighten its sanctions against UNITA, aimed at preventing the illicit flow of arms and the smuggling of petroleum into UNITA-controlled areas, and the sale of diamonds by UNITA. Angola's diamond fields have earned Savimbi and UNITA some $500 million annually.[19] These financial resources together with Savimbi's lust for power and disdain for democracy explain his recurrent stalling of peace negotiations and his war actions, to the detriment of his country's potentially rich economy, causing more deaths and suffering in the Angolan population.

In the continuing civil war, humanitarian action is necessarily limited and subject to reversals. In spite of all the obstacles, UNICEF and other UN agencies, the International Committee of the Red Cross, bilateral donors and NGOs give assistance to the government. Aid includes deliveries of food, seeds and tools; care and counselling of victims of trauma and abuse, and basic health care services; safe water and sanitation; supply of items for shelter; support for education; campaigns to alert the population to the perils of living in one of the most heavily mined countries of the world; and difficult negotiations with UNITA to gain access to all children in need. The Lusaka Protocol, an ill-applied peace agreement signed in November 1994 by the Angola government and UNITA, stipulates, *inter alia*, that 60 000 UNITA soldiers be demobilized in camps. The first camp opened in November 1995. In an unusual mandate for UNICEF, the agency, in coordination with the UN Department of Humanitarian Affairs, worked together with several UN agencies and international NGOs to assist the demobilization process. It allowed UNICEF to reach children through an assistance given to all former soldiers and their families. It also gave UNICEF a better understanding of the problem of child soldiers, a grave issue not limited to Angola.[20]

In April 2000, UNICEF was able to protect 634 000 children from polio by completing an emergency vaccination campaign in response to a local polio outbreak. WHO, UNICEF and Rotary International supported the government in the National Polio Immunization Days (NID) campaign. Three immunization rounds were carried out between June 1999 and May

2000, covering a total of 2.7 million children. With UNICEF's help, Angola was revising its juvenile justice system. Drop-In Centers and a foster parent placement system were established for children who have been separated from parents because of the conflict.

The Kosovo crisis

During the wars between 1991 and 1995 in the Former Yugoslavia, civilians, including children and women, became principal targets and victims. The wars were characterized by grave violations of human rights and humanitarian law. Hundreds of thousands of people were displaced from their homes and fled to neighbouring provinces or countries. During the refugee exodus from Kosovo between March and June 1999, UNICEF's programmes focused on refugee and internally displaced children and women in camps, collective centres and host families. UNICEF promoted the creation of child-friendly environments, providing adequate facilities for children's educational and recreational development and their psychosocial recovery and supported health care. In November 1999, UNICEF estimated that about half of the 517 000 Kosovar refugees in Albania, Macedonia and Montenegro were children under the age of 15.

The focus of UN humanitarian agencies, UNICEF, WHO and the UNHCR, was emergency health intervention and clothing. However, none of the agencies involved anticipated the scale of the refugee exodus.

The UNICEF Office remained operational during the NATO campaign. After the campaign, UNICEF worked to meet the needs of internally displaced persons, including children, by providing disinfectants, clothes, shoes and hygiene items. The agency delivered some 60 metric tonnes of medical supplies, including emergency health kits (containing essential drugs for respiratory illnesses, oral rehydration salt for diarrhoea, water testing kits, chlorine, children's blankets and clothing), generators and essential drugs. UNICEF also established a Social Welfare team to counsel at-risk pregnant women in five key hospitals. UNICEF managed the caseload of abandoned babies in Pristina hospital in cooperation with Save the Children. The agency also helped rehabilitate kindergartens, established monitoring systems for disabled children, trained facilitators and care providers, and delivered clothes and toys. Nearly 400 of Kosovo's 1000 primary schools were severely damaged or destroyed during the conflict. UNICEF funded the repair of more than 45 schools and provided school furniture, teaching aids, school kits and textbooks for some 55 000 primary school children (out of 300 000).

An estimated 1 million landmines, thousands of unexploded cluster bombs and other devices are scattered across wide areas of Kosovo.

UNICEF, the lead UN agency in landmine awareness, initiated a massive campaign to alert Kosovars, including children, to their dangers.[21]

East Timor

A set of agreements was signed in New York on 5 May 1999 between Indonesia and Portugal to finally resolve the status of the former Portuguese colony, annexed by Indonesia as its 27th province in 1974. The two governments entrusted the UN Secretary-General with organizing and conducting a 'popular consultation' in order to ascertain whether the East Timorese people accepted or rejected a special autonomy for East Timor within the Republic of Indonesia. In June 1999, the Security Council established the UN Mission in East Timor (UNAMET) to carry out the consultation and oversee a transition period after the vote. In a climate of high tension, the voters decided on 30 August 1999 by a 78.5 per cent majority to reject the proposed autonomy and begin a process of transition towards independence.

Following the announcement of the result, pro-integration militias, supported by the Indonesian security forces, launched a campaign of violence, looting and arson throughout the whole territory. Many East Timorese were killed and as many as 500 000 were displaced from their homes, about half leaving the territory, in a number of cases by force. Some 75 000 were estimated to be under the age of five. In September 1999, the Security Council authorized a multinational force (INTERFET) under Australian command to restore peace and security in East Timor and to facilitate humanitarian assistance operations. On 19 October 1999, the Indonesian People's Consultative Assembly formally recognized the result of the consultation.

UNICEF had been operating in both East and West Timor since 1982. The agency was forced to evacuate on 5 September 1999 and its office was subsequently destroyed. It re-established its presence on 20 September in Dili and was then designated as the lead UN agency for health in East Timor.

In July 1999, UNICEF negotiated a 'Truce for Children' between all parties in East Timor, including the pro-independence and pro-integration movements, with a promise to guarantee children and their families safe access to immunization sites and to promote the campaign among their followers. The Truce allowed the immunization of children against tuberculosis, measles, polio, diphtheria, whooping cough and tetanus. The campaign was coordinated by UNICEF, Médecins Sans Frontières International (MSF) and WHO, with the support of the Catholic Church. Other NGOs participated in the running of the vaccination centres.

As early as 7 September 1999, UNICEF publicly condemned violence in East Timor: 'The indiscriminate targetting of civilian populations in East Timor, in particular children and women, is an outrageous response to the people's free choice for independence.' The agency expressed its extreme concern about the lack of safe havens for thousands of children and women forced to flee internationally protected places, including churches, schools, hospitals and humanitarian premises. It was alarmed about the lack of access to food, water, sanitation facilities and any kind of protection for civilians who had fled to the mountains, or been forced to other parts of the territory, as well as countless others seeking shelter in the besieged UN compound. UNICEF denounced the targeting of UN and humanitarian personnel as a direct breach of international law. It called on the Indonesian authorities to adopt urgent measures to effectively protect and care for children and women and to ensure full respect for humanitarian law and for the provisions of the Convention on the Rights of the Child.

In September 1999, UNICEF started an emergency relief programme for East and West Timor estimated at $5 million and covering activities in water and sanitation, health, nutrition, education and psychosocial services. The programme was planned and carried out in coordination with the UN humanitarian inter-agency mission. Nutritional supplements, blankets, drugs and medical supplies were distributed to help meet the needs of women and children. Other items included water purification tablets, jerry cans and water jugs, tents for temporary medical and educational centres, mosquito nets, sarongs, sleeping mats, education supplies for temporary schools and sets of play items for 'child-friendly spaces'.

Other organizations involved in the UN humanitarian operation on East Timor included the WFP, UNHCR, ICRC, Oxfam, Médecins Sans Frontières, Médecins du Monde, Caritas and Care.[22]

Child soldiers

Current armed conflicts target mainly civilians, including many innocent and vulnerable children.

Olara A. Otunnu, Special Representative of the UN Secretary-General for Children and Armed Conflict, stated in December 1999 that over the previous decade, 2 million children were killed in conflict situations, over 1 million were made orphans, over 6 million have been seriously injured or permanently disabled, and over 10 million have been left with grave psychological trauma. A large number of children, especially young women, have been made the targets of rape and other forms of sexual violence as a deliberate instrument of war. At the end of the twentieth century, there were over 20 million children who had been displaced by war within and outside their countries. Approximately 800 children were killed or maimed by landmines every month. Some 300 000 young persons under the age of 18 were being forcibly recruited and exploited as child soldiers around the world. They are led by their adult commanders to killing, maiming and torture through psychological pressure and the forced absorption of alcohol and drugs. They are often treated brutally, and desertion may lead to imprisonment or even summary execution. When in combat, children are at greater risk than adults because of their relative immaturity, their belief in their own invulnerability. In some countries, girl-soldiers are reported to represent up to 30 per cent of some non-state armed groups. Girls may also be used as cooks or sexual slaves. Orphans and displaced children living in camps are particularly vulnerable to recruitment by armed groups. Surviving child soldiers may suffer from severe physical and psychological problems, in particular through witnessing and/or committing atrocities.[23]

Examples in specific countries unfortunately abound. During the Iran–Iraq conflict (1980–88), child soldiers were used as cannon fodder and as advance troops in mined areas. In Uganda, the Lord's Resistance Army (LRA) has abducted between 5000 and 8000 children since 1995. The Ugandan Ambassador told the US Congress on 10 March 1998 that the LRA, supported by the Sudan government, had abducted 8000 children in the last 36 months to use as soldiers – some as young as eight years old. In Angola, both the government and UNITA underestimate the number of children who participated in the civil war, allegedly because of their knowledge that such practices are both forbidden by international conventions and against the best interests of the children, and their fear of inopportune public exposure in international media. During a visit to Angola by Graça Machel in August 1995, appointed by the UN General Assembly to report on war's effect on children, the government and UNITA each reported 1500 former child soldiers. However, initial headcounts of demobilized soldiers indicate many more. When the UN Department of Humanitarian Affairs surveyed 17 000 demobilized soldiers in only 4 of the 15 demobilization centres in March 1996, it counted more than 1500 under 18 years old. In Sierra Leone, the Revolutionary United Front (RUF), under the leadership of Foday Sankoh with the logistical and financial assistance of Presidents Charles Taylor of Liberia and Blaise Compaore of Upper Volta, has waged a campaign of terror against the government. War methods, in breach of all humanitarian and human rights laws, included targeting mainly civilians, burning houses and their residents, rape, pillage and torture, cutting ears, noses or arms with machetes. At least 20 000 people – most of them non-combatants – have died since the RUF began its fight in 1991. In 1999, the RUF was estimated to have more than 20 000 fighters, as many as half of them abducted children.[24]

According to the Guatemala Truth Commission Report issued in February 1999, during the 36-year-long civil war, children were killed, abducted, forcibly recruited as soldiers and sexually abused. Foetuses were cut from their mother's wombs, young children were smashed against walls or thrown alive into pits where the corpses of adults were later thrown. The disappearances of children, which in some cases included the stealing of infants for illegal adoption, were widespread occurrences. In Colombia, according to the Defensoria del Pueblo de Colombia, the official human rights ombudsman, an estimated 6000 children under the age of 18 were involved in 1999 in the continuing civil war. According to CODHES, an independent human rights monitoring group, 131 children were kidnapped in 1998. Over the past decade, 1 257 000 people have been displaced by the conflict, including 700 000 children.[25]

While the use of children as soldiers in wars is not a new phenomenon, it has steadily increased in recent years, for several reasons. In the first place, most of the recent armed conflicts are civil wars rather than international wars. In the latter, combatants in regular armies could be expected to take heed of humanitarian law and respect the minimum age for recruitment. On the other hand, civil wars are characterized by social breakdown and lawlessness and the involvement of undisciplined autonomous armed groups. Secondly, technological 'progress' has made semi-automatic rifles light enough to be carried by children and simple enough to be stripped and reassembled by them. Furthermore, these weapons are easily available and not expensive: in Uganda, an AK-47 can be purchased for the cost of a chicken. Armed groups recruit children to fill the ranks. Children are considered obedient soldiers, easily led to fight and commit atrocities under the influence of alcohol or drugs and through their love or respect for charismatic leaders and their cause. They are unaware of the real dangers they face: they believe that they are magically protected against the enemy's weapons and are immune to physical injury and death. While children may be coerced to join a force, some volunteer to escape desperate conditions at home, some are attracted by the prestige of wearing a uniform or being an accepted part of a group, or to prove their manhood, or to avenge atrocities committed against their family or community.

International instruments

National laws in the majority of the world's countries set the minimum age for military recruitment and participation in armed conflict at 18. However, a number of countries allow volunteers to be recruited at 15, 16 or 17.[26]

The Convention on the Rights of the Child of 1989, which entered into force on 2 September 1990, defines a child as 'every human being below the age of eighteen years, unless, under the law applicable to the child, majority is attained earlier' (Art. 1). However, Art. 38.3 lowers the minimum age for being recruited into armed forces to 15:

> States Parties shall refrain from recruiting any person who has not attained the age of fifteen years into their armed forces. In recruiting among those persons who have attained the age of fifteen years but who have not attained the age of eighteen years, States Parties shall endeavour to give priority to those who are oldest.

The twenty-sixth international Conference of the Red Cross and Red Crescent held in December 1995 recommended *inter alia* that parties to conflict take every feasible step to ensure that children under the age of 18 years do not take part in hostilities. The Statute of the International Criminal Court adopted in July 1998 but not yet in force maintains 15 as the minimum age. Its Art. 8 (b)(xxvi) includes among 'war crimes' under the jurisdiction of the future court the act of 'Conscripting or enlisting children under the age of fifteen years into the armed forces or using them to participate actively in hostilities'.

In June 1999, the 87th International Labour Conference adopted unanimously ILO Convention 182 concerning the Prohibition and Immediate Action for the Elimination of the Worst Forms of Child Labour, which bans *inter alia* forced or compulsory recruitment of children for use in armed conflicts. For the purposes of the Convention, the term 'child' applied to all persons under the age of 18 (Art. 2 and 3 (a)).

On 25 May 2000, the UN General Assembly adopted two Optional Protocols to the Convention on the Rights of the Child. One, on the involvement of children in armed conflict, requires states parties to 'take all feasible measures to ensure that members of their armed forces who have not attained the age of 18 years do not take a direct part in hostilities' and that persons under 18 are not compulsorily recruited into their armed forces. The Protocol also prescribes that armed groups, distinct from the armed forces of a state, should not, under any circumstances, recruit or use in hostilities persons under 18. States parties are made responsible to take all feasible measures to prevent such recruitment and use, and, more appropriately, to adopt legal measures necessary to prohibit and criminalize such practices (Art. 1, 2 and 4).[27]

UNICEF's policy and programmes

In February 1999, Carol Bellamy described to the UN Security Council the elements of UNICEF's *Peace and Security Agenda for Children*, which goes beyond but includes the specific issue of child soldiers. Its main principles, elaborated further in May 1999, are as follows:

- Peace agreements should include specific reference to the demobilization of child soldiers and their reintegration into society.
- Nations should universally agree to an international requirement that raises the age of military recruitment to 18.
- There must be a dramatic reduction in the availability of small arms and light weapons whose portability is a major factor in turning children into combatants.
- The world must fully implement the global ban on anti-personnel landmines, which continue to kill or maim far more children than soldiers.
- All military, civilian and peacekeeping personnel should receive specialized child-rights training, so that they will understand their legal responsibilities to all children.
- Children should be protected from the effects of international sanctions.
- Special protection must be afforded to all children caught up in armed conflict, disaster, extreme poverty and all forms of violence and exploitation.
- Early warning and preventive action for children should be promoted as the most effective humanitarian strategy.

Finally, UNICEF has challenged the impunity of war crimes and crimes against humanity, especially those committed against children, and promoted the deployment of a fully empowered International Criminal Court.[28]

Among recent programmes, UNICEF and USAID have funded the Support to War-Affected Youth Programme which started in 1994 in Liberia. The Programme, carried out by NGOs in seven countries, caters to former child soldiers and other children affected by the war, a third of whom are girls. The children, aged 9 to 19, spend six to nine months learning skills in reading, writing and mathematics. They also study a trade, such as carpentry, agriculture or graphic arts. Older students learn business skills and may obtain small-business loans and set up cooperatives.

UNICEF and local organizations have supported the Children's Movement for Peace in Colombia. In 1996, 2.7 million Colombian children ranging in age from 7 to 18 took part in a special election which offered them a chance to identify which child rights they deemed most important to themselves and their communities. They overwhelmingly chose the right to survival and the right to peace. In 1999, UNICEF trained and mobilized 100 000 adolescents to advocate in 1000 towns for an end to the civil war. Five million Colombians joined street protests for peace as part of the 'no mas' (no more) campaign. Also in 1999, UNICEF and Save the Children were attempting to trace the identities of children in Eastern Zaire and begin the process of reunification. In Angola, the Democratic Republic of the Congo, Sierra Leone, Sri Lanka and Sudan, UNICEF participated in negotiations for the periodic cessation of hostilities to reach and immunize children.[29]

The role of the United Nations

The direct interest of the UN in child welfare and protection, following the creation of UNICEF in 1946, was first expressed in the Declaration of the Rights of the Child adopted by the General Assembly in 1959, and by the 1974 Declaration on the Protection of Women and Children in Emergency and Armed Conflict. In a resolution of 1975 endorsing ECOSOC's call for the observance of an International Year of the Child in 1979, the General Assembly expressed concern for all aspects of the well-being of children, for their human rights and for their legal and cultural identity. The 1989 Convention on the Rights of the Child was the first holistic international instrument which defined principles, different types of rights and mechanisms for monitoring and implementation. The World Declaration on the Survival, Protection and Development of Children in the 1990s and the Plan of Action for implementing this Declaration which were adopted by the World Summit for Children held in 1990 stressed the necessity to implement their provisions. In December 1993, the General Assembly adopted a resolution by consensus requesting the Secretary-General to appoint an expert, working in collaboration with the UN Center for Human Rights and UNICEF, to carry out a study on the impact of armed conflict on children. The resolution was a recognition by the international community of the catastrophic conditions to which children were exposed, both as targets and perpetrators of the atrocities of war.[30]

The 'Study of the Impact of Armed Conflict on Children' was presented to the General Assembly in November 1996. It was the result of a two-year process of research and consultation undertaken by Graça Machel, the Secretary-General's expert on the subject and a former Minister for Education in Mozambique.

The report says, in part, that in the past decade, around 2 million children have been killed in armed conflict, three times as many have been seriously injured or permanently disabled, and countless others have been forced to witness or even to take part in horrifying acts of violence.

The report calls for a global campaign to stop the recruitment of anyone under 18 into armed forces and to encourage governments and opposition groups to immediately demobilize all such children. It recommends that all peace agreements specifically address the need to demobilize and reintegrate child soldiers back into society. It also called on all governments to support the ready conclusion and adoption of the (then) draft Optional Protocol to the Convention on the Rights of the Child establishing the minimum age of recruitment and participation as 18 years of age.[31]

A General Assembly resolution of December 1996 recommended, in part, that the Secretary-General appoint for a period of three years a Special Representative on the impact of armed conflict on children. UNICEF, UNHCR and the UN High Commissioner for Human Rights and Center for Human Rights were to provide support to him. Mr Olara A. Otunnu (Nigeria) was appointed to this post and his mandate started in October 1997. Mr Otunnu was a former diplomat and a former President of the International Peace Academy in New York. He defined his core activities as follows:

- public advocacy to build greater awareness of the problem and mobilize the international community for action;
- promoting the application of international norms and traditional value systems that provide for the protection of children in times of conflict;
- undertaking political and humanitarian diplomacy and proposing concrete initiatives to protect children in the midst of war;
- making the protection and welfare of children a central concern in peace processes and post-conflict programmes for healing and rebuilding.

In his own words, Mr Otunnu explained that his challenging mandate means that he must fulfil several complementary roles:

I must be an advocate but must also be a catalyst, proposing ideas and approaches that can enhance the more effective protection of children. As well as bringing together key actors to encourage a more concerted and effective response and applauding good work on the ground, I must also be a facilitator, undertaking humanitarian and diplomatic initiatives to unblock difficult political situations and thus facilitate the work of operational actors in the field.

In working to end the recruitment and use of children in conflict, Mr Otunnu has pursued a three-pronged approach: campaigning to raise the age limit for recruitment and participation in armed conflict from 15 to 18, pressing for the immediate mobilization of international pressure on armed groups that are currently abusing children as combatants; and urging parties to conflicts as well as key international actors to address the political, social and economic factors that create an environment that facilitates the exploitation of children in this way.

As one specific policy recommendation, the Special Representative has proposed that child protection and welfare should become an explicit priority in the mandate of every UN peace operation and that a senior Child Protection Advocate should be attached to that operation.

On 25 August 1999, following the General Assembly's lead, the UN Security Council adopted its first resolution to specifically deal with the issue of child soldiers and the victimization of children during war. The Council

> strongly condemns the targeting of children in situations of armed conflict, including killing and maiming, sexual violence, abduction and forced displacement, recruitment and use of children in armed conflict in violation of international law, and attacks on objects protected under international law, including places that usually have a significant presence of children such as schools and hospitals, and calls on all parties concerned to put an end to such practices.

The Council stressed the responsibility of all states to bring an end to impunity and their obligation to prosecute those responsible for grave breaches of the Geneva Conventions of 12 August 1949. It expressed its support for the ongoing work of the Special Representative of the Secretary-General for Children and Armed Conflict, UNICEF, UNHCR and other relevant organizations. The resolution urged parties to a conflict to ensure that the welfare and rights of children are taken into account during peace talks; to take special measures to protect children, particularly girls, from rape and other forms of sexual abuse and gender-based violence during armed conflicts and in their aftermath; and to undertake feasible measures to minimize the harm suffered by children, such as 'days of tranquillity' to allow the delivery of basic necessary services. It also urged states to restrict arms transfers and combat illegal arms flows.

On 22 February 2000, the UN announced the deployment of Child Protection Advisers, who should ensure that the protection of children's rights is a priority concern in peacekeeping operations. The Advisers will also ensure that all personnel involved in peacekeeping operations – both military and civilian – have appropriate training on the protection of children's rights. One Adviser has been assigned to Sierra Leone and two to the Democratic Republic of the Congo. More are expected to be assigned to East Timor and Kosovo. Advisers will be drawn from the ranks of experienced staff in key UN agencies and from relevant NGOs and development agencies with expertise in the protection of children's rights. The first three appointed Advisers were UNICEF officials.[32]

On 25 May 2000, the UN General Assembly adopted the Optional Protocol to the Convention on the Rights of the Child on the involvement of children in armed conflict. This Protocol establishes 18 as the minimum age for direct participation in hostilities, for compulsory recruitment and for any recruitment or use in hostilities by non-governmental armed groups. However, it allows government forces to accept voluntary recruits from the age of 16, subject to certain safeguards including parental permission and proof of age. The US was the eighth country to sign the new agreement on 5 July 2000.

States parties to the African Charter on the Rights and Welfare of the Child have committed themselves also to apply 18 as the minimum age for voluntary and non-voluntary recruitment into armed forces.

In 1998, Tamil rebels promised Mr Otunnu that they would stop recruiting children under 17 and sending anyone under 18 into battle, but in July 2000 it was reported that the rebels had been rounding up boys and girls in their early teens to send them into battle against the Sri Lankan Army. This showed how difficult it is to translate international agreements and commitments into action, particularly when irregular forces are concerned.[33]

Landmines – 'toxic pollution'

According to the Graça Machel report of 1996:

> Children in at least 68 countries are today threatened by what may be the most toxic pollution facing mankind – the contamination by

mines of the land they live on. Over 110 million landmines of various types, plus millions of unexploded bombs, shells and grenades, remained hidden, waiting to be triggered by the innocent and unsuspecting.[34]

Once laid, a mine may remain active for up to 50 years. More than 26 000 people are killed or maimed by landmines each year – 90 per cent of these victims are civilians. Children are particularly exposed. Their natural curiosity leads them to investigate any strange object and, unable to read warning signs, they can easily stray into minefields. While an adult may survive a detonation, even the smallest explosion can be lethal for a child. Children who survive explosions are likely to be more seriously injured than adults, and often permanently disabled. They rarely receive the medical care and rehabilitative therapy they need.

Afghanistan, Angola and Cambodia have suffered 85 per cent of the world's landmine casualties. An estimated 37 million mines are embedded in the soil of at least 19 African countries. The UN Department of Humanitarian Affairs estimates that 9 to 15 million landmines litter Angola, a country of 10 million people. About 70 000 landmine victims are amputees, 8000 of them children under 15 years old.

Banning anti-personnel landmines

UNICEF was the first UN agency to call openly for the banning of the production of landmines. Since 1992, the agency has cooperated with, and provided support for, the International Campaign to Ban Landmines, a coalition of more than 1000 NGOs created in October of that year. The agency initially advocated that such a ban be adopted by strengthening Protocol II governing landmine use of the Convention on Certain Conventional Weapons Which May Be Deemed to Be Excessively Injurious or to Have Indiscriminate Effects (known as the Conventional Weapons Convention). However, the Review Conference of the Convention ended in May 1996 without results.

In October 1996, at the initiative of Canada, an International Strategy Conference on Antipersonnel Landmines was attended by 74 governments, UN agencies and NGOs. The final document of the Conference, the Ottawa Declaration, offered suggestions for global, regional and national action in pursuit of a ban. In December 1997, 122 states signed the Convention on the Prohibition of the Use, Stockpiling, Production and Transfer of Anti-Personnel Mines and Their Destruction. For its work in making the treaty a reality, the coalition of NGOs, including demining and victim-assistance groups, and its coordinator, Jody Williams, were awarded the 1997 Nobel Prize for Peace.

The treaty entered into force on 1 March 1999, following its ratification by 65 states. However, three of the Security Council's permanent members, China, Russia and the USA, have not signed the Treaty.[35]

The action of UNICEF

UNICEF has called for the universal ratification of the treaty and an international commitment to see that every child in a mined area knows proper safety procedures. Carol Bellamy said in March 1999 that the real test lies in seeing that the treaty is fully implemented, that stockpiles are destroyed and that demining proceeds rapidly. She praised the remarkable effects of the anti-landmine movement. According to the International Campaign to Ban Landmines, 10 to 15 million mines had been destroyed from stockpiles and the number of countries involved in producing them had dropped from 50 to 15.

UNICEF has been designated within the UN family as the lead agency to educate and advocate on the landmine issue. Educational campaigns have centred on teaching children about the dangers of landmines and safety procedures to follow in mined areas. For instance, in Afghanistan, educational materials have been distributed to almost a half million persons. In Angola, with Norwegian Peoples' Aid, government agencies and other partners alerted over 600 000 persons in 1999 to the danger of landmines. In Bosnia and Herzegovina, UNICEF has reached all children enrolled in primary schools with mine awareness messages. In Iraq, approximately one million mine awareness exercise books have been distributed, mainly to primary school children, and 4000 Iraqi teachers have been trained in mine safety procedures.[36]

Conclusion

The policies adopted by UNICEF to deal with emergencies and its recent programmes show that the agency has retained a strong humanitarian profile, in parallel to its official classification and role as a development agency. Even if working on sustainable development is more conceptually rewarding that facing short-term emergencies, UNICEF can hardly ignore the damage and suffering caused to children and mothers by emergencies, especially as it is the only UN agency dedicated to this category of persons. UNICEF cannot forget that it was originally founded as an emergency organization for children and its long experience and acknowledged competence in such situations is precious. Furthermore, the sheer number of natural and man-made emergencies has grown in recent years, demanding more international assistance. Finally, the public image of UNICEF lies to a large extent in its role as a humanitarian agency, justifying its calls for financial support.

UNICEF has worked towards the principal goals for its emergency-related cooperation with national and international partners defined in 1996, essentially the survival of the most vulnerable children and women, protection against violence and exploitation, rehabilitation and women's participation in self-development. However, the first goal, ' To prevent the exposure of children to risks by addressing the root causes of conflicts', is over-ambitious. Conflicts may be caused by excessive nationalism, ill-placed national prestige or more concretely by unsolved territorial claims between countries, and, within countries, by political rivalry, long-lasting ethnic or religious hatreds, economic disparities, social ills and other factors. The continuation of unnecessary and costly external or internal conflicts may be caused by the same reasons as those which started the conflict, with the support of external 'friends', suppliers and their resources, and the purchase of yet more weapons. Within the UN family, the UN Security Council is the body in charge of trying to prevent or resolve conflicts, which in turn depends on the active cooperation of its members. Knowing the limits of the Security Council's effectiveness in this field reduces the expectation that a specialized body such as UNICEF can 'address' the root causes of conflict. UNICEF may be aware of these causes, but it has no political legitimacy nor leverage as a peacemaker. Carol Bellamy rightly declared on 12 March 1999: 'Contemporary armed conflicts have their roots in deeply interwined political and economic issues which humanitarian organizations are neither equipped nor mandated to address'.[37] UNICEF's proper role is to advocate for the end of conflicts in view of their damaging consequences for children, and for the respect of humanitarian law as applied to children. The agency has thus promoted or supported NGOs' efforts to stop the use of child soldiers and to ban landmines, through the (NGO) Coalition to Stop the Use of Child Soldiers and the International (NGO) Campaign to Ban Landmines. The negotiation and conclusion of international instruments in both those areas, also effectively supported by NGOs with the cooperation of UNICEF, are positive developments to convince national authorities to take action. UNICEF also helps in promoting the ratification of these instruments by states and in encouraging the monitoring of their implementation by governments. However, NGOs are better placed than UNICEF, an intergovernmental body, to monitor governments' actions, publicize their findings and take to task those governments which fail to be true to their signature.

It is noteworthy that UNICEF has taken a strong position regarding the killing, maiming and other abuses against children during conflicts: not satisfied with offering relief and physical and psychological care to surviving victims, the agency has extended its advocacy to calls for the universal ratification of the Statute of the International Criminal Court and for the end to impunity of war criminals with regard to crimes committed against children through national and international justice. As noted in other chapters, UNICEF is not alone in the field of emergency relief and other fields of work. It works within the realm of the UN family of organizations, under the authority, or at least in cooperation with, the UN Emergency Relief Coordinator at the global level, the Special Representative of the Secretary-General in a specific country or area, the UNDP Resident Coordinators, or the representative of the designated lead UN agency for a specific emergency. UNICEF works together with the WFP on food supply, with UNHCR on child refugees and with WHO on health issues. Liaison is maintained with regional organizations such as the Humanitarian Office of the European Union (ECHO) and the OAS. Cooperation is sought with the ICRC, a pioneer and active partner in humanitarian assistance, together with the Federation of Red Cross and Red Crescent organizations, and with the numerous NGOs providing humanitarian assistance. They include human rights activist NGOs (Amnesty International, Human Rights Watch, etc.) and operational partners (the Save the Children Alliance, Oxfam, World Vision, Handicap International, Médecins Sans Frontières, Médecins du Monde, etc.), national and local NGOs, and international foundations such as Rotary International.

In the same way as WHO has recently shown more international presence in dealing with children's health, children and youth have taken a prominent place on the agenda of the UN General Assembly since the end of the Cold War and following the 1990 World Summit for Children. The UN has not only promoted the negotiation and ratification of such an important international instrument as the Convention on the Rights of the Child, but it has commissioned the Machel Report and authorized the appointment of a Special Representative on the impact of armed conflict on children. Finally, (UN) Child Protection Advisers were deployed in 2000 to ensure that the protection of children's rights was a priority concern in peacekeeping operations. It does not seem that this new interest in children's welfare and protection on the part of the UN should be interpreted as unwanted rivalry with UNICEF and/or a sign of distrust towards the agency: it only shows that the 'international community' has become more aware of children's needs and more concerned about their welfare and protection. The work of Mr Otunnu as the dynamic and effective Special Representative of the Secretary-General on the impact of armed conflict on children, as an advocate and a catalyst, usefully complements, in this specific area, that of Carol Bellamy, by providing a more diplomatic backing to the same themes.

UNICEF was appointed by the UN Secretary-General to be the lead agency within the UN system in two emergency situations, in Kampuchea in 1979 and in Somalia in 1988. In the former case, Labouisse expressed misgivings to Kurt Waldheim about this decision. In both cases, the designation of UNICEF was based on its competence as a humanitarian agency, and in the latter case on the additional prestige acquired by James Grant. In both cases, this designation implied a temporary extension of UNICEF's mandate beyond that of promoting children's welfare and protection only. Both were anomalies in so far as the main component of both operations was food relief, not the preserve of UNICEF. It is therefore unlikely and undesirable that UNICEF should again be designated as lead agency of a UN humanitarian operation associating several UN agencies. On the other hand, the designation of UNICEF as lead agency to educate and advocate on the landmine issue fits in well with its educational mandate in so far as children are the main innocent targets of landmines.

In December 1999, Carol Bellamy complained about 'humanitarian favoritism', i.e a recent pattern in emergency donations that have substantially funded publicized crisis spots while leaving several of the world's most disadvantaged countries wanting. The most underfunded of UNICEF's humanitarian appeals in 1999, by percentage of funding, were for Afghanistan (41 per cent), Angola (36 per cent), the Democratic Republic of Korea (30 per cent), the Democratic Republic of the Congo (43 per cent), Eritrea (22 per cent), Tajikistan (44 per cent) and Uganda (17 per cent). By contrast, Kosovo, Turkey and East Timor all received nearly as much or more than the amounts requested in 1999.[38]

This trend is not specific to UNICEF: public and private donors choose their causes, not only as a result of publicity, but also for political and other reasons. As most donations come from western countries, it is not unexpected that their generosity towards North Korea would be limited. Donors also become reticent about giving more assistance to countries in unending civil war, where national financial and human resources are wasted on costly conflicts (Afghanistan, Angola, Congo, Eritrea). Should the focus not be on promoting peace rather than on pouring aid into a bottomless Danaides barrel? Is international aid feeding conflicts by being taken over by combatants, to the detriment of civilians?

UNICEF, like other intergovernmental organizations, cannot wait for peace to come. The agency has always considered it its duty to bring relief to those in need, whatever the consequences of such a position.

Another dilemma is that of maintaining impartiality and neutrality when one party is clearly mainly responsible for grave breaches of human rights and humanitarian law. Here, UNICEF has to follow the lead of the UN Security Council and General Assembly through their resolutions.

While UNICEF is now primarily a child development agency, its role in emergency action for children and women, in partnership with many other organizations, remains a limited but significant part of its overall mandate.

7
Advocating Children's Rights

For UNICEF, advocacy means not only informing donors and the public about what UNICEF is doing but, more importantly, sending public messages on its policies in an effort to influence national and international decision-makers and obtain the support of public opinion for policies, some of which may, at times, be controversial or opposed by large segments of populations or countries. These policies are either initiated by the agency itself, or are part of a UN interagency campaign, or are the result of campaigns by NGOs. Effective advocacy requires communications and marketing expertise, an area in which UNICEF has long proved its skills. Advocacy is an essential part of all UNICEF programmes: in some cases, the programme is limited to advocacy when the causes are too broad to generate specific operations, or when resources are lacking, or when other organizations, in particular NGOs, assume the operational activities.

UNICEF advocacy is expressed either by the public speeches of its Executive Director, by press releases, by publications, by commissioned research or surveys followed by public reports, by announcements preceding conferences or seminars and resolutions adopted in these meetings, by the public announcements of National Committees, by lobbying chiefs of state, governments, parliaments and intergovernmental fora, by the use of Goodwill Ambassadors, and by the organization of special events (days of tranquillity, 'Day of the African Child').

In Jim Grant's times, campaigns were often based on catchy slogans in specific areas. Since the adoption of the Convention on the Rights of the Child in 1989, UNICEF has integrated these rights in its Mission

Statement. As part of its Mission, adopted by the UNICEF Executive Board in January 1996 (see Figure 2.1):

> UNICEF is guided by the Convention on the Rights of the Child and strives to establish children's rights as enduring ethical principles and international standards of behaviour towards children.

UNICEF was born as a humanitarian organization, then became a development agency. Has it now become a 'human rights' institution with aims similar to those of the Human Rights Commission and of such NGOs as Amnesty International and Human Rights Watch? Or are human rights only a new function added to UNICEF's traditional tasks? Should its advocacy apply equally to all its facets and programmes or should it now stress the promotion of human rights in priority to its earlier more concrete concerns?

This chapter will first review the origin and contents of the Convention and its impact on UNICEF's role. Advocacy on issues related to the Convention not covered in previous chapters, such as gender issues, child labour and modern slavery, will then be considered, ending with two other issues adopted by the agency: advocacy for debt relief and the damage caused to children's survival and health by economic sanctions.

The Convention on the Rights of the Child

The origin of the Convention

NGOs have played a determining role in the drafting and adoption of the Convention, and in earlier attempts to define children's rights, on a universal basis, to protection, care and support. The key role of the founder of Save the Children, Eglantyne Jebb, in drafting and promoting the 'Declaration of Geneva' (see Figure 1.1) has been discussed in Chapter 1. In 1924, the Declaration was adopted by the League of Nations as the 'Charter of Child Welfare of the League of Nations'.

On 20 November 1959, the UN General Assembly adopted the Declaration of the Rights of the Child. The rationale for issuing a separate declaration for children's rights was that 'the child, by reason of his physical and mental immaturity, needs special safeguards and care, including appropriate legal protection, before as well as after birth'.[1]

The non-binding Declaration sets several important principles:

1. *As general principles of protection*: the rights set forth in the Declaration should be enjoyed by every child without discrimination on account of

race, colour, sex, language, religion, political or other opinion, national or social origin, property, birth or other status, whether of himself or of his family; the best interests of the child should be given the paramount consideration; the child should be the first to receive protection and relief; primary responsibility lies with the parents, while society and the public authorities have the duty to care for children without a family.

2. *As legal rights*: right to a name and nationality; right to social security benefits; right to protection against all forms of neglect, cruelty and exploitation and from discrimination; no admission to employment before an appropriate minimum age.

3. *As rights to survival and development*: right to health care, adequate nutrition, housing, recreation and medical services; right to education; right to special care for handicapped children.

There is no specific mention of UNICEF in the Declaration: the agency was included anonymously in the Preamble among 'specialized agencies and international organizations concerned with the welfare of children' whose statutes include special safeguards for children. However, in another resolution adopted on the same day, the General Assembly recognized that 'the aid provided through the Fund constitutes a practical way of international cooperation to help countries to carry out the aims proclaimed in the Declaration of the Rights of the Child'.[2]

In 1979, the International Year of the Child, the Polish delegation initiated a proposal for the drafting of a Convention on the Rights of the Child which would complement the 1959 Declaration by holding governments legally accountable for meeting the obligations that make the rights meaningful. The drafting of the Convention took place in a working group set up by the UN Commission on Human Rights. Government delegates formed the core of the Working Group, but representatives of UN bodies and specialized agencies – UNHCR, ILO, UNICEF and WHO – and NGOs took part in the deliberations. The debates were greatly influenced by the well-organized and technically competent Ad Hoc NGO Working Group, which included among others Defence for Children International (DCI), the Save the Children Alliance, Rädda Barnen, Anti-Slavery International and the International Catholic Children's Bureau.

UNICEF was originally reluctant to join an initiative which would include child protection, a sensitive area where the agency might find itself in confrontation with governments, compromise its tradition of impartiality, and thus jeopardize its global child survival and development programmes. James Grant originally declined to participate in the drafting of the Convention. He also doubted that governments would accept that children had independent rights of their own.

As reported by a UNICEF official,[3] to the frustration of some governments and many NGOs, UNICEF treated the Working Group on the Convention with 'benign neglect' for several years. NGOs and a few UNICEF staff members finally convinced the agency's Executive Board that the agency's full engagement was important for the realization of children's rights and for the quality of the new Convention. UNICEF's attitude was also influenced by its interest in a new category of children's issues, referred to as Children in Especially Difficult Circumstances (CEDC), which included working children, children with disabilities and children in war zones. By 1987, UNICEF was fully engaged in the drafting process in New York. UNICEF field offices supported workshops, conferences and symposia on child rights to stimulate public debate and press for legislative protection for children in all regions of the world.

The final text of the Convention was approved unanimously by the General Assembly on 20 November 1989.[4] Sixty-one countries signed the Convention on 26 January 1990, the first day it was opened for signature. With the receipt of over 20 ratifications on 2 September 1990, the Convention entered into force. In September 1990, the World Summit for Children was held in New York on the initiative of UNICEF and six States (Canada, Egypt, Mali, Mexico, Pakistan and Sweden). The summit encouraged all states to ratify the Convention. By 2000, 191 countries had ratified the Convention. The US and Somalia (a failed state) were the only exceptions.

The main contents of the Convention

The 54-article binding Convention integrates the main principles previously set out by the Declaration: non-discrimination, the need to extend special safeguards and care to the child, the best interests of the child as a primary consideration, the responsibility of parents and society to ensure the child has protection and care. States parties are made responsible for the survival and development of children.

It adds considerably to the Declaration by including the whole range of human rights – civil, political, economic, social and cultural – and fundamental freedoms contained in the Universal Declaration of Human Rights of 1948, in the International Covenant on Civil and Political Rights (ICPR) and in the International Covenant on Economic, Social and Cultural Rights (ICESCR) both adopted in 1966. As an important and controversial innovation, the Convention establishes the right of the child to be an actor in his or her own life, and a right of participation in all decisions affecting him or her. For the first time at the international level, a child is defined as every human being below the age of 18, unless, under the law applicable to the child, majority is attained earlier.

To the rights to a name and nationality and to social security have been added the inherent right to life, the right of the child who is capable of forming his or her own views to freedom of expression, thought, conscience and religion, and even the rights of the child to freedom of association and freedom of peaceful assembly.

The child has specific rights of protection: protection of the law, through appropriate legislative, administrative, social and educational measures, from arbitrary or unlawful interference with his or her privacy, family, home or correspondence, from all forms of physical or mental violence, injury or abuse, neglect or negligent treatment, maltreatment or exploitation, including sexual abuse, from the illicit use of narcotic drugs, from economic exploitation and from hazardous work. A minimum age for admission to employment should be provided. States should provide measures to prevent the abduction of, the sale of or traffic in children. No child should be subjected to torture or other cruel, inhuman or degrading treatment or punishment. Neither capital punishment nor life imprisonment without possibility of release should be imposed for offences committed by persons below the age of 18. No child should be deprived of his or her liberty unlawfully or arbitrarily. Children should be protected by international humanitarian law as applicable to them in armed conflicts and as refugees. States should refrain from recruiting any person below the age of 15 into their armed forces. Special measures concern the adoption of mentally or physically disabled children.

UNICEF's (and WHO's) input may be recognized in Article 24 regarding the need for preventive health care and the following specific measures to be taken by states: to diminish infant and child mortality, to develop primary health care, to combat disease and malnutrition, and to promote health care for mothers, health education and the advantages of breastfeeding. Recommendations concerning the development of family planning education and services, and the abolition of traditional practices prejudicial to the health of children, are controversial or even unacceptable in a few countries on social, religious and/or traditional grounds. UNICEF's influence is also seen in the recognition of the right of children to education and the responsibility of states to make primary education compulsory and available to all (Article 28), as well as a reference to the needs of children living in exceptionally difficult conditions.

The Convention establishes a Committee on the Rights of the Child for the purpose of examining the progress made by states parties in achieving the realization of the obligations that they have undertaken when they ratified the Convention. The Committee consists of ten experts 'of high moral standing and recognized competence' in the field covered by the Convention, who serve in their personal capacity. They are elected by states parties, consideration being given to equitable geographical distribution as well as to the principal legal systems. States parties have reporting obligations: they submit to the Committee reports on measures they have adopted which give effect to the rights recognized in the Convention and on the progress made on the enjoyment of these rights. Their first report is submitted within two years of the entry into force of the Convention for the state party concerned, and thereafter every five years. Unlike the Convention on the Elimination of Racial Discrimination (CERD) and the Convention against Torture, the present Convention has no provisions for hearing complaints or for initiating investigations when violations are suspected or reported.

The UN specialized agencies, UNICEF and other UN organs are entitled to be represented at the Committee's session at the consideration of the implementation of provisions within the scope of their mandate. The Committee may invite the same UN institutions to provide expert advice and to submit reports. It may also transmit to these bodies any reports from states parties that contain a request, or indicate a need, for technical advice or assistance, along with the Committee's observations and suggestions, if any.

During the drafting of the Convention, some NGOs had envisaged a more central role for UNICEF. One proposal suggested that the specialized agencies would keep UNICEF fully informed of measures they have taken either in response to states parties' requests or within their programmes of action to further the full realization of rights guaranteed by the Convention. Another one proposed that the Committee transmit to UNICEF 'as designated lead agency for children', the reports of states parties as well as the Committee's comments. These proposals were not considered by the Working Group for apparent lack of time. They had met the opposition of a few governments' representatives and the reticence of some specialized agencies. According to an NGO participant, the UNICEF leadership itself seemed less than keen about being charged with a central role in facilitating the implementation of the Convention as a whole.[5]

What role for UNICEF?

The responsibility for implementing the Convention lies with states, while the UN specialized agencies, UNICEF and other UN organs are to

foster its effective implementation and encourage international cooperation in the field covered by the Convention. Even though the Convention
did not designate UNICEF as a central body to assist governments in
implementing its provisions, the agency's decision of 1996 to include in
its Mission Statement that it would be 'guided' by the Convention showed
that the children's agency had of itself assumed a significant role in this
regard, although by no means an exclusive role as other UN bodies and
many NGOs are playing their part.

Perhaps as compensation for its 'benign neglect' in the first years of the
drafting of the Convention, UNICEF has taken a more active role in the
pre-sessional meetings of the Committee on the Rights of the Child, held
the week before the Committee meets. As reported by Oestreich:

> At these meetings UNICEF, other UN agencies, and invited NGOs (but
> no representatives from the reporting countries) consider the reports
> that have been submitted and prepare questions for the formal
> meeting. UNICEF headquarters in New York routinely requests that
> its field offices prepare reports, which are then used at the presessional
> meetings, making UNICEF among the best-informed and more active
> organizations in regular attendance at the sessional meetings ... By
> making country reports and other publications available to the
> Committee, UNICEF has carved out a role for itself as an informal
> monitoring body, albeit not the only agency providing materials to the
> Committee.[6]

UNICEF has received requests for technical advice or assistance either
from the Committee or directly from countries. The agency is regularly
asked by countries for assistance in preparing their reports to the
Committee, assistance which is mainly provided by UNICEF field offices.
In such cases, UNICEF may be placed in the somewhat awkward position
of later commenting on a report which it has helped to produce.

In 1992, UNICEF arranged an inter-agency consultation in Quito
(Ecuador) so that the Committee could learn what other agencies were
doing to promote child rights. The meeting was also attended by
government officials and NGOs.

In 1994, UNICEF provided financial assistance to the NGO Group for
the Convention on the Rights of the Child in Geneva to publish *A Guide
for Non-Governmental Organizations Reporting to the Committee on the Rights
of the Child*.

Internally, the rights-based approach led UNICEF to broaden its scope
to cover all aspects of child well-being, from early childhood care and

development to protection from abuse, exploitation and armed conflict. Programmes have expanded to reach not just infants and young children but also adolescents and youth.

The expansion of the agency's programmes required a planned reorientation of its staff. The Executive Director appointed in 1990 the Consultative Group on Child Rights, an internal, inter-divisional group, to promote the integration of the Convention into UNICEF-assisted country programme activities. In 1993, the Group discussed the need to link implementation of the Convention on the Rights of the Child to the Convention on the Elimination of All Forms of Discrimination against Women, the need for UNICEF to intensify its advocacy against the sexual exploitation of children, and the need for UNICEF to be more vocal when children's rights are flagrantly violated, especially in situations of armed conflict. In 1994, the Group's focus shifted towards specific protection issues, including efforts to revise UNICEF policy and programme guidelines to address child labour and prostitution and other violations of child rights. UNICEF was to provide technical assistance to those governments making legislative reforms in line with the Convention. Training was to be provided to all UNICEF staff, as well as to government and NGO officials, in matters related to the Convention. Programmes increasingly were emphasizing the strengthening of family capacities, gender equality, child participation and children in need of special protection. Finally, in the first quarter of 1998, programming guidelines were finalized and distributed to all UNICEF offices and training initiated.

Externally, UNICEF's role was first to promote ratification by countries, second to publicize and advocate the rights of children and third to support national capacity-building to monitor implementation, in association with many other organizations. UNICEF has actively pursued universal ratification, with the support of its National Committees and many NGOs. It helped accelerate the ratification process through liaison with ambassadors at the UN in New York, through writing letters to heads of state who signed the World Summit Declaration and through lobbying at the World Conference on Human Rights in Vienna held in June 1993. In June 1994, more than 50 Islamic countries attended a UNICEF consultation on the Rights of the Child held in cooperation with the Organization of the Islamic Conference. The meeting focused on states' specific reservations regarding the Convention and possibilities for ratification.

In order to ensure the wide dissemination of the Convention and to create greater awareness of its reporting process, UNICEF, in collaboration with the High Commissioner on Human Rights and the Committee on the Rights of the Child, issued in 1998 the *Implementation Handbook for the Convention on the Rights of the Child*. This article-by-article analysis of the Convention, as interpreted by the Committee during its first six years of work, has been shared with the UNICEF Executive Board, heads of UN organizations and all UNICEF offices, as well as with leading children's rights organizations and experts. The UNICEF resource guide on the Convention reporting process and the *Handbook* are used regularly by UNICEF country offices.

Consultations and capacity-building sessions on the Convention were organized by UNICEF in 1998 in the following regions: Central and Eastern Europe; the Commonwealth of Independent States (CIS) and Baltic States; the Middle East and North Africa; East Asia and the Pacific; and West and Central Africa. This support ranged from assisting in the organization of consultations prior to the preparation of states parties' reports, to follow-up to the Concluding Observations of the Committee on the Rights of the Child. These sessions often led to an overall assessment of the situation of children in the country to identify major areas of concern and promote the development of a national agenda for children's rights, including law reform and policy action.

For example, in Peru, UNICEF helped fulfil the child's right to a name and nationality by supporting training for 9000 public registrars. At the same time, the agency worked with the National Association of Municipalities, educators, women's organizations, police, the country's largest soccer clubs and others to provide free registration for over 100 000 children and adolescents lacking official birth documents. As a result, 24 000 children previously excluded from education were enrolled in school, and the need for registration was given wide publicity.

A successful technique for building national capacity to track progress for children is the Multiple Indicator Cluster Survey (MICS), a low-cost, fast and reliable household survey method developed by UNICEF and several UN agencies. MICS are carried out by government ministries of health and national statistics offices, with UNICEF assistance. In a 1997 UNICEF evaluation of MICS methods in 60 countries, the majority of governments reported that participating in the surveys helped their own capacity to gather and analyse data.

The Child Rights Monitoring Project, initiated by Child Watch International (an NGO) and supported by UNICEF and several other donors over the period 1994 to 1998, has stimulated the development of monitoring activities at the local level in a number of countries. The UNICEF yearly *Progress of Nations* also serves to monitor global and national advances towards the goals set in 1990 by the World Summit for

Children, as a blueprint for action in conjunction with the human rights and development objectives of the Convention.[7]

On 25 May 2000, the UN General Assembly adopted two Optional Protocols to the Convention. The Optional Protocol on the sale of children, child prostitution and child pornography makes it a criminal offence to sell, trade or use children for a variety of purposes including sexual exploitation and pornography. The measure was first proposed by Cuba and Guatemala, among other countries, because of other perceived violations of children's rights, including the selling of organs and forced adoptions, according to the UNICEF representative. With the rapid growth in human trafficking, especially the sale of girls into brothels in Asia, the proposed Protocol gained wide support in the US, Europe and other regions. By July 2000, six countries had signed the Protocol; ten ratifications are required for it to enter into force.[8]

On the Optional Protocol on the involvement of children in armed conflict, see Chapter 6.

The African Charter on the Rights and Welfare of the Child

The African Charter was adopted in 1990 at the 16th Ordinary Session of the Organization of African Unity (OAU) Heads of State and Government held in Monrovia, as the first regional treaty on the human rights of children. In November 1999, the fifteenth country ratified the Charter, allowing it to enter into force. States parties are now required to submit reports to an 11-member African Committee of Experts which will monitor compliance with the Charter.

The Charter acknowledges that most African children continue to live in most critical conditions due to socio-economic, cultural, traditional and development factors, natural disasters, armed conflicts, exploitation and hunger. It also recognizes that on account of the child's physical and mental immaturity the African child needs special safeguards and care. Like the UN Convention, the African Charter recognizes all human beings 18 years of age or below as children. The delay in ratifying the Charter was due to the reluctance of African governments to change local legislation and practice, particularly regarding children's economic and social rights threatening loss of parental control. The protection accorded by the Charter to the girl child was rightly deemed another serious threat to long-established social and religious customs of sexual discrimination.[9]

UNICEF programmes in relation to specific 'rights' of children have been reviewed in previous chapters: health care and family planning in Chapter 4, nutrition and education in Chapter 5. Other specific programmes, also related to the UN Convention, follow.

Gender issues

In the Preamble of the Convention on the Rights of the Child, states parties recognize that the UN has, in the Universal Declaration of Human Rights and the International Covenants on Human Rights, proclaimed and agreed that everyone is entitled to all the rights and freedoms set forth therein, without distinction of any kind, including, *inter alia*, sex. The non-discrimination on the basis of sex is prescribed in Article 2 of the Convention which includes the states' obligation to ensure that the child is protected against such and other forms of discrimination. States also agree that the preparation of the child for responsible life in a free society should adhere, *inter alia*, to a spirit of equality of sexes.

The World Summit for Children held in 1990 was more specific in acknowledging that women in their various roles play a critical part in the well-being of children. Its participants affirmed that strengthening the role and status of women in general and ensuring their human rights will be to the advantage of the world's children. The 1979 Convention on the Elimination of Discrimination Against Women, which entered into force in 1981, had extended the women's rights provisions of the International Bill of Human Rights. Participants at the Summit declared that 'Girls must be given equal treatment and opportunities from the very beginning': however, the present situation is that two-thirds of the more than 100 million children without basic schooling are girls. Responsible planning of family size, child spacing, breastfeeding and safe motherhood will be promoted. Equal opportunity should be provided for the girl child to benefit from the health, nutrition, education and other basic services to enable her to grow to her full potential. The mid-decade review of progress towards the Summit goals emphasized, *inter alia*, the need to adopt gender-sensitive approaches to girls' education, maternal mortality reduction and the elimination of gender disparities in the monitoring of national achievements.

The Fourth World Conference on Women held in Beijing in September 1995 adopted a Platform for Action and the Beijing Declaration which formulated revolutionary advances in women's reproductive health and rights. The Platform recognized that 'the human rights of women include their right to have control over and decide freely and responsibly on matters related to their sexuality, including sexual and reproductive health, free of coercion, discrimination, and violence'. It also called upon governments to eliminate female genital mutilation.[10]

UNICEF policy and activities

The UNICEF mission statement adopted in 1996 states, *inter alia*, that 'UNICEF aims, through its country programmes, to promote the equal rights of women and girls and to support their full participation in the political, social and economic development of their communities'.

Following Beijing, UNICEF identified as priority areas of its action girls' education, adolescent girls' and women's health, and children's and women's rights. Its main activities are in the area of support to research and communications, and advocacy. UNICEF's regional and country offices have supported the preparation of situation analyses of women and girls from the life-cycle perspective. For instance, in India, UNICEF successfully lobbied for the girl-child week, which was adopted by the government in September 1998. This included a national seminar on the status of the girl child. In the Philippines, a National Plan of Action for the Filipino girl child was formulated. A UNICEF-supported study of 1997 showed that it is in families where boys and girls first learn that they have different entitlements and it is also in families that they are socialized into their gender roles. Early in their lives children imbibe a whole view of culture generally based on male dominance and female subordination. This view is reinforced in other institutions such as the church, school and media. The results of this study will be used for the development of appropriate messages and education materials directed at families and communities for behaviour change. In 1998, the country programme focused on issues of girl-children and domestic violence. Sixteen region-based advocacy meetings were conducted on girl children and violence against women and children.

UNICEF is providing technical support to its country offices in implementing a project on 'Meeting the Development and Participation Rights of Adolescent Girls', a project funded by the UN Foundation. Initiated in 14 countries, the project focuses on:

- access to information;
- access to education/learning, health services and recreation;
- life and livelihood skills;
- providing safe and supportive environments;
- providing opportunities to participate in society, in the decisions that affect their lives, and in the project itself.

In 1995, responding to grassroots requests, the Working Group on Girls of the NGO Committee on UNICEF created an International Network for Girls, which had more than 600 members in 90 countries in 2000. Its programmes include education, health, nutrition, child labour and sexual exploitation. UNICEF has initiated or supported, in Asia and Africa, various communication initiatives, such as animated film series, BBC radio series dealing with such issues as son preference, unfair treatment of girls in the family, girls' domestic workload, their lesser access to health and education services, harmful traditional practices such as early marriage and dowry, genital mutilation and sexual harassment.[11]

Violence against women and children

In December 1993, the UN General Assembly adopted by consensus a Declaration on the Elimination of Violence against Women. It defined violence against women as 'any act of gender-based violence that results in, or is likely to result in, physical, sexual or mental harm or suffering to women, including threats of such acts, coercion or arbitrary deprivation of liberty, whether occurring in public or in private life'. This encompasses, *inter alia*:

> physical, sexual and psychological violence occurring in the family and in the general community, including battering, sexual abuse of children, dowry-related violence, rape, female genital mutilation, and other traditional practices harmful to women, non-spousal violence and violence related to exploitation, sexual harassment and intimidation at work, in educational institutions and elsewhere, trafficking in women, forced prostitution, and violence perpetrated or condoned by the state.[12]

In December 1999, UNICEF released *The State of the World's Children 2000*. This report noted a 'pervasive violence', one that runs as a 'subtle context' through the lives of women and children. 'The incidence of violence within a family, though hidden from public sight and statistics, is almost certainly the most persistent ... It trickles down from one generation to the next, turning children reared on violence into violent adults.'

UNICEF's May 2000 edition of the Innocenti Digest, entitled *Domestic Violence Against Women and Girls*, provides a detailed description and analysis of the global 'epidemic' of gender-based violence.[13] The report says that domestic violence against women and girls is a 'global epidemic', one that 'kills, tortures and maims – physically, psychologically, sexually and economically. It is one of the most pervasive of human rights violations ... Violence against women is present in every country, cutting across boundaries of culture, class, education, income, ethnicity and age'. Studies estimate that between 20 and 50 per cent of women have experienced physical violence at the hands of an intimate partner or family member. Although violence against women can vary in nature according to country and region, in most areas of the world, specific groups of women are more vulnerable to violence, including minority groups, indigenous and migrant women, refugee women and those in institutions and detention, women with disabilities, female children, and elderly women. The UNICEF report claims that gender-based violence against female children is particularly alarming. 'In many countries, the discrimination that leads to the neglect of girl children is the greatest cause of sickness and death among girls between the ages of two and five years'. This discrimination leaves girls with inferior access to nourishment and medical assistance, and girls are therefore at greater risk of mental or physical disability, often even death. Types of violence may begin with a sex-selective abortion and includes, aside from physical beatings and other more visible forms of violence like acid throwing and honour killings, forced malnutrition, lack of access to medical care and school, forced prostitution and bonded labour. The report notes the relationship between domestic violence and the spread of HIV/AIDS. Combined with female infanticide, these discriminatory practices towards girls have resulted in what the report calls the 'missing millions' of women and girls. 'An estimated 60 million women are simply missing from the population statistics. In other words, there are 60 million fewer women alive in the world than should be expected.' These missing millions are absent primarily in South Asia, North Africa, the Middle East and China.

While all countries are guilty of discrimination against women to varying degrees, Afghanistan under Taliban rule is a blatant example of government-sponsored, official sex discrimination amounting to violence against girls and women in the areas of education, employment and health. Since 1995, the Taliban regime has banned girls from attending formal schools and restricted women from the teaching profession. Women are restricted from social activities and most forms of employment that involve contact with men other than husbands or relatives. The health sector is the only area where women are allowed to work. Male doctors are prevented from treating female patients. Private clinics are prevented from accepting female in-patients. A woman's physical and mental health and her access to health care are jeopardized by the restrictions on her movements, her mode of dress, her presence in public places and use of public transport. According to a UNICEF report, these measures resulted in a significant decrease in antenatal care coverage, tetanus immunization and assisted delivery of children. Restrictions on women have impacted on children: less than 10 per cent are fully immunized, and 20 per cent who are six to 35 months of age are severely malnourished. Carol Bellamy visited Afghanistan in April 1998 and reported that UN humanitarian agencies working in the country were seriously concerned, in part, over the official discrimination against women and girls. On 6 April, the Security Council said, *inter alia*, that it was 'deeply concerned at the continuing discrimination against girls and women and other violations of human rights as well as violations of international humanitarian law in Afghanistan'. In a report submitted to the April 2000 session of the UN Human Rights Commission, the Sri Lankan jurist R. Coomaraswamy called the life of Afghan women a 'nightmare without equivalent in the world and a shock for mankind's conscience'. In spite of these conditions, UNICEF continues immunization campaigns, support to feeding centres and provision of nutritional supplements, safe drinking water and sanitation systems. In partnership with other organizations, UNICEF is also promoting a community-based maternity health programme in the country.[14]

In a recent report, the UN Development Fund for Women (UNIFEM) said that 'All of these forms of violence are associated with power inequalities: between women and men, between children and their caregivers, as well as with growing economic inequalities both within and between countries'.[15]

According to recent information compiled by UNICEF on Bangladesh, reported attacks on women – often by men they had rejected – rose from 47 disfiguring assaults in 1996 to more than 200 in 1998. In India, more than 6000 'bride burnings' or other dowry deaths were reported in 1997. Also in 1997, about 300 women in one province in Pakistan were reported killed in the name of saving a family's honour. The US State Department, in its annual survey of human rights published on 25 February 2000, reported that there were about 10 000 cases of female infanticide in India annually, not counting an unknown number of abortions performed to prevent the birth of a girl.[16]

UNICEF calls for a series of measures to reduce this toll:

- enacting legislation and ending impunity for perpetrators: by 2000, 44 countries have adopted specific legislation on domestic violence, of which 12 are in Latin America;
- training the judiciary to be gender-sensitive, as carried out in Costa Rica, India and the USA;
- setting up women's police stations, staffed with multi-disciplinary female teams (Sao Paolo, Brazil).

UNICEF is involved in inter-agency campaigns on violence against women in Latin America and the Caribbean, Africa and South Asia. Its partners include, among others, UNFPA, Save the Children and other international, national or regional NGOs. UNICEF produces information material on the equal rights of girls including video dramas and assists in the printing of posters. The agency runs training workshops on legislation and women's rights for judges, public prosecutors, police and lawyers and awareness and training workshops in schools (Bolivia).

Female genital mutilation (FGM)

FGM is a specific instance of violence against girls and women, with the aggravating fact that its damaging effects on women's integrity are lifelong and cannot be reversed.

As defined by WHO, FGM comprises 'all procedures involving partial or total removal of the external female genitalia or other injury to the female genital organs whether for cultural, religious or other non-therapeutic reasons'. FGM is often referred to as 'female circumcision'.[17] Depending on the type and severity of the procedure performed, FGM may involve immediate and/or long-term adverse consequences detrimental to the physical, psychosexual and psychological health of the persons undergoing the mutilation. In cultures where it is an accepted norm, FGM is practised by followers of all religious beliefs as well as animists and non-believers.[18] It is usually performed by a traditional practitioner with crude instruments and without anaesthetic. The age at which FGM is performed varies from area to area. It is performed on infants a few days old, female children and adolescents, and occasionally on mature women.

FGM is mostly practised in 28 African countries, and to a lesser extent in Asia and in the Middle East. It has also been imported by immigrants from these countries to Europe, Australia, Canada and the USA. In 2000, the number of girls and women who have undergone FGM was estimated at between 100 and 140 million. It is estimated that each year, a further 2 million girls are at risk of undergoing FGM.

The concern of UN organizations in FGM was relatively slow and initially cautious, no doubt in view of the strong religious and cultural connotations of the practice, and their fear of political reactions from a number of their member states.

WHO supported the Working Group on Female Circumcision, which was formed in 1977 by members of 20 NGOs with an African woman as its coordinator. UNICEF entered the scene in the 1980s, in concert with other UN agencies.

In March 1980, a joint WHO/UNICEF consultation on female circumcision, held in Alexandria, Egypt, stressed the need that 'outsiders' should exercise extreme caution, lest their well-intended efforts to help eradicate female circumcision be construed as 'interference', leading to a counter-productive reaction. It was suggested that work in this area should be taken by and through nationals whenever possible, with programmes adapted to each country according to the level of awareness and type of practice. The participants agreed that female circumcision is a public health problem which can be successfully approached through primary health care programmes.

In August 1982, WHO made a formal statement of its position to the UN Commission on Human Rights as follows:

- Governments should adopt clear national policies to abolish the practice, and to inform and educate the public about its harmfulness.
- Programmes to combat it should recognize its association with extremely adverse social and economic conditions, and should respond sensitively to women's needs and problems.
- Involvement of women's organizations at the local level should be encouraged, since it is through them that awareness and commitment to change must begin.

WHO also expressed its unequivocal opposition to any medicalization of the operation, advising that under no circumstances should it ever be performed by health professionals or in health establishments.

In 1984, WHO, UNICEF and UNFPA organized a seminar in Dakar which promoted the establishment of national committees in all countries where female circumcision was practised, and set up an Inter-African Committee to act as a bridge between the groups, working among the people and the outside supporters of their work. A Regional Workshop on Women, Health and Development, jointly sponsored by the same agencies in November 1984, was held in Damascus, Syria. Its participants asserted that women's groups and NGOs had proved to be more effective than individual community workers or health personnel in persuading women to abandon the practice. Parallel efforts to also convert and convince men were recommended.

UNICEF has joined WHO in its finding that FGM violates the human rights of girls and women, causes health hazards and is an act of violence. In 1994, an Executive Directive was sent to UNICEF field offices urging them to take action to eliminate FGM. UNICEF developed and distributed to its offices the 'Strategic Framework and Programming Guidelines to Eliminate Female Genital Mutilation' in 1995.

In 1997, UNICEF joined UNFPA and WHO in issuing a joint statement in support of global, national and community efforts for the elimination of FGM[19]. The statement confirms the universally unacceptable harm caused by FGM, and issues an unqualified call for the elimination of this practice in all its forms. While noting that FGM continues as a deeply rooted traditional practice, the statement maintains that culture is in constant flux, capable of adapting and reforming. The clear position of the three agencies was thus presented in the hope that this harmful practice will end when people understand the severe health consequences and indignity it inevitably causes.

FGM was designated as one of UNICEF's programme priorities for 1998–2000 in countries where the practice is prevalent. UNICEF's strategy for ending FGM includes advocacy to governments to enact and implement legislation banning the practice and to support international and national NGOs combating FGM. Laws against FGM have been adopted in Burkina Faso (1997), Côte d'Ivoire and Togo (1998) and Senegal (1999). On 6 May 1999, participants of the Regional Workshop on the Fight against FGM in the member countries of the West African Economic and Monetary Union adopted the Ouagadougou Declaration. It affirmed the determination of the Inter-African Committee to collaborate with other partners, NGOs and associations for the total elimination of FGM by the year 2010. It recommended, *inter alia*, the creation of national networks of religious and customary leaders as well as networks of traditional and modern communicators with a view to setting up subregional networks.

Obstacles are enormous and progress is slow. Political will is often weak or hostile to change. In some African countries, FGM remains the door to 'dignity', identity and community acceptance, from generation to generation.

One West African Minister of Health shocked the donor community at a conference sponsored by the NGO Defence for Children International in 1991 by declaring: 'We will not tell our people to stop practising our culture because that's where we get our votes and that is where we get our bread.'

Early in 2000, the President of Gambia criticized those who work to eliminate FGM and told a group of Muslim elders that his country will not ban the practice. In Guinea, government and NGO activities continue despite a recent declaration by a group of religious leaders that FGM is mandated by Islam, but recommending that the least severe form be practised. This recommendation is opposed by all anti-FGM organizations.[20]

Child labour

Child labour is another issue which is not a preserve of UNICEF: UNICEF shares it mainly with the International Labour Organization (ILO), with WHO in the health area and with many NGOs. In this domain, ILO exercises its statutory fact-finding, normative and monitoring role, while UNICEF has an important role to play in both advocacy and field work. One ILO programme is addressed to the progressive elimination of child labour.

The ILO estimates that, in 2000, of the 250 million working children between the ages of 5 and 14, nearly 120 million work full time. In sub-Saharan Africa, 41 per cent of all children work; in Asia and Latin America approximately 21 per cent. In absolute terms, Asia has the largest number of child labourers, accounting for 61 per cent of the world's total, while 32 per cent are in Africa and 7 per cent in Latin America. Of children around the world who do not attend school, 14 to 17 per cent are working 49 hours or more per week, and 11 to 13 per cent are working 56 hours or more per week. The employment of very young children is a particularly alarming problem. ILO surveys show that in some areas up to 20 per cent of economically active children are under the age of ten. Of the 'invisible' child domestic workforce, 90 per cent are girls, most are 12 to 17 years old, and some work 15-hour days. Some 30 million children are working in Latin America and the Caribbean – many of them in hazardous jobs – and about half of them are under the age of 15. The ILO reports that many children work in risky places like coal mines, porcelain and missile factories, and sugar cane and tobacco plantations. The majority of children work in domestic service and agriculture. Only 25 per cent of adolescents between the ages of 13 and 17 in urban areas and 15 per cent in rural areas attend school.

More than 1.5 million children in Colombia, nearly 19 per cent of the child population, work at tasks ranging from the production of drugs to prostitution. Only 26 per cent of Colombian children have access to health services, and less than 29 per cent earn the legal minimum wage. Many working children have elevated levels of lead and mercury in their blood, wounds or injuries caused by various forms of violence, infections like tetanus, and deformation of the skeleton caused by carrying heavy loads. In addition, Colombia's working children suffer from respiratory problems and are exposed to sexual abuse.

In developing countries, child labour is an outgrowth of profound poverty, entrenched cultural habits and government neglect or incapacity. It is both caused by and results in a lack of education for the children, preventing them from acquiring qualifications for adult employment. According to an ILO official, 'It's an issue of socioeconomic development, better income distribution, social mobilization ... We can't just say, "this is a problem of lack of education or health or social assistance". We have to develop a number of integrated approaches'.[21]

Industrialized countries also use child labour without the excuse of widespread profound poverty. According to a Human Rights Watch report issued in June 2000, hundreds of thousands of child farmworkers, most of them Latino, are labouring under dangerous and gruelling conditions in the USA. They often work 12- to 14-hour days, and risk pesticide poisoning, heat illness, injuries and life-long disabilities. The international rights group advocates that US laws should be changed to protect the health, safety and education of all children.[22]

UN and ILO Conventions

States parties to the 1989 Convention on the Rights of the Child 'recognize the right of the child to be protected from economic exploitation and from performing any work that is likely to be hazardous or to interfere with the child's education, or to be harmful to the child's health or physical, mental, spiritual, moral or social development'. In particular, states parties should provide for a minimum age or minimum ages for admission to employment; for appropriate regulation of the hours and conditions of employment; and for appropriate penalties or other sanctions to ensure the effective enforcement of this right.

The ILO Convention No. 138 – the 1973 Convention Concerning Minimum Age for Employment – has determined the following minima:

General minimum age	*Light work*	*Hazardous work*
In normal circumstances:		
15 years or more	13 years	18 years (16 years
(not less than compulsory school age)		conditionally)

Where economy and educational facilities are insufficiently developed:

14 years	12 years	18 years (16 years
		conditionally)

While this Convention has influenced national law and practice, there has been a growing international consensus that more attention needs to be given to the most intolerable or extreme forms of child labour to protect children from especially hazardous occupations, industries and activities. This led to the adoption of Convention No. 182, the 'Worst Forms of Child Labour Convention, 1999', by the ILO International Labour Conference in June 1999.

The Conference recognized that child labour is to a great extent caused by poverty and that the long-term solution lies in sustained economic growth leading to social progress, in particular poverty alleviation and universal education. In spite of this recognition, governments which ratify the Convention are obligated to take immediate and effective measures to secure the prohibition and elimination of the worst forms of child labour as a matter of urgency, the term 'child' applying to all persons under the age of 18. These 'worst' forms are identified as follows (Art. 3):

(a) all forms of slavery or practices similar to slavery, such as the sale and trafficking of children, debt bondage and serfdom and forced or compulsory labour, including forced or compulsory recruitment of children for use in armed conflict;

(b) the use, procuring or offering of a child for prostitution, for the production of pornography or for pornographic performances;

(c) the use, procuring or offering of a child for illicit activities, in particular for the production and trafficking of drugs as defined in the relevant international treaties;

(d) work which, by its nature or the circumstances in which it is carried out, is likely to harm the health, safety or morals of children.

An accompanying Recommendation (No. 190) prescribes, *inter alia*, giving special attention to younger children, the girl child and the problem of hidden work situations in which girls are at a special risk.

The ILO International Programme on the Elimination of Child Labour (IPEC) is the world's largest technical cooperation programme on child labour. IPEC was launched in 1992 with funding from Germany and currently leads an alliance of nearly 90 countries in the battle against child labour. The programme, supported by 22 donors, guides and supports national initiatives in policy making and direct action.

For instance, the ILO and the Pakistan Carpet Manufacturers and Exporters Association reached an agreement which would remove all child labourers under the age of 14 from work in the carpet industry, and prevent other children in that age group from doing such work. The agreement was signed in Islamabad on 22 October 1998.[23]

The role of UNICEF

UNICEF has both an advocacy and an operational role in this area, in association with and complementary to the leading role of the ILO.

The Mission of UNICEF (see Figure 2.1) does not refer specifically to child labour, but the agency's required guidance by the Convention on the Rights of the Child includes the protection of children's rights from economic exploitation or harmful work.

In 1986, its Executive Board approved a child labour policy that gave rather general criteria to define the exploitation of child workers. It was determined that children were being exploited if:

• they were working full time at too early an age;
• they were working too many hours;
• their work exerted undue physical, social or psychological stress;
• they were working and living on the streets under bad conditions;
• they were working for inadequate pay;
• they were working at jobs with too much responsibility;
• their work hampered access to education and was detrimental to their full social and psychological development;
• they were performing work that could undermine a child's dignity and self-esteem.

Within the framework of the Convention on the Rights of the Child, UNICEF has acted on two fronts. It supports activities that protect working children from abuse and it advocates for the gradual elimination of exploitative child labour.

In September 1994, educators and child labour experts representing the ILO, UNICEF and the World Bank elaborated a strategy of universal primary education as a key to removing children from exploitative situations. For such a strategy to be successful, the quality and relevance of primary education needs to be improved and some compensatory measures for family incomes need to be established.

In May 1995, UNICEF issued guidelines for the procurement of goods on national and international markets to ensure that its own purchasing policy was consistent with its stand on child labour.

UNICEF country offices in Asia have worked with the ILO, the government and employers to try to find ways to encourage the attendance of working children at school. The Rugmark Foundation, set up in 1996 and supported by UNICEF, aims to eliminate child labour from the carpet industry by identifying and certifying factories that do not employ under-age children. UNICEF and the Nepal Rugmark

Foundation joined forces in 1997 to provide child carpet workers with 'non-formal' schooling through local NGOs. UNICEF pays for the schooling as well as for the running of the Rugmark offices, staff salaries and promotional campaigns. A similar UNICEF-Rugmark programme has been initiated in India to help loom workers attend school, and the Indian Human Rights Commission has started its own programmes to promote compulsory primary education and elimination of child labour. UNICEF National Committees were involved in the two international conferences on child labour held in 1977. NGOs are also active in combating child labour. Some 400 NGOs, humanitarian associations and regional movements have joined the South Asian Coalition Against Children's Slavery.[24]

The dilemma

The use of trade sanctions and consumer boycotts on goods produced by child labour has stimulated public debates and raised controversies. While the 'worst forms of child labour' are to be totally condemned, the abolition of child work may lead to worse distress and worse exploitation of children. If the economic situation of their family so requires, children may then be forced to earn illegally, invisibly, in circumstances of greater vulnerability.

In 1994, employers of Bangladesh textile factories dismissed 50 000 children, following a proposed US law forbidding the import of clothing made by children. Some of the unemployed children had been reduced to begging or to engaging in prostitution.

A movement of working children and adolescents was created in Latin America in the 1970s, 'Niños y Adolescentes Trabajores', or 'Nats'. It started in Peru and spread to numerous other Latin American countries in the 1980s, then to West Africa and to India in the 1990s. It is developing in other Asian countries such as Thailand. The Nats are supported by such NGOs as ENDA in Africa, Manthoc in Peru and 'Concerned For the Working Children' in India. The Nats are opposed to the minimum age for work and protest against boycotts of goods they produce for export. They ask the UN to make a distinction between the exploitation of children and the other forms of work which contribute to their development. They stress the positive aspects of employment: it gives them self-confidence, a know-how and money for food. At the same time, the Nats want to be respected, have a decent salary and time breaks from work, and have access to education and health care.[25]

Purchasing slaves in Sudan

In January 1999, Christian Solidarity International (CSI), a Swiss human rights NGO set in Zurich, announced that it had recently 'redeemed' in South Sudan 1050 black slaves, most of them women and children, at a cost of $50 per person for their freedom. Since the beginning of its programme in 1995, CSI has freed 5942 slaves. Slavery is a long-standing practice in Sudan and a few other countries. Sudan's civil war, which has killed two million people in more than 16 years and displaced four million, has also involved the abduction and subsequent exploitation of children and women from the area of Bahr El Gazal in southern Sudan, as an instrument of the war. The Islamic government in Khartoum has been fighting the animist and Christian South in its quest to impose Sharia, or Islamic law, on the entire country. Muslim raiders sweep through southern villages, burn houses, loot food and livestock, kill the men and abduct women and children to use as domestic slaves, forcing their islamization. According to UNICEF, more than 19 000 have been abducted since 1989. However, the Sudanese government rejects the charge of slavery, a 'myth' invented by the West.

UNICEF has vigorously opposed the 'well-intentioned effort' of a number of privately funded groups to purchase the freedom of individual slaves. In statements issued in 1999, Carol Bellamy has first declared that efforts to end the slave trade must be pursued until the 'abhorrent' practice is eradicated. The Convention on the Rights of the Child requires states parties' governments to take all appropriate measures to prevent the abduction, sale of or traffic in children for any purpose and in any form. Second, Bellamy considers that freeing slaves with cash payments to their captors will not end the practice. On the contrary, it has added a profit motive to other factors which allow the trade to flourish. As a matter of principle, UNICEF does not engage in or encourage the buying or selling of human beings. UNICEF believes the main effort should be directed at enlisting the support of the warring parties in ending the armed conflict and all its practices. Bellamy rightly added that 'in virtually all instances, contemporary armed conflicts have their roots in deeply intertwined political and economic issues which humanitarian organizations are neither equipped nor mandated to address'.

John Eibner, head of CSI, replied: 'It is very difficult to understand why UNICEF should say that our activities are intolerable.' Charles Jacobs of the Anti-Slavery Group in Boston, which raises money to support CSI, added: 'What is intolerable is to leave these women and children in the hands of brutal captors.' Reed Brody, from Human Rights Watch, agreed that buying back slaves could 'fuel a market in human beings'. However, he pointed out that although human rights groups and the UN have long called for humanitarian monitors in Sudan to trace and free children, no action has been taken. CSI also rejected another contention of UNICEF that redeeming slaves helped prolong civil war by giving combatants cash for arms and ammunition. CSI said that it pays with Sudanese pounds to avoid introducing dollars in the region, which could be used for arms purchases.

James Jacobson, head of Christian Freedom International, after several visits to Sudan, reluctantly turned away from slave redemption as a tactic. He had identified three problems with this well-intentioned activity. First, the financial incentives of slave redemption are so powerful in Sudan, one of the world's poorest nations, that they encourage the taking of slaves. Second, these incentives may provoke hoaxes. Finally, the way the UN distributes food acts as a magnet for slave raiders.

While ending the Sudan civil war remains a primary responsibility for the government and the rebels, with appropriate pressures from other governments, the UN and the OAU, UNICEF still attempts to cooperate with the government of Sudan and, among others, the UN Office of the High Commissioner for Human Rights (OHCHR), to achieve the following objectives:

- a firm commitment, from all those directly and indirectly responsible, to end the slave trade in Sudan;
- freedom of movement for international verifiers;
- full support for a retrieval, tracing and reunification programme; and
- A specific plan and provision of free access to document all phases of a full-scale effort to bring the slave trade to an end, to free its victims and to restore them to their rightful communities and families.[26]

Advocating debt relief

In a statement issued in July 1999, UNICEF urged debt relief for Ecuador. Why should the child's agency be concerned with an economic issue which, at the international level, mainly concerns the industrialized countries, the World Bank and the International Monetary Fund (IMF)?

Carol Bellamy justified UNICEF's interest in debt relief in a statement delivered to the Geneva 2000/Copenhagen +5 Summit Conference held in July 2000:

The under-investment in basic social services that we are witnessing is, in part, a consequence of the crippling debt burden that weighs on many low- and middle-income countries, some of which are spending as much as three to five times more on debt service than on basic social services.

To spend such sums on external debt when tens of millions of children lack access to basic education, primary health, adequate food and safe drinking water is not only morally wrong – it is also poor economics.[27]

UNICEF's concern over the effect of economic factors and decisions on children's survival, health and development is not new. UNICEF has been advocating 'adjustment with a human face' since 1983 when social indicators started to reflect the negative consequences of structural adjustment programmes in many of the developing countries' poorest communities. A concrete UNICEF initiative was to help debt-ridden countries to discharge some of its debts by substituting action on behalf of children. In exchange for an agreed equivalent in local currency, which would be made over to an approved UNICEF programme, a commercial bank would cancel an amount of debt owed by the debtor government or sell it at a heavily discounted rate. Pioneered in Sudan, by 1995 the experiment was applied successfully in eight other countries: debt with a face value of $199 million had been converted into local currency worth $53 million for an expenditure of $29 million.

An idea then promoted by James Grant, the 20/20 Initiative was launched at the 1994 International Conference on Population and Development held in Cairo, and pursued the following year at the World Summit for Social Development held in Copenhagen. It builds upon the mutual obligations in the Convention on the Rights of the Child for both rich and poor countries to come up with adequate resources for basic social services for human development. The Initiative suggests as a guiding principle that developing countries commit 20 per cent of their budget, and donor countries 20 per cent of their official development assistance (ODA), to build and buttress these services.[28]

A 1998 study of 28 developing countries by UNICEF and UNDP revealed that 19 countries spent more on debt servicing than on basic social services. UNICEF supports the Heavily Indebted Poor Country Initiative, launched by donors in 1996 to reduce the debt of poor countries with good policies. 1996 was the first year when the World Bank and the IMF have forgiven debt. The Group of 7 agreed at its meeting in Cologne (Germany) held in June 1999 to a debt-relief plan that would cancel about $15 billion of debt owed to them by some of the world's poorest countries. Additional debt relief contingent on the countries' future economic reforms could bring the total relief to $65 billion, and more if other industrial countries participate. However, the total debt of developing countries is approximately $2000 billion.

The UNDP Poverty Report 2000 recalls that responsive and accountable institutions of governance are often the missing link between anti-poverty efforts and poverty reduction: governments accountable to the people, democratic institutions, civil peace, and the reduction or abolition of corruption are all necessary components of anti-poverty campaigns, a prerequisite to debt reduction. For instance, $30 billion of international aid have been diverted through corruption in Africa.[29]

Indiscriminate economic sanctions

UNICEF has also taken a strong position against indiscriminate economic sanctions ordered by the Security Council as a non-military means of pressure against internationally condemned governments.

For instance, following the military coup in Haiti in September 1991, the Security Council imposed economic sanctions on the country in an ill-focused effort to restore democracy and human rights. According to UNICEF, over the three years of sanctions, the rate of malnutrition for children under five increased from 27 per cent to over 50 per cent in many health institutions. Sanctions caused employment and food production to plummet and also provoked inflation, which raised the cost of drugs and other essential items. Primary school enrolment dropped almost 25 per cent. A six-member mission from the Harvard Center for Population and Development Studies went to Haiti in July 1993 and included a visit to Maissade in the Central Plateau. Save the Children had already reported from this rural area of 45 000 people that from 1991 to 1992, when sanctions were being enforced, child mortality increased by up to 64 per cent. They reported that between 1990 and 1993 there had been a parallel increase in the proportions of children who were moderately and severely malnourished. In addition to shortages of food, Haitians also suffered from the deterioration of health services. Field interviews by the Harvard team revealed that shortages of drugs, supplies and electrical power had led to breakdowns in primary health care. The immunization coverage declined: between 1991 and 1992, the proportion of deaths attributed to measles increased from 1 per cent to 14 per cent. With the lifting of sanctions and the return of President J.B. Aristide to Haiti in October 1994, a six-month-long measles eradication campaign, supported by UNICEF, immunized almost 3 million children between the ages of 9 months and 14 years, raising coverage to 95 per cent of children by August 1995. In comparison, only 20 per cent were covered in 1993. Many of those immunized also received vitamin A capsules and a dose of polio vaccine provided by Rotary International.

The Harvard team recommended that the international community sharpen its approach to sanctions. First, it should focus more precisely on the real targets: the military and their elite supporters – freezing overseas bank accounts, withdrawing commercial air traffic and denying visas. Second, it should take measures specifically to protect the poor. These would include guaranteeing free movement of life-saving supplies, especially of food and medicines; ensuring access to water, shelter and clothing for vulnerable groups, particularly for mothers and children; closely and impartially assessing and monitoring the welfare of innocent populations; and safeguarding aid from misuse and diversion.

UNICEF also found that the balance sheet of several years of sanctions against Iraq showed a minimum of political dividends against a high human price paid primarily by women and children. The food rationing system provides less than 60 per cent of the required daily calorie intake, the water and sanitation systems are in a state of collapse and there is a critical shortage of life-saving drugs. According to UNICEF studies, because of chronic malnutrition and a shortage of medicine, 500 000 more Iraqi children have died under sanctions than would have been expected from pre-war trends. According to a joint UNICEF-Iraqi survey issued on 12 August 1999, Iraqi children were dying at twice the rate they did before Baghdad's invasion of Kuwait led to the Gulf War and UN economic sanctions. Carol Bellamy said the UN embargo and the Iraqi regime were both to blame for the precarious state of children's health. On 4 August 2000, Human Rights Watch, Save the Children (UK) and four other NGOs urged the UN Security Council to address the grave humanitarian consequences of the sanctions it imposed on Iraq ten years before. The NGO group also recognized that the Iraqi regime bears a large share of the blame for the crisis.

The UN Secretary-General has recognized the problem. In January 1995, he described sanctions as a blunt instrument. 'They raise the ethical question of whether the suffering inflicted on vulnerable groups in the target country is a legitimate means of exerting pressure on political leaders whose behaviour is unlikely to be affected by the plight of its subjects.'[30]

Conclusion

Advocacy permeates all UNICEF's programmes: in some cases, advocacy *is* the programme. Advocacy for the cause of children is generally well-received, although some themes have met well-expected obstacles. While the agency was initially hesitant to add the protection of children's rights to its earlier functions as an emergency agency and then as a development agency, its necessary support for the Convention on the Rights of the Child has broadened its responsibilities and exposed it to occasional dissent or opposition. Other causes adopted by UNICEF, outside the boundaries of the Convention, have caused questions as to their relevance to the agency's mandate.

UNICEF has not been designated as the monitoring instrument of the implementation of the Convention by member parties: this task has been entrusted to the Committee on the Rights of the Child. However, the agency plays a useful role in promoting the ratification of the Convention by countries, by its surveys and studies in the Convention's domain, by its participation in pre-sessional meetings of the Committee of the Child, and generally by its advocacy of all the clauses of the Convention. In its advocacy for the Convention, UNICEF, like human rights organizations, has had to lose some of its impartiality, a problem also faced by UNHCR in armed conflict situations. But UNICEF cannot be 'impartial' in fighting against maternal and infant mortality or for family planning, for breastfeeding, for education. Its strong advocacy for the equal rights of women and girls, for the education of the girl child and for the protection of girls and women against violence has placed UNICEF in the position of champion against long-entrenched customs and traditions, sometimes based on religion and culture.

UNICEF has taken a strong position against gender-based violence, which involves the girl child, girls and women of all ages. However, the agency is not the 'lead agency' for women: it should restrict its concern to children and mothers, a wide-enough field of action. Female genital mutilation affects mostly girls and has a damaging impact on the health of women throughout all their lives. UNICEF has properly and courageously associated its efforts with other organizations in combating this form of violence. The open or hidden opposition to the campaigns against female genital mutilation, which oppose, on the one hand, medical knowledge, public health concerns and care for the integrity of a woman's body, and, on the other hand, an imperative cultural require-ment for a woman's identity and community acceptance based, in some areas, on mistaken religious beliefs, shows strikingly that a position on such an issue cannot be even and impartial: it cannot even tolerate the compromises offered in some quarters.

Economic constraints, not religion, as well as tradition and the wish of children to support their families and be active participants in the economic life of their community have proved obstacles to anti-child labour campaigns. In the view of opponents to international child labour legislation, the abolition of child labour would not only disrupt the economy and increase production costs, but it would also cause worse distress and worse exploitation of children. According to governments and industry leaders in developing countries, the demands by industrialized countries that firms in developing countries respect age minima and other restraints are only covers for protectionism. On the other hand, there are some suspicions that the Nats movement in South America may be manipulated by employers. In any case, there should be no argument against the abolition of the worst forms of child labour. The implementation of anti-child labour laws should be applied progressively, with financial compensation for the families and with assurances that education facilities are available. The assistance of NGOs, here as in other operational programmes, is particularly necessary.

In terms of interagency cooperation, child labour is another area where UNICEF shares responsibilities with another UN agency, in the same way that WHO and UNICEF are both active in child health. The ILO is clearly the lead agency in the implementation of Conventions No. 138 – the 1973 Convention Concerning Minimum Age for Employment – No. 182 – the 1999 Worst Forms of Child Labour Convention – and Recommendation No. 190. While WHO is responsible for public health policy and UNICEF is charged, in general, with operational activities in this area, in the area of child labour the ILO is responsible both for policy (the Conventions) and monitoring, while UNICEF retains an important advocacy role and a role in negotiating such agreements as those of the Rugmark programme. Cooperation between the ILO and UNICEF are required at all stages of policy implementation, in order to avoid the unncessary and wasteful rivalry which has often occurred in the past between WHO and UNICEF in the health field.

The vigorous stand taken by UNICEF to condemn the purchase of Sudanese slaves should be applauded both on moral and practical grounds. This well-intentioned practice is unfortunately counterproductive, as it would tend to encourage, rather than stop, the slave trade. It is acknowledged that the alternative, to negotiate with and convince both the Sudanese government and the rebels to stop slavery, is not expected to bring results soon. Slavery in Sudan is in part linked with the everlasting civil war, a war that neither side seems prepared to stop, and in part related to a long tradition with religious undercurrents – a few Arab tribes claim that the Koran gives them the right to make slaves out of blacks in South Sudan. Even though UNICEF's objectives in

Sudan will not be reached soon, the agency should continue its efforts in this direction.

International economic matters such as debt relief fall within the domain of the World Bank, the IMF, creditor countries and banks: UNICEF's advocacy to reduce the debt of developing countries can only be justified by the impact of debt repayments on social services, which, in turn, affect children's health and development. There is, however, no evidence that debt relief will automatically benefit social services, unless debt relief is made conditional on the allocation of additional budget credits to education, health, nutrition, water supply, etc. with adequate monitoring. The 1995 Sudan programme depended on the goodwill of commercial banks, convinced by UNICEF, to allow a portion of debt to be credited to a UNICEF-approved programme. This commendable initiative could, however, only include a minimal portion of the total debt of all developing countries, a self-indicted economic handicap well promoted by industrialized countries and national and international banks.

UNICEF has shown courage, not always appreciated by the US, in commissioning studies of the impact on children's survival and health of economic sanctions imposed by the Security Council on countries or governments guilty of non-compliance with orders decided upon by the Council, as a means of pressure for forcing their compliance, or as a factor to overthrow a non-democratic leader. In principle, as a UN body, UNICEF should follow policies and directives issued by the UN General Assembly and the Security Council. While the agency cannot interfere with political positions and decisions taken by the Security Council, its findings concerning the negative impact of economic sanctions on such vulnerable groups as children and mothers, groups which are of direct concern to UNICEF, are or should be a useful element of judgement for decision-makers. On the other hand, sanctions are not the only cause of damage imposed on the life, health and development of those groups: political leaders are primarily responsible for not taking appropriate measures to protect in priority those vulnerable groups by ensuring that they may benefit from even scarce resources, food and medicines. The recommendations of the Harvard mission to Haiti are well taken and should be considered by the Security Council members, even if many obstacles would hamper their implementation.

UNICEF's advocacy for the rights of the child has certain limits. The agency cannot adopt the same methods as such human rights NGOs as Amnesty International or Human Rights Watch. As an intergovernmental organization, its public appeals rarely denounce a particular government, with the noted exceptions of Afghanistan and Sudan. UNICEF needs the cooperation of governments for many of its campaigns, for instance its immunization campaigns. Rather than 'shaming' governments, the agency generally chooses to call for reform or improvement of legislation and policy and for the implementation of practical remedies.

Advocacy is an essential part of UNICEF's identity and image, and one of the conditions for its effectiveness. However, UNICEF cannot be all things to all people – it cannot espouse all 'good' causes. As for economic sanctions, there may be a need for refocusing on the primary purposes of the creation of UNICEF, i.e. advocating for the welfare of children and mothers.

8
Internal Management Issues

UNICEF, as well as WHO, has long enjoyed the reputation of being one of the most effective and professional UN agencies. As WHO was losing this credit in the 1980s but regained some lustre with a new Director-General in 1998, UNICEF cannot take for granted that its mission will forever protect it from fair or unfair allegations of poor management or ill-use of its resources. UN organizations are particularly at risk, in view of the charges of politicization, bureaucratization, inefficiency and even corruption levelled against some of them by conservative groups in the US and by press reports in western countries over the last 30 years.

UNICEF, with almost 60 years of activities, in a changing environment of new rivals, new technologies, new approaches to development and lesser financial resources, has no choice but to prove to the world, and particularly to its donors, that it is not only surviving, but that it plays an essential role in its own specialized field and has gained a new vitality and a visible effectiveness. To this end, the agency needs to rely on effective management systems and practices, including effective controls, and to provide up-to-date, reliable and transparent reports on the implementation of its programmes and of its budget.

The internal management of UNICEF, whose resources are essentially provided by voluntary and not by obligatory budgetary contributions, is watched by the main donors, and in particular the US, the UK, the Nordic countries, the Netherlands and other European Union countries, thus providing an 'automatic' external control with the potential but very real threat of the decrease or withdrawal of voluntary contributions.

External auditors, with the support of internal auditors, exert a formal control over the agency's finances and management.[1] The UN Joint Inspection Unit provides, on request or at its own initiative, independent inspection and evaluation of the efficiency of the services and the proper use of funds of participating organizations, including UNICEF.[2] In addition, UNICEF has, from time to time, called on the services of independent, private-sector management firms to assess its management policies and practices. Finally, the agency has recently asked its staff to comment freely on their morale and their assessment of its management leadership and practices.

Assessments, criticisms and recommendations

A first management survey was carried out in 1975 over a period of a year by a team from the Scandinavian Institutes for Administrative Research (SIAR), at the initiative of the Executive Director of UNICEF.[3] Staff groups participated in the survey and the approach was that of joint problem-solving. The title of the SIAR report was complimentary: 'The strengthening of the best traditions of UNICEF', i.e. 'its ability to combine a down-to-earth practicality with far-reaching analysis, its flexibility without losing sight of the ultimate goal and its highly motivated and very able staff led by a non-bureaucratic management'. Based on the survey's recommendations, UNICEF worked towards the following objectives:

- strengthening of the field organization;
- promoting the exchange of knowledge and experience among field staff and between the field and headquarters;
- improving coordination and communications within headquarters;
- reinforcing and professionalizing the personnel function;
- improving financial and budgetary controls and monitoring.

In a report issued in 1986,[4] the Joint Inspection Unit, in a backhanded compliment and clear criticism, stated:

> Although UNICEF is far from being the most mediocre management model within the UN system, the increase in indirect costs relating to its activities and its structures continues to be troubling. Like many efficient enterprises, UNICEF has substantially modernized its equipment and its methods, yet the anticipated gains in administrative productivity barely seem to offset corresponding increases in costs relating to documentation, monitoring, research and training, organization and support.

The Unit found that UNICEF ranked among the UN agencies with the worst support cost:programme ratio. The Inspectors recommended restructuring of the secretariat, selective monitoring and follow-up on programme implementation by the regional offices; like the budget cycle, the cycle of Executive Board and committee sessions should be made biennial.

In 1987, the US conservative Heritage Foundation questioned the competence and integrity of UNICEF operations partly on the basis of the September 1986 Report of the UN's Board of Auditors.[5] The auditors found numerous instances of financial mismanagement, delinquent accounting and failure to comply with both General Assembly and UNICEF regulations. As one instance, two additional office buildings were acquired by the agency in Niamey, Niger and Port-au-Prince, Haiti in 1985 at a cost of $424 367, although no appropriation had been provided in either the original or the revised budget estimates for 1984–85. This and other irregularities prompted Joseph Reed, then US representative to the Economic and Social Council, to warn that the US ...

> is seriously concerned by the result of the audit of UNICEF's accounts for 1985 ... We agree with the view of the Advisory Committee [on Administrative and Budgetary Questions] that the responses of UNICEF officials to the issues raised by the Board were less than satisfactory and that the UNICEF management had not attempted to deal with these matters in a serious manner.

The *Backgrounder* also raised questions about the 'cozy connections' between UNICEF officials and officials of the US government, in particular State Department officials who were highly supportive of both increased US funding for UNICEF and the incumbent management. The *Backgrounder* still recognized that UNICEF, 'unlike many other UN agencies', had done its job with competence and dedication. However, if it was to retain its effectiveness, greater financial and budgetary accountability and increased management and personnel control were clearly necessary.

Comments made by the UN Advisory Committee on Administrative and Budgetary Questions (ACABQ) on the report of the Board of Auditors for the biennium ending 31 December 1991[6] showed frequent 'concern' about various aspects of UNICEF management: lack of effective management of staff personal accounts, in particular improper controls arising from the non-compliance with relevant UNICEF rules and procedures, cumbersome manual recording and lack of coordination; UNICEF's inability to detect and report over-expenditures to donors during the implementation of projects; decrease of programme implementation from 80 per cent in 1990 to 69 per cent in 1991; and irregularities under inventory management in field offices.

ACABQ expressed its serious concern that the examination of the annual report of the Office of Internal Audit on the status of implementation of its recommendations showed 'a catalogue of recurring internal control weakness, already reported in internal audit reports', which implied that most of the identified weaknesses were not resolved. The Committee was of the view that the lapses reported in the internal audit reports generally pertained to non-adherence to established procedures, rather than the lack of effective procedures, which implied that UNICEF did not effectively enforce its own procedures. The Committee agreed with the internal audit recommendation endorsed by the Board that heads of office should be held personally and fully accountable for less than adequate performance of duties in their areas of authority.

Finally, the Committee was concerned about the Board's finding of 12 cases of fraud and missing office equipment in the biennium 1990–91, as well as increasing losses of office equipment through pilferage at UNICEF headquarters. Although UNICEF said that it was taking remedial measures to protect property, these measures were clearly inadequate in view of the heavy financial losses incurred by the UNICEF country office in Kenya (see below).

The 1994 management study

In 1994, in response to both internal and external changes, the UNICEF Executive Board requested that a management review be undertaken to examine opportunities for clarification of the UNICEF mission, a more effective organization structure, improved transparency and account-ability, better management processes and procedures, and a more productive interface with the UN.

The external environment was characterized by rapid change and shrinking official development assistance. Internally, over the years, the agency's staff and budget had grown rapidly and its mandate had expanded considerably, following the World Summit for Children and the near universal ratification of the Convention on the Rights of the Child. The management review was entrusted to the consultant firm Booz-Allen & Hamilton. The study received Grant's full cooperation and support. In its report, the consultants commended the consistently high performance levels of UNICEF but found that some of the agency's business processes had been neglected or did not have adequate resources.

The study found that the traditional UNICEF strength of using decentralized country programmes was being undermined by increased centralized management of the mid-decade goals. The consultants found large staff discontent focused on processes, not on aims: 82 per cent of the staff wanted change. The study also found a 'phantom organization' of temporary staff and consultants, vastly outnumbering those in UNICEF core posts. The study recommendations focused on the need to clarify the UNICEF mission; strengthen the agency's response in emergencies; adapt global goals to country and local situations within a framework of global standards; clarify accountabilities organization-wide and improve transparency; strengthen the supply function, financial systems and information resources management; improve human resources processes; and enhance private sector fund-raising.[7]

Fraud and losses in Kenya

UNICEF lost approximately $10 million, out of its $37 million budget for 1993 and 1994, to serious fraud and mismanagement in its Kenya country office. The first irregularities were uncovered by a UNICEF auditor during an unannounced visit to Nairobi in October 1994. A full-scale audit began in January 1995. The auditors found $500 000 in unpaid bills, and identified more than $1 million lost through fraud. The fraud included payments for non-existent services, double billing, bogus contractors, and insurance claims for non-existent medical treatments. An additional loss of $8–9 million was due to 'gross mismanagement', including spending beyond the authorized budget, failing to oversee contract services and using UNICEF vehicles for personal purposes. The audit found chaotic conditions in the office, with 'gross violations of UNICEF rules and regulations', a 'lack of operational, financial and administrative controls', and 'widespread fraud and wastage'. Implicated were both international and national staff, but the main responsibility seemed to lie with the two successive Directors of the Kenya country office.

The investigation revealed that 'the office environment was corrupt' and that 'there was poor staff integrity' and 'biased recruitment'. There was 'collusion with staff and banks, suppliers and non-governmental organizations' and with the two directors, who were suspended without pay. The fraud was probably facilitated by the doubling of the office's budget in that period, caused by the drought and influx of refugees from Somalia. The office's staffing had increased from 71 to 254.

The newly appointed Executive Director, Carol Bellamy, declared: 'This is a serious blow to UNICEF . . . This kind of behaviour is just totally unacceptable.' She promised to make management changes a top priority.

As a result of the first audit, 23 staff had been summarily dismissed. All cases had been referred to the Kenyan authorities with the evidence of fraud for criminal investigation. The first case went to trial in late October 1996.

UNICEF internal auditors undertook a follow-up audit in September 1996. By mid-November, all but 10 of the 67 audit recommendations originally made had been fully carried out. The UNICEF programme was more focused, with only six components and a corresponding reduction in the number of projects. The number of staff had been reduced from 254 in January 1995 to 78 in November 1996. A new operations officer with a strong audit and operations background had been recruited. The closure of a warehouse in November 1996 had both eliminated control risks and secured economies, resulting in savings of $10 000 a month. All items had been sold by public auction, donated or recycled. The UNICEF Regional Office for Eastern and Southern Africa was to undertake quarterly checks to ensure that internal controls were operating effectively. More generally, UNICEF assured that oversight of all field offices had been strengthened. Internal auditors, when selecting field offices to visit, were to take into account the type of risk factors that had been evident in the Kenya country office.[8]

Other audit reports

The first public report of the Office of Internal Audit (1997)

In 1997, the Executive Board welcomed a proposal by the Executive Director to issue an annual report to the Board on internal audit activities. The Office of Internal Audit (OIA) submitted its first report, on its 1997 activities, to the Executive Board in 1998.[9]

The OIA identified 109 entities within UNICEF on which it should report, including 95 field locations. Each year, these entities are assessed, using risk assessment criteria, to ensure that audits target areas of higher risk. An Audit Risk Model, developed in 1997, uses both subjective and quantitative variables as risk attributes. One of the OIA's approaches is to use local public accountants to support in-house teams and to contract national and international accounting firms, under supervision, to undertake assignments requiring special expertise.

By the end of 1997, the OIA had 15 audit staff. During the year, the OIA undertook 39 audits, including examinations at 29 field offices, reaching some 30 per cent of the total number of field locations, thus meeting its target. Among its findings and recommendations were: there should be vigorous screening of NGOs before cash assistance is approved; there is a need for improved control of greeting card operations in a number of countries; in a few cases, expenditure on fund-raising was high in relation to revenue secured; there was a need to ensure that UNICEF equipment supplied to counterparts was not put to 'other uses'; payments in cash were to be reduced in one country office. The standards of internal control in the offices visited by the OIA in 1997 varied from good to weak, the reasons for weak controls being often related to 'adverse local conditions' and the small size of some sub-offices.

While this first annual report was a worthy attempt at more administrative transparency, the report often referred to 'efforts' being made to improve performance rather than giving details on actual measures adopted and implemented; it also lacked such financial data as are provided in external auditors' reports and precise indications as to the locations of offices with weak internal control. Diplomatic reserve vs. national administrations and/or protection of the secretariat vs. its Executive Board and the agency's constituencies?

The Board of Auditors' Report (1998)

This report,[10] covering the biennium ended on 31 July 1997, was more trenchant than that of the internal auditors. On management issues, the Board noted the low level of country programme implementation, 72 per cent in 1996, 78 per cent in 1997. Its common causes were identified as frequent changes in counterpart ministries, inadequate monitoring, low government support to UNICEF programmes, unrealistic phasing of allotments, and weak communications between field offices and headquarters on details of agreements concluded with donors. The Board noted that the existing evaluation methodologies and guidelines did not fully meet the needs of sectors such as child rights programmes, capacity-building, participation and new modes of cooperation.

The UNICEF Field Manual requires field offices to ensure that arrangements have been made to transfer responsibility for UNICEF supplies and equipment to the government and that a government official sign the government receipt as formal evidence that UNICEF has delivered supplies and equipment as previously agreed by the government. Based on a test examination, the Board was not able to confirm that programme supplies valued at some $3 million delivered by UNICEF had reached the intended recipients in five countries.

Following consolidation of UNICEF's headquarters from three into two buildings, the agency incurred a total liability of $3.8 million, which could have been avoided if a termination clause had been inserted in the initial lease agreement between UNICEF and its landlords and if the move had been effectively planned. The Board deplored the extensive engagement of consultants without competitive bidding and the payment against contracts without submission of the required evaluation reports.

During the same biennium (1996–97), 54 cases of fraud and presumptive fraud were reported to the Board – 42 of these cases involved staff members. In 30 cases, UNICEF suffered losses of $777 342. However, the administration had not determined responsibility in a fraud case in a field office involving falsification of records resulting in an estimated loss of $445 000. The Board was concerned about the low recovery rate of the amounts in those fraud cases and reiterated its recommendation in its previous report that headquarters strengthen its monitoring of the operation of internal control systems in field offices through prompt and effective investigation of indications of mismanagement.

The Management Excellence Programme (MEP)

This programme was initiated in 1995 as a direct follow-up to the Booz-Allen & Hamilton findings and recommendations. It was designed to address internal performance issues. Its objectives were 'to strengthen accountability at all levels of the organization, to institutionalize best management practices and standards of behaviour for all UNICEF staff, and to make systems improvements to support oversight and control'. The Executive Director intended to implement change through broad staff participation, and to start to transform the internal management culture itself. The UNICEF management reform was to be part of the larger reform process affecting the entire UN system of organizations, as formulated by the Secretary-General's reform plan.[11]

With the approval of the Executive Board, functions were redefined at country, regional and headquarters locations. The role of UNICEF representatives was reaffirmed as one of leading, implementing and monitoring the progress of country programmes, together with governments, UN agencies and other partners. Key programmatic, budgetary and oversight functions were transferred from headquarters to regions. Programme functions carried out at headquarters were redefined to focus on setting standards, providing leadership and state-of-the-art knowledge on the main areas of UNICEF work, guiding programme policy formulation and strategies, and disseminating best practices and lessons learned both within UNICEF and from external sources. By 1997, the headquarters structure was streamlined from 19 to 15 divisions. Regional

Inspired by the ideals enshrined in the United Nations Charter, the Universal Declaration of Human Rights, the Convention on the Elimination of All Forms of Discrimination Against Women and the Convention on the Rights of the Child, We, the staff of the United Nations Children's Fund, commit ourselves to the following fundamental principles and professional standards, and agree to be individually and collectively accountable for applying them in our everyday work and actions.

Our first commitment is to act in the best interests of children.

We believe we must demonstrate integrity, truthfulness and honesty in all our actions. We pledge to make responsible use of UNICEF resources, knowing we are entrusted as custodians to safeguard them and use them wisely.

We respect the dignity and worth of every individual and will do our utmost to promote and practice understanding and tolerance to foster respect for diversity, be it of gender, religion, culture, creed or race.

We will foster a climate of impartiality, fairness and objectivity and assure the equitable application of UNICEF regulations, rules and policies. We will create a work environment that is sensitive to the needs of all staff.

Those of us privileged to hold positions of authority have a greater obligation to set the highest standards and to uphold them by personal example. At every level we aspire to optimal achievement, and value the contribution of every staff member.

We acknowledge the importance of sound judgement, initiatives and leadership and will pursue and recognize excellence and productivity.

We are willing to listen to different opinions and willing to learn and grow to contribute our individual best to UNICEF.

We will facilitate participation and promote teamwork within UNICEF and extend that same spirit of collaboration to all our external partners, realizing that only through effective communication and cooperation can we best fulfil our mission.

We affirm our loyalty to the United Nations Organization and promise to place the interests of the international organization above our own. As international civil servants, we are proud to share the broad vision of the Organization and will work indefatigably for the realization of its goals.

Note: UNICEF Guiding Principles complement the United Nations Report on Standards of Conduct in the International Civil Service 1954 (COORD/CIVIL SERVICE/5, 1986 edition) which we affirm as the foundation for our conduct.

Source: UNICEF internal document.

Figure 8.1 UNICEF Guiding Principles for staff commitment and conduct

offices were reorganized and regional management teams established to support the new accountabilities. The Regional Office for Europe was restructured to serve as the focal point for managing relations with National Committees for UNICEF. Headquarters was reorganized to focus on strategic, policy and oversight functions. The Executive Director made it a priority to establish a stronger performance culture based on 'personal accountability', where management standards are applied and each staff member is held accountable for performance and use of UNICEF resources. UNICEF Guiding Principles for staff commitment and conduct were adopted (see Figure 8.1).

New management information systems were introduced: the Programme Manager System (PROMS), the new Financial and Logistics System (FLS), the Human Resources module of the UN Integrated Management Information System (UNIMIS-HR) and programme knowledge networks. A new human resources strategy was adopted, including a career management system.

All offices are required to prepare country programme management plans at the beginning of each five-year programming cycle, and annual programme and management plans. By 1997, over 70 per cent of UNICEF offices had undergone training introducing staff to the basic principles of work process management, people skills, control self-assessment and PROMS.

In Bangladesh, for example, where previously 73 staff worked in four sub-offices in addition to the main office in Dhaka, in 1997 30 staff worked in 18 field locations, with all administration managed centrally by the country office in Dhaka.

Overall efficiency gains achieved from the reorganization of headquarters functions and structures helped UNICEF to maintain a zero-growth support budget, both in the revised budget for 1996–97 and the approved budget for 1998–99. In the biennium budget review for 1998–99, UNICEF reduced support budget costs by $33 million, mostly in headquarters locations, and redirected these amounts to provide new support budgets for 25 country offices and the absorption of other increases due to inflation. During this period, costs in headquarters locations were reduced by 8 per cent in real terms.

Staff cuts and the morale issue

In August 1997, UNICEF announced that, as a consequence of major reductions in resources amounting to about $100 million, 949 posts would be abolished, while 509 new posts were to be created: the net loss would be about 400 positions. A staff representative questioned the rationale for downsizing, suggesting a more effective use of the agency's existing resources. Forty-four appeals which had been lodged by UNICEF staff in 1996 to the Joint Appeals Board or the UN Administrative Tribunal cost the agency close to $25 000 in each case, to a total of more than $1 million. Staff representatives felt that staff insecurity had created anxiety and an undercurrent of distrust and hostility, particularly towards the Human Resources department.[12] At the end of 1999, the *UNICEF Staff News* published the responses of 22 UNICEF staff members in interviews on the culture of UNICEF and staff morale.[13] The contents of the issue were offered, not as a scientific survey, but as a snapshot of the views of a diverse group of UNICEF staff, and as the beginning of a dialogue 'that must be continued if UNICEF, in the midst of change, is not to leave its staff behind'. Extracts follow.

Criticisms were addressed to the current leadership, in contrast with the vision and infectious enthusiasm of Bellamy's predecessor, James Grant: 'The top management is very authoritarian and dictatorial, very temperamental'. 'Carol Bellamy is very smart, a quick learner, and has a good sense of humour. But she has no vision at all'.'There is an arrogance about UNICEF's management'. 'I think a lot of what Carol and the staff around her have done, in terms of defining responsibility, is brilliant. We've come a long way. The big question, of course, is where do we go with it ?' 'The leadership has a very North American perspective. We're not likely to do anything that wouldn't be approved by CNN'. 'Carol has suppressed UNICEF's independence'. UNICEF had become more rigid, more bureaucratic. The abolition of permanent appointments had created a feeling of insecurity.

There were also positive comments: 'I like my job and I'm grateful to have a job at the UN ... The people in my section are so committed to their jobs ... we work well together in this office, and we do feel like a family'. 'Most of us work late, and we mostly don't even write down the overtime'.

Positive and negative comments were given on the Management Excellence programme: 'From a field perspective, Management Excellence has made a difference. There's better reporting, better money management, and very tough audits, which I think we need in this very competitive world'. 'Management Excellence hasn't had any positive effect that I can see. You can argue that we have reduced the number of posts, therefore saved money, and that we have brought in some quality people. My reply to that is, why didn't we use the human resources we already had?' 'The whole process [drafting the Mission Statement and Guiding Principles] was seen in my field office as just one more of those silly headquarters imperatives'. 'Field staff are complaining about how much time they have to spend on running PROMS rather than getting on with their work'. 'Now we have become more efficient, more business-like; strictly from a management point of view, it may be better. But we lose opportunities for people to feel a part of the organization'. 'Some of us feel that we have become too much a compliance-oriented organization, rather than a judgement-exercising organization. We have become much more risk-adverse'. 'UNICEF is now part of the corporate world mentality'.

Dissatisfaction was also expressed on programme issues: 'What's painful for many staff is that we seemed to happily give up the edge in a lot of areas, to other organizations. Where is the high-level advocacy, where is the constituency building, where are the friends of UNICEF?' 'UNICEF's cutting edge in development has lessened because of a shift to the rights perspective ... Rights are important, but there are still the basic needs of people'.

Some comments included recommendations: 'We need ways to break down barriers'. 'We have to feel confident that we have an organization that is remarkable, very precious, but has its problems'. 'There also has to be compassion from management; they have to recognize that staff are having a difficult time, that they need reassurance'.

A staff member who had recently talked to staff worldwide found:

> Staff are still – by and large – proud to work for UNICEF, proud of the ideals UNICEF stands for. But staff generally feel at an impasse. They say we need to focus more on our mandate and do a better job of helping kids, but that we need the necessary training and skills to make us better contributors to this end. They say they want less bureaucracy and better teamwork, less hierarchy, and more respect for the work and yes, feelings, of all staff members. They want more inclusiveness and recognition that we all are working together to make one thing happen ...

Carol Bellamy reacted quickly to the morale problem expressed in the interviews published in *UNICEF Staff News*. In a memorandum of 24 January 2000 to headquarters directors and regional directors, she wrote, in part:

> I urge you to give priority attention to the issue of staff morale in your division/office ... I would like you to personally take the lead and involve chiefs of section, as well as staff representatives, in analyzing and better understanding those issues impacting on staff morale. I would like you to identify two or three actions that can be taken to address some of the more pressing problems ... in the coming year. This matter is central to the achievement of our goals.

At a General Staff Meeting held on 8 February 2000 in New York, Bellamy announced the formation of a 'Reference Group on Staff Morale', consisting of seven headquarters and field staff members. The Group would try to identify good practices already in place in the agency and in other UN agencies and the private sector, and to monitor the implementation of divisional and regional plans and to keep management informed of progress and constraints. She said that she was taking a decentralized rather than a top-down approach.

Conclusion

No large organization can entirely avoid management faults, errors and failings, and, to a varying extent, abuse of its resources and fraud. Poor performances by business firms are sanctioned by the market. UN organizations may be exposed to public criticisms, leading in turn to reduction of budgetary contributions. In the case of UNICEF, its financing by voluntary government and private contributions is particularly sensitive to the periodical assessments made by internal and external control bodies, and their reflection in public debates and the press.

However, the counterproductive temptation, often found in other UN bodies, to hide, dismiss or gloss over the organization's errors or sins only leads to more inquiries and harsher criticisms. UNICEF has been wise in requesting external management firms to carry out independent surveys of its programmes and internal management. These usefully complement the statutory internal and external audit reports. UNICEF has also been wise in publishing internal audit reports, a practice rejected by most other UN organizations. Carol Bellamy has also reacted wisely in taking seriously staff criticisms expressed freely in the *UNICEF Staff News* and in creating a monitoring body to try to identify the main problems and possible solutions.

Management surveys and audit reports have identified, over the years, many problems of different financial scopes which the agency tried to resolve, but the Kenya scandal, in revealing that large corruption and abuses had been carried out with impunity in a UNICEF country office for several years, created a salutary shock for the agency's top management. It revealed major deficiencies in management supervision and control of field programme activities both at the regional and headquarters levels.

This crisis, together with budgetary shortages, amply justified the 'management-oriented' leadership of the newly appointed Executive Director, Carol Bellamy. Budget and staff cuts were decided, better controls were established, and the staff was to become accountable for its actions. In particular, the need for tough audits was recognized, as well as the need for prompt and effective sanctions against staff members guilty of abuse of UNICEF's resources or fraud. Auditors have also insisted on the need to apply better efforts to the recovery of stolen goods and funds.

Has this new management style created a staff morale problem? While recognizing that succeeding a charismatic leader like James Grant was a challenge on its own, it is likely that the new emphasis on a 'lean organization', requiring downsizing, and the use of business-inspired management techniques may have antagonized part of the staff. Change is originally resented in most organizations, and top UNICEF management may not have paid enough attention to the need to listen to the staff and to their feelings, reactions and proposals. A similar, albeit not identical, situation of 'staff malaise' has been found in WHO, following the energetic restructuring measures taken by the new Director-General, Gro Harlem Brundtland, after her election in May 1998. In UNICEF, the staff also had to adjust to the extension of its original humanitarian and development role into a new mission, that of promoting the rights of the child, a new territory which had to be explored and mapped.

To start with, the reality and extent of the staff malaise should be further explored. The comments and interviews published in the *UNICEF Staff News* concerned only a small number of staff: a more comprehensive, systematic and representative survey of staff views and attitudes should be carried out at UNICEF headquarters and in regional and field stations, and renewed periodically.

In the meantime, UNICEF should reassess its recently adopted management techniques to ensure that their cost (time, paperwork) do not exceed their expected benefits. These benefits should be clearly explained to all the staff, but management should be open to criticisms, proposals for improvement or for substitute methods. Is PROMS a useful technique, or just a gadget? Is it appropriate and credible to introduce a 'career management system' when posts are being abolished and staff retired? Communications should be improved between headquarters and field staff, and more direct contacts should be arranged between top management and staff at all levels.

In management terms, UNICEF has many strengths: a well-defined mission, appealing humanitarian objectives, a large world consensus that the agency plays a useful role, its reputation for flexibility, its willingness to learn, a decentralized structure, a (generally) motivated staff, a decisive Executive Director. Top management should therefore be able to face this challenge, among others: how to find a better balance between effective management methods and the restoration of a feeling of belonging to a successful team in the difficult task of promoting children's rights worldwide.

9
UNICEF's Challenges

UNICEF is usually considered as both the best-managed and the better-known and appreciated UN agency, not only because of its humanitarian mandate for children and women, but because of the drive of its leaders and the visibility of most of its activities.

A Danish report issued in 1996 identified UNICEF's comparative advantages as follows:

> Despite certain deficiencies, UNICEF must be considered one of the most important and best functioning of the UN organizations in the field of development assistance. Its target group, choice of sectors and strength of implementation at district and local level has in most developing countries given the organization a central, multilateral presence in the social field, both in terms of operations and in 'advocacy'/spokesman functions.
>
> UNICEF also plays an important role in the area of emergency aid. It is often singled out as one of the organizations which manages 'to get the help to its destination'. There is no doubt that strong representation in the field and experience of development activities commend the organization in this respect.
>
> UNICEF is a particularly relevant organization in the area of poverty reduction ... UNICEF's target group comprises relatively weaker social groups of women, children and youth. UNICEF has a broad social development objective, and it works within relevant social sectors such as health, nutrition, education and water and sanitation. Finally, with its strong national representation and as a logistically strong implementing organization, UNICEF is in direct contact with beneficiaries.[1]

Indeed, UNICEF has impressive strengths: a well-defined mission; attractive objectives shared, at least formally, by North and South governments and populations; strong constituencies in most countries, including public opinion support; strong leadership and committed staff; a decentralized structure, with country programming and implementation; a reputation for flexibility and adaptability; strengthened audit and control systems. On the basis of its broad mandate for children, UNICEF Executive Directors have often had access to chiefs of state or governments, while most UN specialized agencies are linked only with their respective technical ministry (health for WHO, labour for the ILO, etc.), another advantage publicizing its policies and having them adopted.[2] Contrary to some other UN organizations, UNICEF has benefited from initiating or accepting external independent evaluation surveys of its programmes and management, which have enabled the agency to adjust to new challenges in giving satisfaction to its main donors while increasing its 'transparency'.[3]

UNICEF's merits have been recognized, first by a Nobel Peace Prize in 1965, then, within the UN family, by its designation as lead UN agency in Kampuchea in 1979, in Somalia in 1988, as lead UN agency to educate and advocate on the landmine issue in 1999; and, in the same year, as lead UN agency for health in East Timor.

The target group

UNICEF's original mandate was to work for the benefit of children and adolescents of countries the victims of aggression, of countries receiving assistance from UNRRA, and 'for child health purposes generally'.[4] The agency's original focus was on children and mothers.

A multi-donor evaluation of UNICEF carried out by the governments of Australia, Canada, Denmark and Switzerland in 1991–92[5] stated that the promotion of women in development required programmes that met both the practical and the strategic gender needs of women. Meeting the latter required activities that address all three roles of poor women: reproduction, production and community management. The report noted that UNICEF, so far, had focused on women in their reproductive role as mothers.

The Danish report of 1996 argued that the mother/child focus ignored the interrelationship in the development process that exists between children's and young people's problems and between mothers' and other women's problems. While not demanding that UNICEF became primarily a women's organization, Denmark opposed the traditional tendency towards a narrow focus, which made UNICEF less relevant to the broader concept of population policy represented by reproductive health and rights.

However, without denying the primary importance of an effective population policy through family planning, this broader approach has been entrusted to UNFPA, and it appears wise for UNICEF to keep to its more basic functions, which focus on the child and necessarily his/her mother. On the other hand, UNICEF has rightly emphasized the importance of girls' education as an essential condition for the empowerment of women as decision-makers in sexual and reproductive matters.

A child is defined in the Convention on the Rights of the Child as a person under the age of 18, unless national laws fix an earlier age of majority. UNICEF has therefore properly extended its initial focus on infants and young children to adolescents.

Intervention strategies

According to the multi-donor evaluation of UNICEF of 1991–92, three basic intervention strategies cover the bulk of UNICEF's programming activities, across sectors and in both development cooperation and emergency response:

1. Support to the delivery of specific social services through a series of well-defined technical interventions aimed at the largest possible number of beneficiaries, often implemented through vertical structures but which increasingly UNICEF seeks to integrate in service packages.
2. Capacity-building for sustained programme delivery, with a focus on systems development in government, organized training and other forms of capacity building, management support at all levels of government, and public participation in operations and maintenance, including through cost-sharing.
3. Empowerment of target group members through transfer of knowledge and skills, promotion of target group organizations and public participation, advocacy on human rights of children and women, and alliances with organizations of civil society which represent the interests of target group members and are accountable to them.

The report found that, over the previous decade (the 1980s), UNICEF had placed increasing emphasis on support to public service delivery. The use of capacity building had been limited, while empowerment had been stronger in the form of advocacy and alliance building than in direct empowerment of children and women. The report also noted that the three intervention strategies were not mutually exclusive.

Operational interventions

UNICEF is perhaps best known for its programme of Universal Child Immunization, which has seen impressive results. In particular, UNICEF and WHO are now expecting that the world will be certified polio-free in 2005. The initiative is a typical example of a working alliance of many partners. Spearheaded by WHO, Rotary International, the US Centers for Disease Control and Prevention and UNICEF, it has the support of national governments, private foundations, development banks, donor governments, the International Red Cross and Red Crescent movement, corporate partners and millions of volunteers. Most other large UNICEF programmes are carried out or supported by many partners at the national and international levels.

Also as a result of the immunization programme, by the end of the 1990s deaths due to measles have been reduced by 65 per cent globally and deaths from neonatal tetanus are down by more than one quarter. Despite such progress, some 12 million children under five years old still die annually of readily preventable causes.

In the area of nutrition, another well-based and well-advertised programme of UNICEF, it is estimated that some 12 million children no longer risk mental retardation due to iodine deficiency in their diet, and blindnesss due to vitamin A deficiency has been reduced significantly. However, malnutrition still retards the physical and mental development of some 160 million children. In the field of education, in spite of an increase in the number of children in school, the number of school-age children who have no access to primary education is estimated to be 130 million, and girls are still the vast majority. In spite of a 10 per cent increase in the number of people having access to clean water since 1990, basic sanitation is still unknown to more than 3 billion people.

UNICEF's programmes for the survival, protection and development of children will need a long and sustained effort as progress in health, nutrition, education and other social services are linked to political, economic and social factors over which UNICEF has no power: poor governance, corruption, civil or external war, ethnic or religious strife, population explosion and natural catastrophes. The role of UNICEF is therefore to convince leaders of the value of its programmes, and of their relationship to the economy and to their own popularity. UNICEF itself recognized that 'There are no shortcuts to lasting social change, but remarkable progress is possible when governments commit themselves to the realization of children's rights'. UNICEF has called for significant changes in the allocation of public sector investments, the political will and renewed efforts to resolve conflicts, to combat HIV/AIDS, to overcome discrimination and violence and to help poor families, and especially women, to care for and protect their children.[6]

Advocacy

Advocacy has been one of the more successful tools used by UNICEF over the years to advertise its policies, initiate its own programmes, form alliances and try to convince governments and the general public of the value of its views.

UNICEF contributed to give the World Bank's structural programmes a 'human face', by stressing the social consequences of these programmes for the poorest population groups, a position that has been recently forcefully expressed by a variety of NGOs in Seattle and Budapest.

Among other issues, UNICEF has taken a clear position on breastfeeding, child labour, the sale and trafficking of children, child prostitution, gender-based violence, female genital mutilation, child soldiers and Sudanese slave redemption. Its combat against HIV/AIDS, together with UNAIDS, WHO and other partners, has, however, been unclear on such an effective prevention measure as the use of condoms. Its present policy of passive reserve on this issue should be reconsidered.

Has UNICEF tried to 'embrace' too much when advocating for debt relief, or denouncing the impact of economic sanctions at the risk of trespassing on other organizations' mandates, of opposing influential governments and of being exposed to manipulation? Such issues are not only economic, but involve political decisions to be taken by the UN Security Council, the World Bank, the IMF and creditor countries. Even if it can be argued that giving debt relief and lifting economic sanctions would free income in developing countries, there is no guarantee that leaders of those countries would use these resources for social aims, including support to children's and women's causes.

As UNICEF insists rightly on its own independence and autonomy in order to maintain its own image, it is fair to ask that the agency remains firmly within its own domain.

Some of UNICEF's rhetoric appears excessive and thus empty. For instance, UNICEF proposes three significant outcomes for children, as part of a global pact to be adopted by the international community and governments, 'because within them lies the key to breaking persistent cycles of poverty'.[7] These priority outcomes are:

1. Infants start life healthy and young children are nurtured in a caring environment that enables them to be physically healthy, mentally alert, emotionally secure, socially competent and intellectually able to learn.
2. All children, including the poorest and most disadvantaged, have access to and complete basic education of good quality.
3. Adolescents have opportunities to fully develop their individual capacities in safe and enabling environments and are helped to participate and contribute to their societies.

Certainly such conditions are desirable parts and results of development efforts. It is not, however, credible that they constitute 'the key' to breaking persistent cycles of poverty. The real keys are, again, good governance, civil peace, proper distribution of national income, economic growth, and effective public health and education systems. UNICEF can contribute to the reduction of poverty within its own domain, but governments and the financial institutions hold the main keys to this major issue.

Monitoring of human rights

In the normative area, the ratification by 191 countries of the Convention on the Rights of the Child, and the ratification by 161 countries of the Convention on the Elimination of All Forms of Discrimination against Women, are major achievements. UNICEF is playing an active role in the pre-sessional meetings of the Committee on the Rights of the Child: it is now an informal monitoring body to the Committee, together with other organizations. While some countries may have signed and ratified these Conventions without any intention to enforce them, or to enforce parts of them, as for all human rights treaties, ratification provides legal grounds for national and international human rights NGOs to encourage governments to amend their legislation and practices in accordance with the standards set by the Conventions, and to publicly denounce violations. Additionally, it enables citizens to make legitimate legal claims against their authorities' rejection of the clauses which have been formally approved or against their inaction in the face of blatant violations.

According to Hammarberg,[8] the most important achievement of the Convention is that governments have been encouraged to give children's issues political priority. Countries have undertaken comprehensive reviews on the situation of children in relation to their obligations under the Convention. A few countries have amended their legislation accordingly, and some have established Ombudsmen for Children or other structures to monitor independently how the authorities treat children. International organizations, governments and NGOs have focused on vulnerable groups such as child labourers, child prostitutes and children in armed conflicts.

Is there a contradiction between the rights approach adopted by UNICEF and development strategies? The basic issues of children's survival and development, health, nutrition, education and sanitation are contained in articles of the Convention as 'rights': they should be strengthened, not weakened, by a rights approach. However, as an example, immunization protects children from death or illness – it does not guarantee that the whole range of their rights will be promoted and protected by their government.

More generally, the adoption by UNICEF of a 'rights approach' raises the question of the agency's role and image. The multi-donor evaluation has rightly recalled that UNICEF is a favoured partner of the governments of developing countries because of its general effectiveness in providing supplies and equipment, facilitating financial assistance and providing programme advice in often neglected sectors. Before the Convention, UNICEF tended to concentrate its support on activities that are 'above politics' (e.g. advocacy on child survival as a moral imperative) and 'below politics' (its operational activities). It is now viewed as the single most important advocate of child rights worldwide. In advocating for the rights of the child and of women on the basis of ratified Conventions, UNICEF may lose its humanitarian and provider image by changing into a 'critical partner' to governments, with the obligation to monitor and address violations of these international legal instruments.

UNICEF being seen as a critic of governments' policies and practices may affect its relationships with national and local authorities and its operational efficiency. UNICEF's Executive Director rejected, in 1993, the suggestion that the agency should play an 'openly critical' role, which might result in the loss of its comparative advantage and harm the achievement of its objective, i.e. to improve the respect of children's and women's rights. He advocated what could be called (by the author) a 'soft approach'. He explained that UNICEF had used methods which allow it to collaborate constructively with governments when confronted with particularly sensitive questions. UNICEF applies its own planning procedures, such as the consultation process leading to the analysis of the situation in a country, procedures not applied by other international organizations and NGOs. In the view of UNICEF, these procedures are a positive way of directing the attention of governments to certain facts calling for changes in policies and programmes concerning the rights of children and women.[9]

Future focus of UNICEF's work

According to a report issued in 1999, UNICEF will still emphasize the importance of protecting children from various forms of preventable deaths.[10] However:

> The future UNICEF agenda will place early childhood care and development and equal access to good quality basic education as the global centrepiece of its strategy to reduce poverty and realize the rights of children. On a more selective basis, the organization will support specific programmes for adolescents, especially focused on preventing HIV/AIDS and developing their skills to cope with life's challenges ...
>
> UNICEF and the UN system must work to convince national governments and the international community that investing in children's well-being and protecting their rights are the surest way to regain momentum for human development, to build cohesive societies and to make a quantum leap in positive social change within one generation.

This statement essentially maintains UNICEF's focus and range of programmes planned and implemented since the adoption of the Convention on the Rights of the Child. The only important innovation is the agency's interest in adolescents, a well-justified concern.

UNICEF is now engaged in broad consultation with Members of the Executive Board, UN agencies and governments on both a proposed global agenda for children beyond 2000 and the UNICEF contribution. A special session of the General Assembly will examine in 2001 the results of a decade of action for children following the World Summit for Children. The purpose of this mobilization is to generate new momentum and political commitment to human development goals, giving priority attention to children.

Conclusion

This book has tried to give concerned readers a summary of some of the past and current issues that UNICEF has faced and will face in the coming decades, without any attempt to cover all subjects at length. This selected summary and the views expressed necessarily reflect the interests, experience and bias of the author, with the support of other sources and a few former colleagues in the UN system.

Some of the key questions were raised by delegates to the 1998 Annual Session of the UNICEF Executive Board:[11]

1. Delegates underlined the gap between UNICEF commitments and challenges. They concluded that it would be impossible to achieve the World Summit goals in the present environment of declining resources. In their opinion, member states should take more responsibility to mobilize the necessary resources.

   This recalls that UNICEF is dependent on voluntary resources and has to adjust its budget and programmes to income actually received. It reinforces the view that UNICEF needs to focus more on its essential functions, the survival, protection and development of children and mothers, without trying to be an all-purpose organization.

2. Important suggestions were made by delegates concerning the strategy of determining which message would ultimately influence government resource allocations, including: (a) information on the results or impact of programme interventions was a more powerful argument than information on needs alone: the 'needs' argument was no longer satisfactory; (b) stressing that the goals and targets – whether for the World Summit for Children or the Development Assistance Committee (of the OECD) – were still valid; and (c) demonstrating whether UNICEF in particular could make a measurable difference in the situation of children.

These suggestions will no doubt be seriously considered by UNICEF, notwithstanding the principal difficulty of identifying UNICEF's own contribution to children's survival, protection and development when the main responsibility for their welfare lies with governments and so many other organizations are playing their part. This difficulty is shared by many other global organizations, whose 'action' is often concerned with defining and disseminating valid policies, trying to convince recipient governments that they should adjust accordingly their laws and practices, and trying to obtain funds from public and private sources. In UNICEF's case, its direct contribution and its results are more easily identified in emergency aid and in its health, nutrition, education and sanitation programmes than in its advocacy work, which still remains indispensible in the area of the promotion of children's rights. It is perhaps appropriate to end this book on UNICEF's twenty-first century dream for children:

It is a world where children survive to experience childhood as a joyous experience – a world of play, of learning and of growth, where they are loved and cherished, where their health and safety are paramount, where their gender is not a liability, where they can indulge their natural curiosity and expend their boundless energy in a just and peaceful environment – and where they have every opportunity to grow and develop into caring and responsible citizens.[12]

Too many children and women are still living in poverty and suffering from disease, lack of education, hunger, violence and discrimination. While the UNICEF dream should inspire all those who work with and for children, it will take more than a century for this dream to come true in all countries of the world. In the meantime, the work of UNICEF and other humanitarian and development agencies is more than ever necessary, whatever the obstacles and the frustrations.

Notes

IHT   = *International Herald Tribune*
UNGA = United Nations General Assembly

Preface

1. *IHT*, 23 August 1999.

Chapter 1   The Creation of UNICEF

1. P. Macalister-Smith, *International Humanitarian Assistance – Disaster Relief Actions in International Law and Organizations* (Geneva: Martinus Nijhoff/ Henry Dunant Institute, 1985), pp. 10–12. See also Y. Beigbeder, *The Role and Status of International Humanitarian Volunteers and Organizations, The Right and Duty to Humanitarian Assistance* (Dordrecht, Boston and London: Martinus Nijhoff, 1991), chapters 1 and 2.
2. *UN Journal of the Economic and Social Council*, no. 25, 13 June 1946, Annexe B.
3. Beigbeder, op. cit., pp. 186–97, and SCF documentation.
4. SCF Information Sheet 15, Eglantyne Jebb, Founder of Save the Children, December 1993.
5. The life of Dr Rajchman is related in Marta A. Balinska's *For the Good of Humanity. Ludwik Rajchman, Medical Statesman* (Budapest: Central European University Press, 1998). Rajchman's role in the creation of UNICEF is described in Chapter XIII. See also A. Manuila (ed.), *EMRO, Partner in Health in the Mediterranean, 1949–1989* (Alexandria, Egypt: WHO, Regional Office for the Eastern Mediterranean, 1991), pp. 15–18.
6. M. Black, *The Children and the Nations, the Story of Unicef* (New York: UNICEF, 1986), p. 30.
7. Black op. cit., pp. 4, 24, 25, 29.
8. John Charnow, *Maurice Pate, UNICEF Executive Director, 1947–1965*, UNICEF History Series, Monograph XIII (New York: UNICEF, 1989), p. 9.
9. Res. 103: *The Rehabilitation of Children and Adolescents of Countries Which Were Victims of Aggression*, in George Woodbridge, *UNRRA, The History of the United Nations Relief and Rehabilitation Administration* (New York: Columbia University Press, 1950), pp. 167–8, 306–7.
10. Balinska, op. cit., p. 203.
11. Res. E/187/Rev.1 was adopted: Off. Rec. of the Second Part of the First Session of the General Assembly, Third Committee, Summary Record of Meetings 24 October–12 December 1946, Annex 15a, *Establishment of an International Children's Emergency Fund*.
12. Ibid., Annex 15b, *Resolution relating to the establishment of an International Children's Emergency Fund, Report of Sub Committee 1, Rapporteur: Dr L. Rajchman (Poland)*.

13. Woodbridge, op. cit., p. 509. See also K. Karunatilleke, *Le Fonds des Nations Unies pour l'Enfance (FISE-UNICEF)* (Paris: Pedone, 1967) pp. 70–1.
14. Charnow, op. cit., pp. 10, 28.
15. Res. 318 (IV), 2 December 1949.
16. UN Doc. E/1682, May 1950, paras 18, 20, 21, and E/CN.5/L.57, April 1950 – WHO Res. WHA1.120, July 1948 and WHO Doc. A2/35, 27 May 1949.
17. UN Doc. E/1678, E/CN.5/221.
18. UN Doc. A/1411. The Summary records are in the *Official Records of the General Assembly, Fifth Session, Third Committee*, 6, 9, 11, 13, 16, 18 October 1950.
19. The draft resolution, as amended, was finally adopted on 18 October 1950 by 43 votes to 8 (Netherlands, Norway, Sweden, South Africa, USA, Canada, Denmark, Liberia), with 1 abstention. According to a testimony by Ratko Pleic, a former Yugoslav member of the UNICEF Executive Board, a former UNICEF and WHO official, the Yugoslav amendments were supported by the Yugoslav delegates' intensive lobbying with delegates of many countries, including the US and the UK, with the support of UNICEF officials. Mrs Betty Jacob, from UNICEF, was particularly effective both with the State Department in Washington and in New York: interview with R. Pleic in Geneva on 8 October 1999.
20. ECOSOC Res. 495 (XVI), draft Res. A/L.163.
21. WHO Constitution, Art. 2 (l).

Chapter 2   An Expanding Mandate

1. See UNGA Res. 2582 (XXIV) [1969], Doc. E/ICEF/590 [1969], UNGA Res. 3408 (XCXX)[1975], Doc. E/ICEF/673[1980], E/ICEF/701[1983], E/ICEF1985/12.
2. The main facts in this chapter, for the period 1946–95, are based on UNICEF, 'Fifty years for children' in *The State of the World's Children, 1996* (Oxford: Oxford University Press for UNICEF, 1996), Chapter II. See also Maggie Black, *The Children and the Nations, The Story of UNICEF* (New York: UNICEF, 1986), and Black, *Children First, The Story of UNICEF, Past and Present* (Oxford: Oxford University Press for UNICEF, 1996).
3. John Charnow, *Maurice Pate, UNICEF Director, 1947–65*, UNICEF History Series, Monograph XIII (New York: UNICEF, 1989), II, 'Maurice Pate: The person and his experience – at the heart of UNICEF, a profile of Maurice Pate'.
4. The UNICEF mission in Poland closed in December 1950, and the mission in Czechoslovakia in March 1951. See Black (1986), op. cit., pp. 56–61.
5. *Declaration of the Rights of the Child*, Proclaimed by the General Assembly of the United Nations on 20 November 1959 (Resolution 1386 (XIV)).
6. Res. 1391 (XIV), 20 November 1959.
7. Charnow, op. cit., pp. 38–40.
8. Thomas George Weiss, *International Bureaucracy, An Analysis of the Operation of Functional and Global International Secretariats* (Lexington/Toronto/London: Lexington Books, 1975) p. 129.
9. Charnow, op. cit., p. 3.
10. K. Karunatilleke, *Le Fonds des Nations Unies pour l'Enfance (FISE-UNICEF)* (Paris: Pedone, 1967), pp. 254–5.
11. *Henry R. Labouisse, UNICEF Executive Director, 1965–1979* (New York: UNICEF History Series, Monograph XI, 1998), as well as references in Note 1 above.

12. Comprehensive facts on 'The Crisis in Kampuchea' are in Black (1986), op. cit., chapter 16.
13. Res. 3201 (S-VI) and 3202 (S-VI).
14. WHO Res. WHA32.30 and UN Res. 34/58. The Declaration of Alma-Ata is in WHO Doc. *Health for All Series*, No.1, 1978, reprinted 1983. On the Strategy of 'Health for All', see Y. Beigbeder, with the collaboration of M. Nashat, M.-A. Orsini and J.-F. Tiercy, *The World Health Organization* (The Hague/London/ Boston: Martinus Nijhoff, 1998), pp. 21–9. A disagreement arose between UNICEF and WHO when the working document for the conference was prepared. UNICEF recommended that a country's primary health care would be more effectively attached to the head of government or another organ with intersectoral responsibility, rather than leaving the health ministry, often low in the hierarchy, to seek the participation of other concerned ministries. WHO insisted that primary health care should be attached to the Ministry of Health, in accordance with WHO's constitutional links (E. J. R. Heyward, '1978 International Conference on Primary Health Care in Alma Ata' (unpublished manuscript), July 2000).
15. UN Res. 31/165 and 36/197.
16. Alba Zizzamia, *NGO/UNICEF Cooperation: A Historical Perspective*, UNICEF History Series, Monograph V (New York: UNICEF, 1987), pp. 37–40.
17. Interview with Canon Moerman in Geneva, 15 March 2000.
18. Monograph XI, op. cit., pp. 5, 19, 20, 24, 79.
19. Black (1986), op. cit., pp. 408–12; 'James P. Grant: A Remembrance. The man who said "Why not?" ', in 1995 UNICEF Annual Report, pp. 8–9; and references in Note 1 above.
20. See Beigbeder, op. cit., pp. 75–83. The World Health Assembly resolution which approved the marketing code recommendation was WHA34.22, 21 May 1981. See also R. A. Brooks, 'UNICEF, Beware – Dangerous Shoals Ahead', The Heritage Foundation, Washington, DC, 30 August 1983.
21. *The State of the World's Children 1996*, op. cit., pp. 59–60.
22. Black (1996), op. cit., p. 43–4.
23. UNICEF Annual Report 1989, pp. 12–13, 1996, p. 41.
24. Beigbeder (1998), op. cit., pp. 137–8. The 'cold chain' ensures that the quality and effectiveness of vaccines are maintained through refrigeration at constant set temperatures, without interruption, from production to actual vaccination.
25. Larry Minear, *Humanitarianism Under Siege, A Critical Review of Operation Lifeline Sudan* (Trenton, NJ/Washington, DC: Red Sea Press/Institute on Hunger and Development, 1991), p. xi. Danida gave a more negative assessment of UNICEF's role in the Operation: 'Some organizational empire-building and even self-promotion characterised UNICEF during the operation, creating a situation of considerable bitterness and even resentment among partners in the field': *Case Study of 11 Agencies in Kenya, Nepal, Sudan and Thailand, Effectiveness of Multilateral Agencies at Country Level*, Danida [Danish] Ministry of Foreign Affairs, COWIconsult, 1991, 2.10.
26. UNICEF handout, 'The World Summit for Children: Questions and Answers'. *The Economist* (and other realist analysts) had serious doubts about the effect of the expected self-congratulatory consensus of the World Summit: '... most children die either because their rulers and would-be rulers fight each other for power, as in Afghanistan, Mozambique, Ethiopia and so on. Or they die

because their leaders are too weak, too self-interested, or (most often) simply too ill organized, to set a framework for preventing those deaths … Summiteers may feel good when they give their blessing to global solutions and calls for more development aid. But national action is what does the children good' (29 September 1990).

27. *The New York Times*, 19 September 1991.
28. Black (1996), op. cit., pp. 227–8, 233
29. *UNICEF Annual Report 1997*, p. 39. 30
30. *U.N. Observer and International Report*, February 1995, p. 3. Criticisms of UNICEF are in Brooks, op. cit.
31. *IHT* and *Le Monde*, 12 April 1995, and UNICEF *Information Newsline*, 11 July 1999. On the US pressures to appoint Bellamy, see Boutros Boutros-Ghali, *Unvanquished, A U.S.–U.N. Saga* (New York: Random House, 1999), pp. 227–31.
32. Y. Beigbeder, *The Internal Management of United Nations Organizations: The Long Quest for Reform* (London: Macmillan (now Palgrave), and New York: St. Martin's Press (now Palgrave) 1997), pp. 88, 108–9.
33. *Health Strategy for UNICEF*, Doc. 1995 E/ICEF1995/11/rev.1.
34. 'Medium-term plan for the period 1998–2001', Doc. E/ICEF/1998/13, 8 July 1998.
35. 'Renewing the United Nations: A Programme for Reform, Report of the Secretary-General', UN Doc. A/51/950, 14 July 1997, par. as. 153–4; see also Mary Riddell, 'Bill Clinton is said to be "mad about her", but the head of Unicef is strapped for cash in her global fight against child poverty (interview with Carol Bellamy)', *New Statesman* (1996), 27 February 1998, pp. 28–9.
36. Res. 53/128.

Chapter 3 Structure and Finances

1. Doc. E/ICEF/48, p. 4: see K. Karunatilleke, *Le Fonds des Nations Unies pour L'Entance (FISE-UNICEF)* (Paris: Pedone, 1967), p. 121.
2. UNGA Res. 57 (I), 1946, 802 (VIII), 1953, 417 (V), 1950, 1038 (XI), 1956, 36/244, 1982.
3. UN Doc. A/C.2/46/7 of 31 October 1991.
4. Res. 48/162, 'Restructuring and revitalization of the United Nations in the economic, social and related fields', 20 December 1993.
5. 1995 UNICEF Annual Report, p. 93.
6. See Y. Beigbeder, (*The Internal Management of United Nations Organizations: The Long Quest for Reform.* (London: Macmillan (now Palgrave), and New York: St. Martin's Press (now Palgrave), 1997), pp. 155–7. Staffing statistics are in 1996, 1998 and 1999 UNICEF Annual Report(s).
7. UN Doc. A/5270, 1962.
8. B. Urquhart and E. Childers, *A World in Need of Leadership: Tomorrow's United Nations – A Fresh Appraisal* (Uppsala: Dag Hammarskjöld Foundation, 1996), pp. 76, 87–92.
9. Ibid., p. 50; WHO Res. EB97.R.10 of 23 January 1996; and revised Rule 52 of Rules of Procedure of the WHO Executive Board, in WHO, *Basic Documents*, 41st edn (Geneva: WHO, 1996), pp. 156–7.

10. 1997 UNICEF Annual Report, p.6; M. Koivusalo and E. Ollila, *Making a Healthy World: Agencies, Actors and Policies in International Health* (Helsinki, London and New York: Stakes/Zed Books, 1997), p. 47.
11. 'A life with UNICEF – Issue 2'; interview with Rolf Carriere by Monte Leach, for Share International, 17 March 1999, http://www.selfempowermentacademy.-com
12. Information on National Committees is found in Doris Phillips, *A Historical Perspective on National Committees for UNICEF in Europe*, UNICEF History Series, Monograph II, 1986, in UNICEF Annual Reports and in Reports of National Committees. See also *The State of the World's Children 1996*, Panel 13, p. 68. National Committees are active in 29 European countries, Australia, Canada, Hong Kong, Israel, Japan, New Zealand, the Republic of Korea and the US. In 2000, 191 NGOs were in consultative status with UNICEF.
13. Phillips, op. cit., pp. 5, 14, 18.
14. Information based on the 'Recognition Agreement' between UNICEF and the Irish National Committee for UNICEF signed in October 1994.
15. 1990, 1996, 1999 UNICEF Annual Reports.
16. The United Kingdom Committee for UNICEF, *1996–97* and *1997–98 Annual Reviews*.
17. *1997 UNICEF Annual Report.*
18. 'UNICEF Canada in Action', http://www.unicef.ca
19. Information on NGOs is found in: Alba Zizzamia, *NGO/UNICEF Cooperation: A Historical Perspective*, UNICEF History Series, Monograph V (New York: UNICEF, 1987); *Partnership in Action, UNICEF and NGOs working together for children*, UNICEF (undated); UNICEF Annual Reports.
20. UNGA Res. 57 (I) and 417 (V).
21. 1998, 1999 UNICEF Annual Reports.
22. Information on Goodwill ambassadors and celebrities is based on: *The State of the World's Children 1996*, p. 61, and UNICEF Annual Reports; on Audrey Hepburn, see A. S. Moore's article in *People Weekly*, 29 March 1993.
23. See 'UN Special', Geneva, November 1998, *New York Times*, 25 October 1998; *Le Point*, 27 August 1999.
24. Information on funding is found in the UNICEF Annual Reports, and the Annual Report(s) of the Executive Director to the UNICEF Executive Board. See also 'UNICEF Financial Report and audited financial statements for the biennium ended 31 December 1997 and Report of the Board of Auditors', Doc. A/53/5/Add.2, Supplement No.5B, 29 July 1998. Data on 1998 are in 1999 UNICEF Annual Report, 'Report of the Executive Director: progress and achievements against the medium-term plan', Doc. E/ICEF/1999/4 (Part II), 22 April 1999, and on 1988 in UNICEF Annual Report 1989.
25. UNGA Res. 53/215; WHO budget in http://www.who.int/aboutwho
26. 1999 UNICEF Annual Report, p. 27. On the greeting card programme, in addition to UNICEF reports, see W. Olcott, 'Helping the children; for 45 years UNICEF has raised millions to help needy children throughout the world. A growing greeting card program is the cornerstone of its fund-raising effort', *Fund Raising Management*, June 1991.
27. Doc. E/ICEF/1998/13, 8 July 1998.
28. 'UNICEF Newsline', 14 December 1999; WHO Press Release, WHO/75, 7 December 1999.

29. UN Doc. A/51/950, 14 July 1997, para. 214.
30. UNICEF Information, Executive Speeches, 16 April 1999. One such activity is 'Change for Good' under which airline passengers offer their spare change to UNICEF. Under the 'Trick-or-Treat for UNICEF' programme, US and Canadian children go from door to door with the trademark orange collection boxes on Hallowe'en, collecting more than $100 million.
31. UNGA Res. 49/22, 23 December 1994.

Chapter 4   Children's Health: the Main Programme

1. UNGA Res. 57 (I), I.(c).
2. See M. Black, *The Children and the Nations: The Story of UNICEF* (New York: UNICEF), 1986, p. 493 and Table 3.2 in the present book.
3. UNGA Off. Rec. Third Committee, 18 October 1950, p. 103.
4. Ibid., 16 October 1950, p. 96.
5. Res. WHA1.120, July 1948. The joint enterprise for BCG immunization between UNICEF and the Scandinavian Red Cross, called the 'International Tuberculosis Campaign', was approved by the UNICEF Executive Board in March 1948, at the initiative of Rajchman. Vaccinations began in Europe, then in Africa, Asia and Latin America. By 1951, on completion of the campaign, 30 million children had been tested for tuberculosis and at least 14 million had been vaccinated in 23 countries: see Marta A. Balinska, *For the Good of Humanity: Ludwik Rajchman, Medical Statesman* (Budapest: Central European University, 1998), pp. 210–14.
6. See WHO Doc. A2/35, 27 May 1949, 'Report by WHO members on the assumption by WHO of responsibility for UNICEF health projects, and on the functioning of the Joint Committee', 'UNICEF/WHO Relationships, Note by the [WHO] Director-General', WHO Doc. EB13/WP1/12, 21 January 1954.
7. Res. EB7.R60 and WHA4.16.
8. Res. WHA7.50.
9. Res. EB25.R30.
10. Res. EB8.R11 and EB42.R5, WHO Doc. EB99/22 Add.1, 2 January 1997, 'UNICEF/WHO Joint Committee on Health Policy'.
11. UN Doc. E/ICEF/1997/19, 27 May 1997, 'UNICEF/WHO Joint Committee on Health Committee'.
12. WHO Doc. EB99/22 Add.1, 2 January 1997, A52/26, 14 April 1999.
13. UN Doc. A/53/1, par. 127. See also Sue Collinson, 'UN and Health Briefing Note, Global coordination of UN health activities: What are the formal mechanisms?', No. 2, October 1995, p. 3, London School of Hygiene and Tropical Medicine.
14. J.A. Walsh and K.S. Warren, 'Selective primary health care. An interim strategy for disease control in developing countries', *New England Journal of Medicine* 301, (1979), pp. 967–74. We are indebted to M. Koivusalo and E. Ollila's *Making a Healthy World*, for their assessments on PHC in their chapter 8. Our Figure 4.2 reproduces most of their Box 8.3, p. 115.
15. G. Walt, 'WHO under stress: Implications for health policy', *Health Policy*, 24, 1993, p. 137.
16. WHO Doc. WHA36/DIV/4, 3 May 1983, paras. 19–23, and Doc. WHA39/DIV/4, 6 May 1986, paras 2–3.

17. J. Ling, 'One million children with a chance to live' (interview with J. Grant), *World Health*, Jan.–Feb. 1987, p. 12.
18. Black, op. cit., p. 38.
19. 'Information and attitudes among health personnel about early infant-feeding practices', *WHO Wkly Epidem. Rec.*, no. 17, 1995, pp. 117–20.
20. 'UNICEF's recommended length of exclusive breastfeeding', Note prepared by Lida Lhotska and Helen Armstrong, 22 November 1999, http://www.bftopic-s.org/docs/doc2.hcm
21. See WHO 'Promotion of sound infant and young child feeding practices', http://www.who.int/nut/activities.htm, pp. 21, 27, 28; *The World Health Report 1998*, WHO, Geneva, p. 69; *BMJ*, vol. 316, 11 April 1998, pp. 1103–4; 'Breaking the Rules, Stretching the Rules 1998, A Worldwide Report on Violations of the WHO/UNICEF International Code of Marketing of Breastmilk Substitutes', IBFAN, 1998, p. iii.
22. WHO 'Promotion op. cit., 'pp. 21–2; 1997 UNICEF Annual Report, pp. 39–40.
23. UNAIDS, 'Report on the global HIV/AIDS epidemics, June 1998', pp. 48–9; 1999 UNICEF Annual Report, p. 15; *IHT*, 20 August 1998.
24. WHO Press Release, 28 October 1999.
25. See Res. WHA40.27, May 1987.
26. Black, op. cit., p. 205.
27. http://www.unicef.org/wsc/plan.htm
28. 1995 UNICEF Annual Report, p. 57; 1996, pp. 38–9; 1997, p. 19.
29. D. Maine and A. Rosenfield, 'The Safe Motherhood Initiative: Why has it stalled ?', *American Journal of Public Health*, vol. 89, no. 4, April 1999, pp. 480–2.
30. See Koivusalo and Ollila, op. cit., pp. 52–4.
31. E/ICEF/1988/13, decision 1988/3.
32. E/ICEF/1992/L.20, p. 35.
33. WHO Doc. JCHP28/91/21, p. 29.
34. 1998 UNICEF Annual Report, p. 14.
35. On Senegal, 'L'initiative de Bamako dope les soins primaires', in L. Diallo, S. McKeown and I. Wone, *Forum mondial de la Santé*, vol. 17, 1996, pp. 417–20; on cost recovery, *The World Health Report 1998*, p. 159.
36. Statement of Carol Bellamy on 8 March 1999: http://www.unicef.org/exspeeches/99esp3.htm
37. Res. WHA27.57, May 1974; WHA29.63, May 1976; WHA31.53; May 1978; see also Y. Beigbeder, with Nashat, M. Orsini, M.-A. and Tiercy, J. F., *The World Health Organization* (The Hague, London and Boston: Martinus Nijhoff, 1998), pp. 137–140.
38. The Advisory Group had been appointed to advise WHO on its EPI – see WHO Doc. WHO/EPI/GEN/94.1, 1994. See also WHO, *Feature*, no. 127, September 1988; *The State of the World's Children 1993*, p. 16.
39. T. M. Hill, 'The promise of CVI (Children's Vaccine Initiative)', *World Health*, March–April 1993, pp. 26–7.
40. Black (op. cit., p. 44) reported that J. Grant had persuaded President Betancur to back the National Vaccination Crusade; see also 1985 UNICEF Annual Report, p. 14. On 'days of tranquillity', see Black, op. cit., pp. 46–7.
41. Res. WHA41.28, May 1988; WHO Press Releases: WHO72, 3 December 1999, WHO/1, 6 January 2000. At the end of 1999, ten priority countries accounted for most of the world's polio cases: Afghanistan, Angola, Democratic Republic

of Congo, Somalia and Sudan – countries at war, and Bangladesh, Ethiopia, India, Nigeria and Pakistan – reservoirs where transmission is particularly intense. See also S. Hasina, 'A priceless legacy', *The Progress of Nations 1999*, UNICEF, pp. 9–11.

42. Y. Beigbeder, 'Another role for an NGO: financing a WHO programme, Rotary International and the eradication of poliomyelitis', *Transnational Associations*, 1, 1997, pp. 37–43.

43. WHO Press Releases: WHO/55, 11 October 1999, WHO/75, 7 December 1999.

44. Doc. E/ICEF/1900/P/L.39, 8 March 1990, p. 3.

45. W. Muraskin, 'Origins of the Children's Vaccine Initiative, the Intellectual Foundations' and 'the Political Foundations', *Soc. Sci. Med.*, vol. 42, no. 12, 1996, pp. 1703–19, 1721–34.

46. 'Declaration of New York: The Children's Vaccine Initiative', 10 September 1990, UNICEF House.

47. See UNICEF Annual Reports; *State of the world's vaccines and immunization*, WHO/UNICEF, Geneva, 1996, pp. 11–25; WHO Fact Sheet No. 169, June 1997; WHO Press Release WHO/78, 30 October 1997. See also http:// www.unicef.org/gavi/gavi6/htm

48. H. Gavaghan, 'L'OMS enterre l'Initiative pour les vaccins de l'enfance', *Biofutur*, May 1999, p. 14.

49. See http://www.who.int/gpv-aboutus/gavi and http://www.unicef.org/newsline/ gavi.htm The World Health Assembly endorsed the objectives of the Global Alliance for Vaccines and Immunization in Res. WHA53.12 of 20 May 2000.

50. See WHO Press Release, WHO/66, 23 November 1999; UNICEF, *The Progress of Nations 1999*, pp. 17–25; Beigbeder (1998), op. cit., pp. 140–7.

51. *IHT*, 6 July 2000. However, the blame for refusing to confront the AIDS pandemic should also be assigned to governments. As reported by W.W. Furth, a former WHO Assistant-Director-General, in the 1980s most governments in Africa and Asia refused to acknowledge the seriousness of the AIDS problem in their countries and grossly under-reported new AIDS cases to WHO. He recalled several statements by African and Asian public health officials and diplomats who dismissed HIV and AIDS as problems for Europe and North America, not for them (*IHT*, 12 July 2000). The Soviet health authorities were also among the deniers. South African President Thabo Mbeki launched another controversy in July 2000 by denying the scientifically proved causality link between HIV and AIDS (*Le Monde*, 11 July 2000).

52. UNICEF Annual Report 1989, pp. 20–1.

53. Koivusalo and Ollila, op. cit., p. 186; P. Lefevre, 'Vatican revokes UNICEF gift in reproductive rights dispute', *National Catholic Reporter*, vol. 33, no. 5, Nov. 22, 1996, p. 5. See also Black, op. cit., pp. 208–10.

54. 'Report on the global HIV/AIDS epidemic, June 1998', UNAIDS/WHO, 1998, pp. 32, 37; *Popline, World Population News Service*, May–June 1999.

55. 1998 UNICEF Annual Report, p. 23; 1999, p. 15; *IHT*, 6 July 2000.

56. See http://www.who.int/chd/pub/imci/unicef/imci.htm

57. Doc. E/ICEF/1995/11/Rev.1, 13 July 1995, pp. 1, 3.

58. The 'Potantico Retreat, Enhancing the Performance of International Health Institutions', held 1–3 February 1996, was sponsored by the Rockefeller Foundation and organized by the Social Science Research Council and the Harvard Center for Population and Development Studies: pp. 33–4.

59. See, for instance, WHO Press Release WHO/20, 8 April 1989, 'WHO recognizes child abuse as a major public health problem', and Resolution of the World Health Assembly, WHA51.22 on 'Health of children and adolescents', which has created two working groups, one on the young child, the other on the adolescent, with a view to streamlining WHO activities in the area of child rights.

Chapter 5   Nutrition, Education and Sanitation

1. See   http://www.unicef.org/wsc/declare.htm   and   http://www.unicef.org/wsc.plan.htm
2. *The World Health Report 1998. Life in the 21st century: A vision for all* (Geneva: WHO, 1998), p. 154.
3. See M. Black, *The Children and the Nations: The Story of UNICEF* (New York: UNICEF, 1986), p. 493 and Table 3.2 in the present book.
4. J. Charnow, *Maurice Pate, UNICEF Executive Director, 1947–65*, UNICEF History Series, Monograph XIII (New York: UNICEF: 1989), pp. 29–30.
5. See http://www.wfp.org/info/Intro/Info.html
6. 1995 UNICEF Annual Report, pp. 16–17.
7. WHO, *In Point of Fact*, no. 88, May 1995.
8. *The Work of WHO 1990–1991*, WHO, 1992, p. 46; http://www.fao.org/wfs/final/rd-e.htm and http://www.fao.org/wfs/finalspe.htm
9. WHO, *In Point of Fact*, no. 88; *The World Health Report 1998*, pp. 74–5.
10. See http://www.fao.org
11. UNICEF Executive Board Decision 1990/91.
12. 1990 UNICEF Annual Report, p. 20; S. Pennington, 'The pinch of salt solution', *Geographical Magazine*, vol. 67, no. 7, July 1995, pp. 32–4; 1999 UNICEF Annual Report, p. 8; WHO Press Release, WHA/17, 25 May 1999.
13. *The Progress of Nations 1999*, UNICEF, 1999, p. 12; http://www.unicef.org/newsline/99pr11.htm – See also *The World Health Report 1998*, p. 73.
14. *The State of the World's Children 1999, Education*, UNICEF, 1999, pp. 1–19.
15. *Popline*, January–February 2000, p. 2.
16. Black, op. cit., p. 493, and Table 3.2 in the present book.
17. Black, op. cit., pp. 219–20, 237; P. Pridmore and D. Stephens, *Children as Partners for Health: A Critical Review of the Child-to-Child Approach* (London and New York: Zed Books, 2000).
18. Black, op. cit., p. 227.
19. In November 1987, Federico Mayor (Spain) was elected to succeed A. M. M'Bow.
20. See note 1 above.
21. Doc. E/ICEF/1999/14, 30 March 1999.
22. See J. Vickers, *Development Education in UNICEF*, UNICEF History Series, Monograph I (New York: UNICEF, 1986) and interview with J. Vickers, 19 November 1999.
23. French National Education Doc. B.O. No. 18, 6 May 1999.
24. See 1998 UNICEF Annual Report, pp. 19, 27; 1999 UNICEF Annual Report, p.11.
25. WHO Fact Sheet No. 112, March 1996; WHO Press Release WHO/43, 23 May 1997; *UNICEF Strategies in Water and Environmental Sanitation – Executive Board – Plans, Policies and Strategies*, Doc. E/ICEF/1995/17, 13 April 1995.

26. Charnow, op. cit., p. 49.
27. *Henry R. Labouisse*, UNICEF Executive Director, 1965–79. New York, 1988. UNICEF History Series Monograph XI, pp. 35–6.
28. Black, op. cit., p. 493 and Table 3.2 in the present book.
29. *UNICEF Strategies*: see note 25 above.
30. *The First Ten Years of the World Health Organization* (Geneva: WHO, 1958), p. 297; *The Second Ten Years of the World Health Organization, 1958–1967*, (Geneva: WHO, 1968), p. 255.
31. WHO *Press Release* WHO/43, 23 May 1997.
32. This section is summarized from *The State of the World's Children 1996* published for UNICEF by Oxford University Press, 1996, p. 52.
33. *IHT*, 11 November 1998, article by Barry Bearak; see also http://www.unicefusa.org/alert/emergency/bangladesh.html and WHO Fact Sheet No. 210, February 1999 and http://www.cyberbangladesh.org/arsenic.htlm.
34. Doc. E/ICEF/1999/9, *Progress report on follow-up to the World Summit for Children*, 5 April 1999, paras. 32–5.
35. UN Doc. E/CN.4/1999/49. The Rapporteur's intervention was on 8 April 1999.
36. Doc. E/ICEF/1999/9, para. 43.
37. For instance, UNICEF was not cited in a partnership linking national and local governments with the World Bank and a large French water management firm to bring electronic-card water delivery to a rural region in South Africa. See Brett Kline, 'Clean Water Transforms Life for South African Villagers', *IHT*, 7 April 2000.

Chapter 6   Natural and Man-Made Emergencies

1. UN Doc. A/54/1, *Report of the Secretary-General on the Work of the Organization*, 1999, Introduction and Chapter III.
2. In Carol Bellamy's address to the 50th Annual Sesssion of UNHCR, 4 October 1999; see http://www.unicef.org/exspeeches/99esp12.htm
3. Henry R. Labouisse, *UNICEF Executive Director, 1965–79*. New York, 1988, UNICEF History Series Monograph XI, pp. 50–2.
4. UNICEF Executive Board res. 1992/21.
5. Doc. E/ICEF/1996/10 (Part II), 29 February 1996, par. 54–5.
6. Doc. E/ICEF/1997/7, 11 November 1996, 'Children and women in emergencies: strategic priorities and operational concerns for UNICEF'.
7. *UNHCR REFWORLD*, pp. 128–130, 131–8.
8. Doc. E/ICEF/1997/5, 11 November 1996.
9. UNICEF Annual Reports *1991–1994*.
10. P. Willetts, (ed.), *Pressure Groups in the Global System* (London: Pinter, 1982), p. 100.
11. Y. Beigbeder, 'The French Doctors', in *The Role and Status of International Humanitarian Volunteers and Organizations: The Right and Duty to Humanitarian Assistance* (Dordrecht, Boston and London: Martinus Nijhoff, 1991), pp. 257–73, 380–3.
12. See http://www.unicef.org/newsline/99pr4.htm and http://www.unicef.org/africafloods/main.htm

13. See http://www.undp.org/dpa/index.html; http://www.unicef.org/newsline/ 00pr30.htm; *Le Monde*, 20 April 2000; *IHT*, 20 and 24 April 2000; *Newsweek*, 24 April 2000.
14. http://www.unicef.org/africadrought/main.htm
15. R. C. Kent, *Anatomy of Disaster Relief: The International Network in Action* (London and New York: Pinter, 1987), pp. 137–8.
16. Beigbeder, op. cit., pp. 264–5.
17. 'Famines shouldn't be occurring in Ethiopia again', by M. Ahmed, UNICEF representative in Ethiopia and in Japan, *IHT*, 20 April 2000.
18. See http://www.unicef.org/newsline/99pr31.htm – *The State of the World's Children 1996*, p. 24.
19. See UN Press Releases: SC/6616, 23 December 1998, and SC/6846, 18 April 2000; and United Nations Associations of the United States of America, *A Global Agenda, Issues before the 52nd General Assembly of the UN*, pp. 44–6.
20. See http://www.unicef.org/features/feat171.htm
21. 'UNICEF helping Kosovo Children deal with trauma', Public Diplomacy Query, USIA UN Correspondents, 14 April 1999; http://www.unicef.org/ kosovo/index.htm; http://www.unicef.org/kosovo/donrep.htm; http:// www.unicef.org/kosovo/videos/htm.
22. UN Background on East Timor – UNTAET; http://www.un.org/peace/etimor/ UntaetB.htm; http://www.ur.org/peace/etimor99/sr2010.html; http://www.u-nicef.org/newsline/99pr25.htm, newsline/eastt.htm, newsline/99pr39.htm
23. 'Preparing Tomorrow: Working with Civil Society for the Protection of Children affected by Armed Conflict, Remarks' by Olara A. Otunnu, Under-Secretary-General, Special Representative of the Secretary-General for Children and Armed Conflict, World Civil Society Conference, 8 December 1999, Montreal. See also *Stop Using Child Soldiers*, Coalition to Stop the Use of Child Soldiers, published by Rädda Barnen on behalf of the International Save the Children Alliance, 2nd edn, November 1998. The Coalition includes Amnesty International, Defence for Children International, Human Rights Watch, Jesuit Refugee Service, the Quaker United Nations Office, Geneva, Rädda Barnen (Swedish Save the Children), Terre des Hommes, World Vision, the African and the Latin American Coalitions to stop the use of child soldiers. The Coalition cooperates with the International Red Cross and Red Crescent Movement and UN agencies and bodies, including UNICEF and UNHCR. See also 'For Angola's former child soldiers, peace brings uneasy calm' by Damien Personnaz, http://www.unicef.org/features/feat171.htm
24. *Newsweek*, 29 March 1999; *IHT*, 23 August 1999, 8 May 2000.
25. 'UNICEF hails Guatemala truth commission report', http://www.unicef.org/ newsline/99pr7.htm; 'UNICEF calls for protection of children in armed conflict', http://www.unicef.org/newsline/99pr17.htm On Sudan, J. Fisher-Thompson (USIA Staff Writer), 'Sudan cited as behind child abduction in Northern Uganda', Doc. 75, Public Diplomacy Query 75, 13 March 1998.
26. At age 15, Iraq and Japan; at age 16, Belgium, Chile, India, Iran, Pakistan and the United Kingdom among others; at age 17, Angola, France, Germany, Israel, the United States, among others. Uganda recruits volunteers 'exceptionally' at age 13: November 1998 data in *Stop Using Child Soldiers*, op.cit., p. 13.
27. UNGA Res. 54/263, 25 May 2000.

28. Statement of Carol Bellamy to the Executive Board of UNICEF, 19 January 1999: http://www.unicef.org/newsline/99pr18.htm 16 May 1999; http://www.unicef.org/exspeeches/99esp12.htm.
29. *UN Chronicle*, vol. 34, no. 1, Spring 1997, p. 8(1): 'The sinister strangeness of silence?'; 1998 UNICEF Annual Report, p. 15; 1999 UNICEF Annual Report, p. 13; http://www.unicef.org/newsline/99pr18.htm
30. UNGA Res. 1386 (XIV), 1959; 3318 (XXIX), 1974; 3406 (XXX), 1975; 44/25, 1989; 48/157, 20 December 1993.
31. http://www.unicef.org/graca/summry.htm The full Machel report is in UN Doc. A/51/306, 26 August 1996. It was acknowledged in the preamble of UN General Assembly Res. 51/77 II, 12 December 1996.
32. See UNGA Res. 51/77 II, paras 35–9; UN Security Council Res. 1261, 25 August 1999; 'Executive Summary, Children in War: the Many Faces of Suffering, Report to the UNGA by the Special Representative of the Secretary-General for Children and Armed Conflict, Mr Olara A. Otunnu', 26 October 1999; UN Press Release HR/4463–PKO/85, 22 February 2000, 'UN announces deployment of Child Protection Advisers, groundbreaking development in UN peacekeeping'. Mr Otunnu is assisted by ten professional and two general services staff members at UN headquarters.
33. See http://www.unicef.org/newsline/00pr44.htm and *IHT*, 7 July 2000, *IHT*, 18 July 2000.
34. See note 31 above.
35. 1998 UNICEF Annual Report, p. 7; J. Tessitore and S. Woolfson, (eds), *A Global Agenda: Issues Before the 53rd General Assembly of the United Nations*, United Nations Association of the USA (Lanham New York, Boulder, Oxford: Rowman & Littlefield, 1998), pp. 81–3. China has recently announced that it will clear some 800 000 landmines from the Sino-Vietnamese border, along with the recent clearing of more than 200 000 mines and unexploded bombs from border areas in Yunnan Province: see http://www.unicef.org/newsline/99pr8.htm
36. See http://www.unicef.org/newsline/99pr8.htm
37. http://www.unicef.org/newsline/99pr10.htm
38. See http://www.unicef.org/newsline/99pr62.htm

Chapter 7   Advocating Children's Rights

1. UNGA Res. 1386 (XIV), Preamble and 10 Principles, 20 November 1959.
2. UNGA Res. 1391 (XIV), 20 November 1959.
3. See Article by M. Newman-Williams (Deputy Director, Programme Director, UNICEF), in *UN Chronicle*, no. 2, 1999, pp. 38–9. See also M. J. Thapa, 'UNICEF and the Convention on the Rights of the Child: the Mandate and the Mission', unpublished paper, UNICEF, 26 October 1995; J. E. Oestreich, 'UNICEF and the Implementation of the Convention on the Rights of the Child', *Global Governance*, vol. 4, no. 2, April–June 1998, pp. 183–98.
4. UNGA Res. 44/25.
5. Thapa, op. cit., p. 17.
6. Oestreich, op. cit., pp. 190–1.
7. Besides the references in notes 5 and 6 above, information in this section is found in *1993 UNICEF Annual Report*, p. 54; *1994 UNICEF Annual Report*,

pp. 39–40; *1995 UNICEF Annual Report*, pp. 33–4; *The State of the World's Children 1996*, p. 67; *1998 UNICEF Annual Report*, pp. 5–6; UNICEF Docs. E/ICEF/1998/4(Part II), paras. 6–7, 13, para. 2.3; E/ICEF/1999/4 (Part I), paras 33–34, 11, para. 46, (Part II), paras 18–20.

8. UN Res. 54/263, 25 May 2000; see http://www.unicef.org/newsline/00pr44.htm and *IHT*, 7 July 2000.

9. See N. Grey-Johnson article on 'African Charter on the Rights of the Child Enters into Force', *International Children's Rights Monitor*, vol. 13, no. 2, May 2000, pp. 24–26.

10. The World Declaration on the Survival, Protection and Development of Children and Plan of Action are in http://www.unicef.org/wsc/declare.htm and /wsc/plan.htm. On the Beijing Conference, see J. Tessitore and S. Woolfson, *A Global Agenda, Issues Before the 51st General Assembly of the United Nations* (Lanham, New York, Boulder, London: Rowman & Littlefield, 1996), pp. 160–161.

11. See http://www.unicef.org/programme/gpp/new/beijing5/girlch.html

12. UNGA Res. 48/104. See also WHO Fact Sheet No. 239, June 2000 on 'Violence against Women'.

13. The report is based on the research of the UNICEF Innocenti Research Center in Florence (Italy), in addition to various other surveys and compilations of information. See http://www.unicef.org/newsline/00pr45.htm – and US Department of State, International Information Programs, Washington File, 28 June 2000, 'Violence Against Women an Epidemic Needing Treatment' by K. Woodrow.

14. See http://www.unicef.org/safe/afghan.htm; also 'Bellamy discusses discrimination against Afghan women and girls' by J. Aita, USIA UN Correspondent, Public Diplomacy Query, Doc. 64, 6 April 1998; *Le Monde*, 22 April 2000.

15. The UNIFEM report on 'Progress of the World's Women 2000' was released at the Beijing+5 Conference.

16. *IHT*, 10 March 2000.

17. See WHO Fact Sheet No. 241, June 2000, 'Female Genital Mutilation', and http://www.unicef.org/programme/gpp/new/beijing5/violence.htm 14 June 2000.

18. A. Manuila (ed.), (*EMRO: Partner in Health in the Mediterranean, 1949–89* (Alexandria, Egypt: WHO Regional Office for the Eastern Mediterranean, 1991), pp. 291–5, has shown that the widespread belief that female circumcision is endorsed by Islam is utterly false. He affirms that there are no religious grounds for female circumcision in Islam, Christianity or Judaism.

19. 'Female Genital Mutilation, A Joint WHO/UNICEF/UNFPA Statement', WHO, 1997.

20. See http://www.unicef.org/programme/gpp/new/beijing5/violence.html The Ouagadougou Declaration is in *International Children's Rights Monitor*, vol. 13, no.1, January 2000, p. 21. See also the *Monitor*, vol. 13, no. 2, May 2000, p. 25, and *Newsweek*, 5 July 1999.

21. *IHT*, 17 March 2000.

22. See *The ILO, What it is, What it does* (Geneva: ILO), pp. 16–18; 'Child Domestic Work', *Innocenti Digest* 5 Florence: UNICEF ICDC, 1999; 'Child Labour Problems Concern ILO', *Popline*, March–April 2000; http://www.hrw.org/reports/2000/frmwrkr/

23. *The ILO, What it is, What it does*, op. cit., p. 18.

24. 'Procurement policy – child labour', UNICEF Executive Directive, CF/EXD/ 1995-007, 23 May 1995; 1995 UNICEF Annual Report, p. 35; 1998 UNICEF Annual Report, p. 26; 1999 UNICEF Annual Report, p. 15.
25. UNESCO *Courier*, May 1999, pp. 24–8.
26. *IHT*, 13–14 March 1999; *Le Monde*, 14 April 1999; *Newsweek*, 3 May 1999. C. Bellamy's statement of 12 March 1999 is in http://www.unicef.org/newsline/99pr10.htm; see also her article in *IHT*, 13 May 1999; see also R. Miniter, 'The False Promise of Slave Redemption', *Atlantic Monthly*, 284, no.1, July 1999, pp. 63–70, and *Le Monde*, 30 October 1999.
27. See http://www.unicef.org/newsline 11 July 1999, and http://www.unicef.org/exspeeches/00esp12.htm See also S. Ramphal, 'Debt has a child's face' in *The Progress of Nations 1999*, pp. 27–9.
28. *1990 UNICEF Annual Report*, p. 6, M. Black, *Children First: The story of UNICEF, Past and Present* (Oxford: Oxford University Press for UNICEF, 1996), pp. 168–9; *The State of the World's Children 2000*, pp. 37–8.
29. *1999 UNICEF Annual Report*, pp. 18–19; J. Tessitore and S. Woolfson, (eds), *A Global Agenda, Issues Before the 54th General Assembly of the United Nations* (Lanham, MA, New York, Boulder, CO, Oxford: Rowman & Littlefield, 1999), pp. 137–8; *Main Messages of UNDP Poverty Report 2000*, at http://www.undp.org/povertyreport/main/main.html; *Le Monde*, 15 April 2000.
30. *The State of the World's Children 1996*, pp. 22–3; *Newsweek*, 31 July 2000; *IHT*, 13 August 1999; hrw-news@igc.topica.com 4 August 2000. The Secretary-General's statement is in *The New York Times*, 6 January 1995.

Chapter 8   Internal Management Issues

1. An Internal Audit Committee advises on internal audit strategies, approves annual audit plans, reviews all audit reports, monitors implementation of audit recommendations, commissions investigations and reviews their findings, and implements corrective and disciplinary action. The Committee is chaired by the Executive Director and includes the Deputy Executive Directors, the Comptroller and several Directors. The Director of the Office of Internal Audit (OIA) provides secretarial support. The OIA is the principal unit for providing independent oversight within UNICEF by assessing the soundness, adequacy and application of systems, procedures and related internal controls. The OIA may also call on specialist outside help and has called on the UN Office of Internal Oversight Services when necessary. The UNICEF financial report and accounts and the report of the UN Board of Auditors are submitted to the UN General Assembly and reviewed by the Advisory Committee on Administrative and Budgetary Questions (ACABQ) and the Fifth Committee of the Assembly (see UNICEF Doc. E/ICEF/ Organization/Rev.3, 24 April 1998).
2. The Joint Inspection Unit, created in 1976, has eleven members, appointed by the UN General Assembly on the basis of equitable geographical distribution. They serve in their personal capacity. According to the statute of the Unit, the Inspectors have the broadest powers of investigation in all matters having a bearing on the efficiency of the services and the proper use of funds. They provide an independent view through inspection and evaluation aimed at

improving management and methods and at achieving greater coordination between organizations: see General Assembly Res. 31/192 of 22 December 1976.
3. See UNICEF Doc. E/ICEF/AB/L.184, and UNICEF History Series, Monograph XI, pp. 65–7.
4. UN Doc. JIU/REP/86/11.
5. The Heritage Foundation, *Backgrounder*, no. 50, 1 September 1987, 'UNICEF's Mounting Troubles'. The issue also referred to a particularly shocking incident for the agency: the discovery in June 1987 of a child pornography ring which involved the Director of the Belgian Committee for UNICEF and 14 other individuals, including a UNICEF employee.
6. UN Doc. A/47/500, 7 October 1992.
7. Recommendations from the Booz, Allen & Hamilton study are given in Doc. E/ICEF/1997/AB/L.1, 11 November 1996; critical issues identified by the study are in Doc. E/ICEF/1998/AB/L.5, 20 March 1998. See also *International Documents Review*, 6 February 1995.
8. See *International Documents Review*, 6 March and 29 May 1995; *IHT*, 27–28 May 1995; *Le Monde*, 15 June 1995; UNICEF Doc. E/ICEF/1997/AB/L.2, 11 November 1996.
9. Doc. E/ICEF/1998/AB/L.7, 26 May 1998.
10. Doc. A/53/5/Add.2, 29 July 1998.
11. Doc. E/ICEF/1998/AB/L.5, 20 March 1998.
12. 'Glasnost at UNICEF as staff address insecurity issue', by D. Winch, *UN Staff Report*, June–July 1997, *International Documents Review*, 15 September 1997; *The InterDependent*, Spring 1998.
13. *UNICEF Staff News*, no. 4, 1999, nos. 1 and 2, 2000.

Chapter 9   UNICEF's Challenges

1. 'Strategies for Individual Organizations, Annex to the Plan of Action for Active Multilateralism', [Danish] Ministry of Foreign Affairs, Danida, 1996, p. 17.
2. The Executive Directors have benefited from the support, advice and initiatives of their senior staff, among them, Charles Egger, Director of UNICEF's office in Paris, then Regional Director in India, then Deputy Executive Director for Programmes; in the 1970s. E. J. R. Heyward, Deputy Executive Director for Operations, introduced into the agency a more skilled public health and nutrition approach and improved the process by which field assessments were upgraded, as well as staff recruitment. In the 1980s, Richard Jolly, by publishing his *Adjustment with a Human Face*, brought the issues of debt and social justice to the fore, which initiated a debate with the World Bank and the IMF; he also had a role in the recruitment of social scientists and economists, bringing UNICEF closer to developing countries, Socialist nations and to the Nordic countries. Credit should also be given to writer-journalist Peter Adamson for the success of the early *State of the World Children Reports*.
3. UNICEF had its own independent, well-funded and skilled Evaluation Office, under the direction of S. S. Basta from 1986 to 1990. Its freedom of expression was rewarded by support and funds from the main donors.
4. UN Res. 57 (I), 11 December 1946.

5. UNICEF Doc. E/ICEF/1993/CRP.7, 27 January 1993.
6. UNICEF Doc. E/ICEF/1999/10, 13 April 1999, and UNICEF Press Release, 'Reaching the last child with polio vaccine', 7 October 2000.
7. UNICEF Doc. E/ICEF/1999/10, 13 April 1999.
8. Foreword by Thomas Hammarberg in J. R. Himes (ed.), *Implementing the Convention on the Rights of the Child: Resource Mobilization in Low-Income Countries*, UNICEF, International Child Development Center, Florence (The Hague: Martinus Nijhoff, 1995), p. vi.
9. UNICEF Doc. E/ICEF/1993/CRP.8, 24 February 1993.
10. UNICEF Doc. E/ICEF/1999/10, 13 April 1999.
11. UNICEF Doc. E/ICEF/1998/6/Rev.1, 1998, paras 75 and 98.
12. Carol Bellamy's opening statement to the annual meeting of the UNICEF Executive Board, 7 June 1999.

Select Bibliography

UNICEF Publications

UNICEF Annual Reports.
Annual Reports of the Executive Director to the Executive Board.
The State of the World's Children (annual).
The Progress of Nations (annual).
Information Newsline.
Executive Speeches.
Facts and Figures.
Home page: http://www.unicef.org
Reports of the UNICEF Innocenti Research Center in Florence, Italy.
Himes, J. R. (ed.), UNICEF, *Implementing the Convention of the Rights of the Child: Resource Mobilization in Low-Income Countries* (The Hague, London and Boston; Martinus Nijhoff, 1995).
UNICEF History Series:
Monograph I: *Development Education in UNICEF*, by Vickers, J., 1986.
Monograph II: *A Historical Perspective on National Committees For UNICEF in Europe*, by Phillips, D., 1986.
Monograph V: *NGO/UNICEF Cooperation: A Historical Perspective*, by Zizzamia, A., 1987.
Monograph VII: *UNICEF and Women: the Long voyage. A Historical Perspective,* 1987.
Monograph VIII: *Water and Sanitation in UNICEF 1946–1986*, 1987.
Monograph IX: *UNICEF in Education: a Historical Perspective*, by Phillips, H. M., 1987.
Monograph XI: *Henry R. Labouisse, UNICEF Executive Director 1965–1979*, 1988.
Monograph XIII: *Maurice Pate, UNICEF Executive Director, 1947–1965*, by Charnow, J., 1989.

Other Publications

Balinska, M. A., *For the Good of Humanity: Ludwik Rajchman, Medical Statesman* (Budapest: Central European University Press, 1998).
Beigbeder, Y., *The Internal Management of United Nations Organizations: The Long Quest for Reform* (London: Macmillan (now Palgrave), and New York: St. Martin's Press (now Palgrave), 1997).
Beigbeder, Y., *The Role and Status of International Humanitarian Volunteers and Organizations: The Right and Duty to Humanitarian Assistance* (Dordrecht, Boston and London: Martinus Nijhoff, 1991).
Beigbeder, Y. with Nashat, M., Orsini, M.-A. and Tiercy, J. F., *The World Health Organization* (The Hague, London and Boston: Martinus Nijhoff, 1998).
Black, M., *The Children and the Nations. The Story of Unicef* (New York: UNICEF, 1986).

217

Black, M., *Children First: The Story of UNICEF, Past and Present* (Oxford: Oxford University Press for UNICEF, 1996).

Boutros-Ghali, B., *Unvanquished: A U.S.–U.N. Saga* (New York: Random House, 1999).

Danida, *Case Study of 11 Agencies in Kenya, Nepal, Sudan and Thailand, Effectiveness of Multilateral Agencies at Country Level*, [Danish] Ministry of Foreign Affairs, COWIconsult, Copenhagen, 1991.

Danida, *Plan of Action for Active Multilateralism*, [Danish] Ministry of Foreign Affairs, Copenhagen, 1996.

Danida, 'Strategies for Individual Organizations', (Annex to the *Plan of Action for Active Multilateralism*), [Danish] Ministry of Foreign Affairs, Copenhagen, 1996.

Dijkzeul, D., *The Management of Multilateral Organizations* (The Hague, London and Boston: Kluwer Law International, 1997).

Karunatilleke, K., *Le Fonds des Nations Unies pour l'Enfance (FISE-UNICEF)* (Paris: Pedone, 1967).

Kent, R. C., *Anatomy of Disaster Relief, The International Network in Action* (London and New York: Pinter, 1987).

Koivusalo, M. and Ellila, E., *Making a Healthy World: Agencies, Actors and Policies in International Health* (Helsinki, London and New York: Stakes/Zed Books, 1997).

Macalister-Smith, P., *International Humanitarian Assistance – Disaster Relief Actions in International Law and Organizations* (Geneva: Martinus Nijhoff/Henry Dunant Institute, 1985).

Manuila, A. (ed.), *EMRO: Partner in Health in the Mediterranean, 1949–1989* (Alexandria, Egypt: WHO Regional Office for the Eastern Mediterranean, 1991).

Minear, L., *Humanitarianism Under Siege: A Critical Review of Operation Lifeline Sudan* (Trenton, NJ and Washington, DC: The Red Sea Press/Institute on Hunger and Development, 1991).

Narvesen, O., *The Sexual Exploitation of Children in Developing Countries* (Oslo: Redd Barna and Norwegian Save the Children, 1989).

Pridmore, P. and Stephens, D., *Children as Partners for Health* (London and New York: Zed Books, 2000).

Tessitore, J. and Woolfson, S. (eds), *A Global Agenda: Issues Before the 51st General Assembly of the United Nations* (Lanham/Boulder/New York and London: Rowman & Littlefield, 1996).

Tessitore, J. and Woolfson, S. (eds), *A Global Agenda: Issues Before the 53rd General Assembly of the United Nations* (Lanham/New York/Boulder/Oxford: Rowman & Littlefield, 1998).

Tessitore, J. and Woolfson, S. (eds), *A Global Agenda: Issues Before the 54th General Assembly of the United Nations* (Lanham/New York/Boulder/London: Rowman & Littlefield, 1999).

Urquhart, B. and Childers, E. *A World in Need of Leadership: To-Morrow's United Nations – A Fresh Appraisal* (Uppsala: Dag Hammarskjöld Foundation, 1996).

Weiss, T. G., *International Bureaucracy: An Analysis of the Operation of Functional and Global International Secretariats* (Lexington, Toronto and London: Lexington Books, 1975).

Willetts, P. (ed.), *Pressure Groups in the Global System* (London: Pinter, 1982).

Woodbridge, G., *UNRRA: The History of the United Nations Relief and Rehabilitation Administration* (New York: Columbia University Press, 1950).

Index